T0210665

Lecture Notes
in Business Information Processing 243

Series Editors

Wil van der Aalst
Eindhoven Technical University, Eindhoven, The Netherlands
John Mylopoulos
University of Trento, Povo, Italy
Michael Rosemann
Queensland University of Technology, Brisbane, QLD, Australia
Michael J. Shaw
University of Illinois, Urbana-Champaign, IL, USA
Clemens Szyperski
Microsoft Research, Redmond, WA, USA

More information about this series at http://www.springer.com/series/7911

Ewa Ziemba (Ed.)

Information Technology for Management

Federated Conference on Computer Science
and Information Systems, ISM 2015 and AITM 2015
Lodz, Poland, September 2015
Revised Selected Papers

 Springer

Editor
Ewa Ziemba
Faculty of Finance and Insurance
University of Economics in Katowice
Katowice
Poland

ISSN 1865-1348   ISSN 1865-1356   (electronic)
Lecture Notes in Business Information Processing
ISBN 978-3-319-30527-1   ISBN 978-3-319-30528-8   (eBook)
DOI 10.1007/978-3-319-30528-8

Library of Congress Control Number: 2016933479

Preface

The present book includes extended and revised versions of selected papers submitted to the 10th Conference on Information Systems Management (ISM 2015) and the 13th Conference on Advanced Information Technologies for Management (AITM 2015) held in Łódź, Poland, during September 13–16, 2015. These conferences were organized as the sub-conferences within the Federated Conference on Computer Science and Information Systems (FedCSIS 2015). FedCSIS provides a platform for bringing together researchers, practitioners, and academics to present and discuss ideas, challenges, and potential solutions on established or emerging topics related to research and practice in computer science and information systems. Since 2012, the proceedings of FedCSIS have been indexed in the Thomson Reuters Web of Science. In addition, FedCSIS full and short papers are included in the IEEE Xplore Digital Library.

ISM 2015 was a forum for computer scientists, IT specialist, and business people to exchange ideas on management of information systems in organizations, and the usage of information systems for enhancing the decision-making process and for empowering managers. It concentrated on various issues of planning, organizing, resourcing, coordinating, controlling, and leading of management functions to ensure a smooth operation of information systems in organizations.

AITM 2015 was a forum for those in the field of business informatics to present and discuss the current issues of IT in business applications. It was mainly focused on business process management, enterprise information systems, business intelligence methods and tools, decision support systems and data mining, intelligence and mobile IT, cloud computing, SOA, agent-based systems, and business-oriented ontologies.

ISM 2015 and AITM 2015 received 54 papers from 14 countries in all continents. After a review process, only 18 papers were accepted as full papers. Twelve papers of the highest quality as ranked by the Program Committee were chosen and the authors were invited to extend their papers and submit them for consideration to the LNBIP publication. Our guiding criteria for including papers in the book were the excellence of the publications indicated by the reviewers, the relevance of the subject matter for the economy, and promising results. Finally, 11 papers were selected for publication in this book. The selected papers reflect state-of-the-art research work that is often oriented toward real-world applications and highlight the benefits of information systems and technology for business and public administration, thus forming a bridge between theory and practice. These papers focus on knowledge management systems, information technology for business and public organizations, and evaluation of information systems.

I would like to take this opportunity to express my gratitude to all those who contributed to the ISM 2015 and AITM 2015 research events. First of all, the authors, whose quality work was the essence of the conference, and the members of the Program Committee, who helped us with their expertise and diligence in reviewing the papers. I am deeply grateful to the program chairs of ISM 2015 and AITM 2005, namely, Witold Chmielarz, Helena Dudycz, and Jerzy Korczak, for their organizational involvement in the events and the evaluation of papers. Many thanks to the chairs of FedCSIS 2015, i.e., Maria Ganzha, Leszek A. Maciaszek, and Marcin Paprzycki, for putting a lot of effort into organizing the big and excellent research event. Their work and commitment were invaluable.

Finally, we hope readers will find the content of this book useful and interesting for their own research activities. It is in this spirit and conviction that we present our monograph, which is the result of the intellectual effort of the authors, for the final judgment of readers. We are open to discussion on the issues raised in this book, and we look forward to the polemical, or even critical, voices as to the content and form.

February 2016   Ewa Ziemba

Contents

Knowledge Management Systems

Knowledge Management Systems

The Evolution of Adaptive Case Management from a DSS and Social Collaboration Perspective

Łukasz Osuszek[1(✉)] and Stanisław Stanek[2]

[1] Center of Excellence, GE Healthcare, 31-864 Kraków, Poland
lukasz.osuszek@ge.com
[2] General Tadeusz Kościuszko Military Academy of Land Forces,
Czajkowskiego 109, 51-150 Wrocław, Poland
s.stanek@wso.wroc.pl

Abstract. The paper outlines the recent trends in the evolution of adaptive case management (ACM). One such trend is for ACM systems to increasingly often include, besides decision support and knowledge management, functionalities that are typical of group work support or social networking. A social ACM (SACM) connects knowledge workers within a collaborative environment and brings business cases, along with supporting components, into a social space, thus turning them into elements of a social network. In addition, SACM offers mechanisms to capture and formalize feedback and interactions. The paper seeks to illustrate ways in which modern-day social networking technology and existing social networks can be exploited by businesses. Since ACM is commonly incorporated into decision support systems (DSS), the paper also attempts to explore the evolution of ACM and DSS from an architectural perspective, making a reference to the DSS architecture described in a prior article by these same authors [1].

Keywords: ACM · DSS · Social networking · Business processes · Case management · Collaboration · Decision support

1 Introduction

What has long been demanded of information systems is that they move away from the prevalent control flow perspective, commonly adopted in the business process management (BPM) area, toward the data perspective [2]. Attempts to meet these expectations have led to the emergence of a new class of information systems built around the approach known as adaptive case management (ACM).

The term "case" represents a generalization of any activity by so called "knowledge workers" (KW), whose efficiency Peter Drucker sees as a principal challenge in the 21st century [3].

State of the art in case management research reveals a gap in examining the effects that Web 2.0 mechanisms deliver in common business applications. The paper attempts to fill this gap, while at the same time supporting a hypothesis that new collaborative tools and DSS components can significantly enhance business results and business agility.

© Springer International Publishing Switzerland 2016
E. Ziemba (Ed.): FedCSIS 2015, LNBIP 243, pp. 3–16, 2016.
DOI: 10.1007/978-3-319-30528-8_1

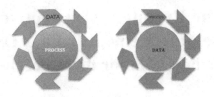

Fig. 1. The classical BPM approach vs. modern ACM.

The specific research question that the paper poses is whether an ACM platform with integrated DSS and social networking capabilities can offer added value to a modern-day business enterprise. Setting off from this question, the article endeavors an in-depth analysis of the research area, seeking to contribute to its scientific investigation.

In an effort to address the research problem, real use cases are used, focusing on the application of social networking and DSS components in deploying ACM to various economy sectors. A descriptive method was, on the other hand, adopted to delineate the extent and outcomes of ACM implementations in modern businesses. Further, qualitative research methods and case studies are utilized both for hypothesis testing and for generalizing beyond the cases being studied.

The first of the following chapters discusses the origins of, and rationale for, adaptive case management. Chapter three looks at ACM from the decision support perspective to outline the benefits of its application in addressing the needs of business managers. The subsequent chapter presents the underpinnings of the latest craze in business case management: social ACM (SACM). Chapter five provides an extended description and a case study illustrating the workings of SACM. The final chapter derives conclusions and implications from the research findings, and delineates paths for further research.

2 The Origins of, and Rationale for, Adaptive Case Management

Unlike in classical BPM, under adaptive case management processes are of dynamic character, since they are not defined until at runtime. To master the unpredictability of processes and hence facilitate process management in contexts where processes are mostly complex and where relevant decisions are affected by a large number of factors, more and more organizations choose to switch to adaptive process management systems [4].

ACM allows perfect visibility and full control of each specific case, whether it is handled by a predefined or an ad hoc process, or by a combination of the two (Fig. 1).

In a dynamic process management environment, operators/managers, i.e. knowledge workers, can be creative and innovative in performing their work, thus contributing to organizational knowledge management and creation (Fig. 2).

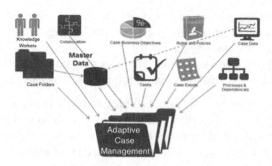

Fig. 2. Adaptive Case components.

To distinguish the role of process operator from that of temporary process participant, under ACM the former has been redefined and termed as the knowledge worker. Prof. Van der Aalst uses the "blind surgeon" metaphor to illustrate the differences between the two [5]. Under the traditional approach to processes, a participant has a partial view of the whole process, usually limited to the step in the process at which the participant is supposed to make a business decision.

The knowledge worker, on the contrary, has a complete insight into information on the case or process. Knowledge workers constitute a new category of specialized staff whose job is, in the first place, to utilize and exchange knowledge in a productive manner. They are responsible for the generation and implementation of new ideas that enable organizations to align their strategies with the increasingly rapid changes taking place in the business environment; they do so, primarily, through searching, exchanging, combining and utilizing knowledge inside as well as outside the organization.

An enterprise that is run in compliance with the ACM concept will be able to seamlessly combine its core activities with an ability to generate and verify innovations daily [6]. Allowing operators to dynamically modify their processes (and business rules, too), the enterprise management system as a whole opens up to creative initiatives from staff at large, while at the same time preventing chaos that could be wrought by uncontrolled changes to the operating properties. In addition, since it possible to examine the outcomes of changes as they emerge, information on which practices and solutions produce the best results and which yield the worst can be appended to organizational collective knowledge. This stands for actual day-to-day improvement and adaptation of business processes, relying on the best knowledge of a large portion of personnel and getting validated through feedback from customers.

The greatest benefit in deploying dynamic ACM-based business process management is that large enterprises can regain agility and responsiveness that makes them capable of operating and competing in a rapidly changing marketplace. Making it possible to actually delegate work and responsibility to process operators without the risk of losing control of the currently running processes, ACM permits large enterprises to manage their knowledge on an everyday basis through:

- creative, proactive experimenting based on continuous, even if modest, changes, introduced by a number of process operators and leading to gradual accumulation and dissemination of knowledge; and
- validation of existing knowledge and elimination of outdated information that no longer meets customers' requirements or competitive challenges.

As a precondition, organizations must be able and ready to adjust their policies and operating properties on an everyday basis as well as to continually update their knowledge on the actual and likely needs of their customers. Adaptive management of business cases is an extension of classical process-based management and an attempt to bring it together with the concept of a learning organization.

One of the cornerstones of ACM is the overarching belief that any organization should continuously expand and process its knowledge on the mechanisms governing its business environment and that this management model is not only more effective but indeed a prerequisite for the ability to keep pace with the unprecedented dynamics of changes in present-day markets and customer expectations. It is often alleged that ACM aims to create a learning organization. Clearly, it streamlines the processes inside an enterprise at several levels, affecting managers as well as personnel.

In the course of its business activity, a company creates, accumulates and validates knowledge, which is then used to evaluate and support business decisions. By this token, an ACM system can use business processes in the following ways:

1. as knowledge sources;
2. as a space for organization-wide, innovation-driven knowledge creation and limited experimentation; and
3. for knowledge preservation and in database building to bypass the need to set up and operate another system.

3   ACM from the Decision Support Perspective

Just like the decision making process itself, the decision context and the process context will change dynamically in the course of decision making as the cases are being handled. From a business perspective, DSS is often regarded as part of ACM. Fischer et al. [7] define the key DSS features as follows:

- developing socio-technical environments to support users and enable them to engage in the process of system development not only at design time but also at use time;
- supporting social creativity by providing the technical and social conditions for the exchange of ideas during discussions, debates, brainstorming, co-creation sessions, and other forms of vivid collaboration;
- combining art and design in the processes of self-realization; and
- use of meta-analysis for comparing, combining, synthesizing, summarizing, specifying, and generalizing of previous studies.

A popular definition of ACM asserts that it is "a collaborative process of assessment, planning, facilitation and advocacy for options and services to meet an individual's holistic needs through communication and available resources to promote quality cost-effective outcomes". Under this definition, ACM can be perceived as a platform comprising a decision support system.

Clyde Holsapple, one of the fathers of the DSS concept, commented that "… DSS architecture does not define what DSS is; rather, it functions as an ontology that gives a common language for design, discussion, and evaluation of DSS" [8]. These insights bring us to the following definition of DSS architecture: "DSS architecture is a general framework that identifies essential elements of a DSS and their interrelationships" [8] (Fig. 3).

Fig. 3. A model of relationships between ACM and DSS

Substantial research conducted by the authors at the request of several business enterprises employing ACM systems indicates that most such systems have similar business goals concerning decision support:

- to support the knowledge worker in making optimal decisions in each and every case;
- to deliver faster and more accurate case resolution; and
- to improve agility by following business rules in deploying decision support.

Within existing decision support systems, the control function is performed via meta-knowledge subsystems (like norms, axioms, ontologies, etc.). The development of a meta-knowledge subsystem is driven by the double loop pattern of knowledge development. The primary feedback loop, which is characteristic of adaptive learning, involves detection and rectification of deviations from the operational norms. The secondary loop, found in the so-called generative learning, is responsible for creative modifications to the operational norms.

Likewise, ACM system users will build up corporate knowledge using IT tools and social mechanisms to bring tacit knowledge (i.e. the staff's expertise and individual experience) to broader use in case processing. It is essential in any DSS project to thoroughly analyze interactions among business owners. As Frederic Adam has it, "[M]anagers are not seen as atoms but as active, purposeful agents. It is possible to visualize the Decision Making Network (DMN) and to investigate what happens within the networks as the organization tackles a Decision Situation" [9].

ACM could be viewed as an IT platform including an integrated decision support system. The DMN can be then identified as a process map that visualizes all possible case states and provides process managers/leaders with a profound insight into the business.

Those having to cope with less structured decision problems will normally need to have a good understanding of the problem solving process and to be familiar with the applicable techniques. Without this know-how, users situated beyond the operational level might not be able to use the system resources efficiently: even if an expert system is activated to provide them with support in choosing the most suitable tools (models) for their problem, the choice has to be ultimately made by the user. Observation reveals that the most common reason why some systems are not used in tactical or strategic problem solving is not the technology itself but the relatively high demand they put on users' competence (knowledge base).

ACM helps manage the unpredictable by enabling knowledge workers to effectively cooperate and share their knowledge, thus improving the functionality of a decision support system.

Users engaged in solving tactical and strategic problems will rather expect the system to become a "partner in problem solving." Interestingly enough, we have found that the lowest skill levels are associated with the highest expectations from the system, including a proactive attitude in assisting the user. Conversely, the expectations of most advanced and creative problem solvers are limited to being offered an efficient technology and a rich collection of presentation tools.

What is expected from the system in such circumstances is, in the first place, adaptability and expandability through appending new decision models. Not only does the DSS have to offer the requisite decision modeling tools but it also needs to be able to instantly integrate (owing to bi-directional data interchange) with dedicated external systems tackling specific business problems.

The ACM model typically includes a special resource containing knowledge related to business processes that is utilized in decision making (decision workflows). Identifying the key business processes and analyzing the decision making processes intrinsic to them makes it possible to accumulate knowledge needed to discover and assess relationships between decisions and their outcomes. This appears critical, in the light of our research, for decision analysis at all levels.

The findings of a survey conducted by the authors indicate that the most frequently used creative problem solving tools include:

- context-sensitive help along with access to historical data and similar cases; and
- group work support tools, such as discussion forums or (widely popular) instant messengers.

4 Social ACM

Social networking functionalities have already been adapted and incorporated into many modern enterprise management systems. As a result, businesses can reap the full benefits of Web 2.0 mechanisms for knowledge sharing and information exchange. What a social ACM essentially does is bring together knowledge workers within a collaborative environment and bring business cases, along with the supporting components (information, knowledge, etc.), into a social space, i.e. turning them into elements of a social network. In addition, it offers a mechanism for capturing and formalizing opinions (feedback) and interactions; this type of information can be converted directly into resource assets (artifacts) or brought to bear on the optimization of process definition. This chapter attempts to showcase the ways that businesses can take advantage of modern-day social technologies and of existing social networks.

At the same time, SACM integrates business process improvement tools and techniques with case management solutions. A social ACM environment can be thus described as a platform for networking that results in the processing of business cases. It lifts the barriers to participation and abandons the role-centeredness of most classical ACM solutions in favor of involving external actors in decision making and collaborative effort – and does so without compromising the core group's key prerogatives.

Considered as SACM enablers, social technologies could be divided into four categories:

- social production via collaborative projects (wikis, Google Docs);
- social networking via "social profile management" (Facebook, LinkedIn);
- social publishing – content sharing and aggregation, e.g. Flickr or YouTube; and
- social feedback – ratings, rankings and commentaries, such as customer product reviews on Amazon.com.

The recent booming of social media and the popular availability of digital communication channels have redefined the traditional ways that knowledge workers approach their work. Since social technologies promote, facilitate and accelerate the flow of information, more emphasis is placed on cooperation between knowledge workers and experts.

Ideally, effective teams should bring together people with three kinds of expertise:

- the "think" component that focuses on uncovering relevant patterns of customer behaviors, sentiments and buying preferences from a vast repository of internal and external data sources;
- the "feel" component that is made up of social media subject matter experts, digital content creators, and customer engagement specialists, who continually maintain communications to facilitate the buying journey; and
- the "do" aspect that focuses on information technologies, systems and infrastructures that empower organizations to engage with customers by onboarding them instantly, minimizing labor-intensive and error-prone business processes, improving customer service levels and anticipating buying sentiments based on real-time predictive analytics [10].

Adaptive case management is designed to facilitate the implementation of dynamic and flexible processes involving these three categories of knowledge. An approach whereby business process owners can directly and immediately begin to apply social networking mechanisms to work with specific business cases – e.g. by creating definitions of immediate solutions and sharing them with colleagues – may mark a real breakthrough in business process management.

SACM helps companies empower their workforce through effective collaboration, engaging with experts and clients, and cultivating trust by focusing on, and taking advantage of, human-centered experiences. One of its greatest strengths is that it gives ample opportunities for ad hoc idea and file sharing. It almost intrinsic to SACM environments to embrace team places where groups can share content and ideas through files, wikis, blogs, calendars, discussion forums, etc. Social software embeds case processing in a social setting, thus enhancing the standard work environment. Applying social software directly to managing business cases is an underpinning principle of what is referred to as Enterprise 2.0 or social case management.

An AIIM (Association for Information and Image Management) study contends that content variety is a key aspect of case management, and that social media can be of relevance in communicating with the young customer as well as in tackling incidents where some actors may be unable to stay online. This may be why social networking tools prove effective in coping with business cases where the process trajectory cannot be predicted or the decision situation is too complex. An example can be found in the Gartner study of Cemex, the giant Mexican concrete manufacturer that was mandated to implement green technologies and alternative fuels. Using a social process, the company was able to identify outliers who had already begun to pioneer such steps and involve them in fostering change throughout the organization [11].

In knowledge discovery and business development contexts, some technologies – such as e.g. wiki – serve primarily to improve communication between employees, customers, and external partners. While some look to finding a social vehicle to change the way their processes engage customers at runtime, others look to doing social mining in order to transform the way their processes work.

A case management paradigm combining social mechanisms with the established BPM toolkit can make a lot of difference to the way business applications handle work. It can not only raise the efficiency of the processing methods being used, but also help expose and swiftly distribute new information, from emergent trends to best practices. Rather than being merely platforms on which to do work, business applications become platforms for innovation.

Social systems mostly draw on existing patterns, but make them more collaborative and often, as a result, alter their nature, triggering profound changes in the way people work. For example, blogs do not just make the writing of newspapers more collaborative, they completely transform the way information is spread; a wiki is not just about getting people to collaboratively write books that are published in the traditional manner, but it is about eliminating the divide between the author and the reader.

Therefore, thinking about social systems in terms of improving ACM application development should be like thinking of using social software to make the writing of newspapers or books more collaborative. This is an approach that might be able to unharness the real power of social software.

4.1   The More Feedback – The Better Business Outcomes

Simply speaking, social ACM can bring more voices into the conversation than would traditional business process management or collaborative case management. The latter would normally involve a small group of people – those actually managing the processes and often referred to as knowledge workers or subject-matter experts. Social ACM, on the other hand, is about bringing in *all* the voices through a network that enables everyone in the organization to see everything and open a dialog to have a say or provide feedback. As Forrester Research Senior Analyst Clay Richardson has it, "… it makes the assumption that the knowledge and innovation is in the business and that you want to get everyone engaged" [11]. Social tools ensure that everyone can get involved if only they wish to: even those who never get to convene with senior management or those who happen to miss a critical meeting can stay on top of recent developments, see what is being changed or suggested, and post comments.

Participation in case processing is social in nature. Knowledge workers are mostly team members who will discuss and collaborate with others and who will want to know other people's thoughts. They will therefore appreciate an opportunity to consult other stakeholders, obtain feedback and exploit their co-workers' ideas in optimizing their actions and processes. Knowledge workers are not to be seen as automatons working on a factory floor, but as humans with social and emotional needs to be satisfied, and with aspirations to learn and progress.

It is for this reason that social networking functionalities and ad hoc collaboration capabilities – such as instant messaging, wikis, discussion forums, etc. – are increasingly often found in ACM and BPM products, added on top of a structured solution to leverage some of its benefits.

4.2   The Challenges and Benefits of Social Case Management

Social case management can be seen as "the practice and process of actively involving all stakeholders (employees and partners as well as customers and prospects) into a business process management endeavor through the use of social software and its participatory cultures" [12]. The most commonly acknowledged benefits of migrating from a traditional case or business process management paradigm to one driven by social networking is the leveraging (via social networking mechanisms) of collective intelligence, expertise and experience in joint design, production, decision making or problem solving. However, few perceive that, compared to old-school business processing, social ACM embraces and impacts a far more complex organizational ecosystem, since it engages a large and heterogeneous group of actors and behaviors, aiming to achieve a higher quantity, quality, variety, and timeliness of contributions [13].

Hence, the following could be said to be the salient features of social ACM:

- use of social technologies and techniques in business process development and improvement: employing social software to aid the development of e.g. case processing applications means that knowledge workers/developers are the ones who take advantage of social media to boost their productivity; and

- collaborative design and iteration of cases: the use of social software in case processing makes a lot of sense as it allows a wider group of stakeholders to influence, and contribute to, process design.

The organizers of the Workshop on Business Process Management and Social Software believe that "… social software is a new paradigm…" and take note of how the business place is transformed by its wider use: "… more and more enterprises regard social software as a means for further improvement of their business processes and business models. For example, they integrate their customers into product development by using blogs to capture ideas for new products and features. Thus, business processes have to be adapted to new communication patterns between customers and the enterprise: for example, the communication with the customer is increasingly a bi-directional communication with the customer and among the customers. Social software also offers new possibilities to enhance business processes by improving the exchange of knowledge and information, to speed up decisions, etc. Social software is based on four principles: weak ties, social production, egalitarianism and mutual service provisioning" [14].

Making the most of social software stands for individuals being able to produce, publish and run their own case management applications. It means collaboration at design phase and all the way through to collective effort using the final product.

5 Case Studies

5.1 Social ACM in Practice

Given the nature of ACM, it should be perceived, almost by definition, as much more open than traditional BPM tools and a lot more adequate for social networking and collaboration.

The workings of social media and collaborative environments can be illustrated with the following examples of actions undertaken by the knowledge worker who embarks on a new case and finds that the available information is insufficient to proceed with the decision process:

- make use of knowledge in the form of external social networking tools (e.g. an Internet discussion forum for law/legal issues);
- use instant messaging to chat with internal subject matter experts and subsequently add the conversation history to case evidence (an artifact);
- search for relevant documents in an internal repository based on a folksonomy and social tagging;
- learning by experience and adaptation, add elements to the process instance (e.g. solution templates, views, process definitions) to optimize case processing;
- utilize content analytics to explore information sources such as social networks (Twitter, Facebook, etc.) with a view to supporting the decision making process; and
- on completing steps like those detailed above, share comments or disseminate the information to make it available to other knowledge workers handling similar cases.

For example, on having handled several similar cases, KWs in the back office might recognize that some software checks appear regularly, so it would be best to include them in a template. At this point, it should be borne in mind that their reasoning on future cases is augmented through learning from previous cases. KWs also understand that if they can make a template available to their colleagues, they will be able to ask their co-workers once in a while to perform the checks for them – and save some time in this way. Therefore, they will search for a case that contains such checks, copy the part into a new template, and edit the template to supply instructions that other KWs can follow. KWs then share their knowledge by publishing that template across the library section for their group, so that other KWs can access it. If a similar case comes up, KWs can copy the template into their case. This example highlights all of the CBR phases at once. In effect, KWs can save some of their time while at the same time sharing their knowledge and providing guidance to the other team members through case patterns/templates.

Users of templates can rate them, tag them, and make suggestions for improvements. A template can be promoted to a policy status in order to gain more visibility to KM. The CBR process ensures that templates are not promoted to policies until they have been reviewed and approved by the participants and parties involved. The same is true of discarding templates/policies that are no longer in use. Hence, none but practically proven cases can become templates, and the set of templates is continually improved: new templates are created on an as-needed basis while obsolete templates are disposed of. This implies that CBR is adapted in iterative cycles, and that the therefore the CBR adaptation process can be seen as a continuous improvement cycle. As a consequence, the template library can be adjusted to new processes and new business situations as necessary. One of the ways in which this can be accomplished is by combining ACM features with the CBR idea to automate a case processing solution.

5.2   Case Management – Decision Support at the Operational Level

An important argument for choosing the ACM approach is that it makes it possible to build and handle processes whose trajectory is not known or pre-defined in advance. Law court cases provide a perfect example – in such cases, users must be able to create and modify tasks within the process at any time. It is such users that are designated as knowledge workers.

The Office of the Attorney General of Texas (OAG) has 25 divisions across the state of Texas, altogether processing hundreds of thousands of cases annually. Prior to the introduction of ACM, case-related documents were stored locally at each of the offices and were not secured before storage. At the same time, processes were far from coherent or consistent, which is highlighted by the fact that summary reports would be compiled manually, with no support from the system whatsoever.

What the Office needed to accomplish in the first place was therefore streamlining the processes operationally and hence increasing the staff's efficiency and productivity by unleashing their the potential. It was hoped that the improvements would result in time and cost savings.

Perceived Benefits. The OAG of Texas has applied an ACM solution to the law domain in handling legal cases (legal matter management), employing it to set up a system for recording and processing information related to cases. Arguably the greatest benefit of the system is that it provides support to the performance of ad hoc activities as well as to tasks that arise dynamically in processing a case. Overall, the solution has streamlined legal matter management by giving each knowledge worker a central access point to all relevant information (pertinent correspondence, official rulings and decisions, etc.) required in processing a case. In addition, the adoption of a uniform system-wide scheme for case naming and classification has facilitated work with case files. The information retrieval system has also been upgraded to include full-text search and natural language processing. The system's key functionalities are:

- a case tracking system;
- a secure central document repository;
- an automated information retention policy; and
- an automated reporting layer.

Business Outcomes. The OAG has achieved a higher level of advancement and maturity by standardizing the case management process through a centralized ACM platform. The platform's deployment has led to an increase in staff productivity. As a further result, task handling at the OAG has become much more efficient. For example, the Office has been able to reduce information access/retrieval times by 97 % – from more than 15 min to around 30 s. Further, the process of identifying, locating and securing data has been accelerated by nearly 99 % (from more than 2 days to 15 min). In addition, the time needed to create a case file has been cut down by 71 %.

6 Conclusions

The new business model associated with ACM proves more effective and capable of satisfying most of the requirements of modern businesses – including support for critical decisions and broad collaboration.

A dynamic management strategy permits concentration and intensification of efforts aimed at supporting decision processes and organizational knowledge building, standing for an ability to respond to even the most extraordinary customer expectations. New business demands are reflected in the evolution of ACM platforms and their components (DSS, collaboration/social networking mechanisms). Modern ACM platforms are therefore evolving rapidly. Owing to their process-orientedness, they offer more possibilities of establishing systemic, institutional ties between a company's core business activities, decision support and knowledge management.

Adaptive management initiatives are frequently undertaken in multi-stakeholder settings, where the most immediate barriers to success prove to be organizational and social: their adaptability is frequently compromised by executive and line managers', as well as process leaders', inability to deliver a timely response to rapid changes in the business environment.

Business applications can drive superior outcomes by taking a work-focused approach that brings to bear whatever technologies are needed to facilitate the work, rather than a technology-focused approach. That is why social ACM should be highlighted as a promising business platform of new generation case management. Adaptive case management, because of its more work-focused mandate, provides a way to incorporate social tools into a business context.

SACM can not only improve the efficiency of the processing methods being used, but also help expose and propagate new information swiftly, from emergent trends to best practices. The combination of social networking and adaptive case management can empower workers and allow organizations to substantially increase staff productivity. Importantly enough, it does so not by turning them into cogs in a machine, but rather by giving them as many opportunities as possible to use their accumulated skills and knowledge, even in areas that might normally be outside the scope of their jobs. At the same time, organizations can increase staff satisfaction, elevate their level of engagement, and boost their sense of contribution as well as their awareness of that contribution.

Collaborative adaptive approaches, on the other hand, underscore flexibility and scalability, or the capability of growing. Community involvement accounts for a sense of ownership and a feeling of accomplishment in working together to solve a problem. This approach offers a path to truly changing the way applications are developed and managed by moving towards an application development process that is user-generated and just-in-time, whereby applications evolve with the needs of the business in real time rather than only at design time.

An enterprise that is run in line with the ACM concept will be intrinsically capable of combining its core business activities with an ability to create and review innovative solutions daily, at the same time mitigating the risks and challenges stemming from business process optimization. For example, since process operators are allowed to change their processes dynamically, the enterprise management system becomes open to creative initiatives from staff at large and there is hardly any risk of chaos arising from spontaneous changes to operating properties. In addition, because it is possible to track the effects of changes as they emerge, information on which practices and solutions deliver the best results and which produce the worst can be immediately appended to organizational collective knowledge. This stands for day-to-day improvements and adaptations to business processes relying on the best knowledge of a large portion of personnel and becoming validated through feedback from customers.

A fundamental principle of ACM is associated with the belief that any organization should continually collect, process and utilize knowledge on the mechanisms governing its business environment, and that such an approach is not only most effective, but simply essential if you want to be able to respond to customers' expectations and keep pace with the rapid changes in today's marketplace. ACM is often said to be focused on building a learning organization. Improvements to an organization's internal processes indeed take place across several dimensions and involve executives and staff alike.

ACM represents state-of-the-art in business process management, comprising integrated subsystems responsible for knowledge management and decisions support. Its superiority has been demonstrated by multiple business case studies.

References

1. Osuszek, L., Stanek, S.: Knowledge management and decision support in adaptive case management platforms. In: Ganzha, M., Maciaszek, L., Paprzycki, M. (eds.) Proceedings of the 2015 Federated Conference on Computer Science and Information Systems, Annals of Computer Science and Information Systems, vol. 5, pp. 1539–1549 (2015)
2. Van der Alst, W.M.P., Berens, P.J.S.: Beyond workflow management: product-driven case handling. In: Ellis, S., Rodden, T., Zigurs, I. (eds.) International ACM SIG GROUP Conference on Supporting Group Work (GROUP 2001), pp. 42–51. ACM Press, New York (2001)
3. Drucker, P.F.: Management Challenges for the 21st Century, p. 157. Harper Collins, New York (1999)
4. Swenson, K.D.: The nature of knowledge work. In: Swenson, K.D. (ed.) Mastering the Unpredictable: How Adaptive Case Management Will Revolutionize the Way That Knowledge Workers Get Things Done. Meghan-Kiffer Press, Tampa (2010)
5. Van der Aalst, W.M.P., Weske, M., Grünbauer, D.: Case handling: a new paradigm for business process support. Data Knowl. Eng. **53**, 129–162 (2005). Elsevier
6. White, M.: Delivering case management with BPM in the public sector: combining knowledge with process. In: Fischer, L. (ed.) 2009 BPM and Workflow Handbook: Spotlight on Government, pp. 65–80. Future Strategies Inc, New York (2009)
7. Fischer, G., Giaccardi, E., Ye, Y., Sutcliffe, A.G., Mehandjiev, N.: Meta-design: a manifesto for end-user development. Commun. ACM **47**(9), 33–37 (2004)
8. Holsapple, C.W.: DSS architecture and types. In: Burstein, F., Holsapple, C.W. (eds.) International Handbooks on Information Systems, Handbook on Decision Support Systems 1 – Basic Themes, pp. 163–190. Springer, Heidelberg (2008)
9. Adam, F.: Experimentation with organisation analyser, a tool for the study of decision making networks in organisations. In: Humphreys, P., Bannon, L., McCosh, A., Migliarese, P., Pomerol, J.-C. (eds.) Implementing Systems for Supporting Management Decisions, pp. 1–20. Chapman & Hall, London (1996)
10. Perry, A.: The value of adaptive case management in the experience economy, thrive: blog for finance professionals, 8th August 2014. http://www.lexmark.com/en_us/solutions/financial-process-automation/blog/2014/08/ (Accessed on 30th November 2015)
11. Earls, A.: Social BPM, collaborative BPM: sorting out which to use when ebizQ, 5th April 2012. http://www.ebizq.net/topics/social_bpm/features/13347.html (Accessed on 30th November 2015)
12. Benefits and Challenges of Social BPM. OpenKnowledge: Digital Transformation Strategy & Consultancy, 31st March 2014. http://www.open-knowledge.it/benefits-and-challenges-of-social-bpm/ (Accessed on 30th November 2015]
13. Pflanzl, N., Vossen, G.: Challenges of social business process management. In: 47th Hawaii International Conference on System Sciences, pp. 3868–3877 (2014)
14. Nurcan, S., Schmidt, R.: Introduction. In: Rinderle-Ma, S., Sadiq, S., Leymann, F. (eds.) BPM 2009. LNBIP, vol. 43, pp. 197–199. Springer, Heidelberg (2010)

Process of Ontology Design for Business Intelligence System

Helena Dudycz(✉) and Jerzy Korczak

Wrocław University of Economics,
Komandorska 118/120, 53-345 Wrocław, Poland
{helena.dudycz,jerzy.korczak}@ue.wroc.pl

Abstract. Business Intelligence systems tend more and more towards semantically rich functionalities. One of the main artefacts to create a semantic network is the ontology. There are many methods describing the procedure of creating ontology for information solutions. The article presents the approach to the conceptualisation of the financial knowledge for a Business Intelligence system. The content of the knowledge is focused on essential financial concepts and relationships related to the management of small and medium enterprises (SME). That includes the illustration of the process of conceptualization of the financial ontology, which can be implemented in the Business Intelligence system.

Keywords: Financial knowledge · Ontology · Financial indicators · Decision support system · Business Intelligence system

1 Introduction

Useful, adequate and easy to interpret information is a key prerequisite in the process of decision-making. However, available information systems concentrate mainly on providing information reflecting semantic relationships between examined economic and financial indicators. In order to facilitate the process of data analysis, the usage of the ontology is proposed as a model of financial knowledge about the analysis of indicators.

The decision-makers of small and medium enterprises (SMEs), in comparison to managers of big companies, may not have access to all essential strategic information. Usually, financial expertise is either not available or too expensive. Big companies have at their disposal strategic consultation and possess standard procedures to solve problems in the case of essential changes in the business environment. For financial and personnel reasons, most SMEs cannot afford these types of facilities. It should be noted that SMEs operate in a definitely more uncertain and risky environment than big enterprises, because of a complex and dynamic market that has much more important impact on SMEs' financial situation than on big companies [1].

In general, most existing Business Intelligence (BI) and Executive Information Systems (EIS) provide various functionalities for data aggregation and visualization. Many reports and papers in this domain underline that decision makers expect new ICT solutions to interactively provide not only relevant and up-to-date information on the

© Springer International Publishing Switzerland 2016
E. Ziemba (Ed.): FedCSIS 2015, LNBIP 243, pp. 17–28, 2016.
DOI: 10.1007/978-3-319-30528-8_2

financial situation of their companies, but also explanations that take into account the contextual relationships.

Our research concentrates on two essential issues: the conceptualization of financial ontology and the use of the semantic network in decision making. The structure of the paper is as follows. In the next section, the functional schema of the BI system with ontology applications is discussed. Section 3 describes the process of ontology development, in particular the actual design of the ontology. This concept of the presented method is based on: (1) a critical analysis of literature, (2) built ontologies of economic and financial indicators, which were realized during the period 2012–2013. A case study in Sect. 4 illustrates an example of design and use of financial ontology. To show the reasoning, a case for explanation of financial data is specified. In the conclusion, the future research directions are indicated.

2 Domain Knowledge in Business Intelligence Systems

The Business Intelligence (BI) system is used for the analysis of all basic areas of an enterprise's activities, such as, e.g., finance and accounting, manufacturing, logistics, marketing, sales, and customer relationships. These applications provide many reports containing valuable information in each statement. Retrieval information from these reports is eased by the use of appropriate forms of its presentation, and of a friendly and easy user interface. Nowadays, decision-makers want not only to look at static reports or even ad hoc reports, but want also easy-to-use tools to assess goals and key performance indicators to identify any chances of advancement and threats of breakdown. The usefulness of the BI system is not related to the amount of generated information, but to the provision of required information at the right moment. These were basic motives for developing and applying a new technology and knowledge representation in the BI system. In the literature, the development of BI systems towards BI 2.0 (using semantic search) is described (see [2–4]). This system is focused on the semantic analysis of data, using data and information from multiple sources (including external sources). One of the main artifacts to create a semantic network is the ontology, because the architecture of BI 2.0 has new components, such as ontologies and service ontologies (see [2]). The ontologies are used to create the necessary knowledge models for defining and explaining functionalities in analytical tools. Using ontologies and semantic networks for a visual interface to support an information search in the BI system may help to reduce the following weaknesses of management information systems (see [4, 5]):

- lack of support in defining business rules for getting proactive information and support in consulting in the process of decision making;
- lack of a semantic layer describing relations between different economic topics;
- lack of support in presenting the information of different users (employees) and their individual needs;
- difficulty in rapidly modifying existing databases and data warehouses in the case of new analytic requirements.

In Fig. 1, a functional architecture of the information system is presented, with ontology applications. Various mechanisms can be seen for extracting source data from transactional systems (ETL), the data warehouse, and external sources. However, the available solutions – in particular the standard analyses, reports and analytical statements generated by the system – are complemented by economic and financial knowledge (most importantly ontologies). This enables a dynamic, interactive analysis of key economic and financial indicators. Such an architecture concept was used in the project InKoM[1] (a wide review of the issue is presented in: [6, 7]). This solution will significantly extend existing BI and EIS functionalities.

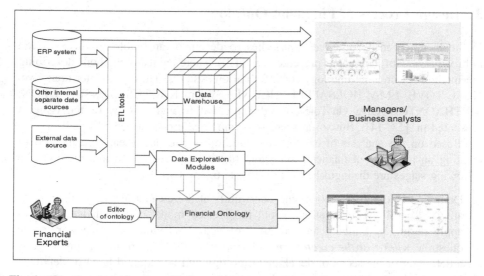

Fig. 1. Functional architecture of information system with ontology applications (source: based on [1, p. 57]).

To support the analysis, SME decision makers need economic and financial knowledge. The scope of required knowledge in the Intelligent Dashboard for Managers was arbitrarily divided by experts into six selected areas, namely: Cash Flow at Risk, Comprehensive Risk Measurement, Early Warning Models, Credit Scoring, Financial Market, and General Financial Knowledge [6].

The system that enables semantic information retrieval should be intuitive to use or easy to understand. For managers, the presentation layer is the most critical aspect of a BI system, since it broadly shapes their core understanding of the data displayed [8]. The basic assumption of navigation is that managers should be able to view focus and

[1] This research was supported by the National Research and Development Centre within the Innotech Pprogram (track In-Tech), grant agreement no. INNOTECH-K1/IN1/34/153437/NCBR/12. The name of this project, called was the Intelligent Dashboard for Managers, which was conducted by a consortium led by the Wrocław University of Economics, Poland, and the other principal member is the company UNIT4 TETA BI Center. The project was realized during the period 2012–2014.

context areas at the same time to present an overview of the whole knowledge structure [9].

The ontology of financial knowledge is the foundation of creating a semantic network. In our project, special attention was paid to the role of the visualization of a semantic network, which is not only a tool for presenting data, but also provides an interface allowing interactive visual information retrieval (see inter alia [10, 11]). Working from the displayed semantic structure of a built-in ontology of financial and economic knowledge, it is possible to interactively choose topics or relations, to change the area of presented details, and to access relevant source data.

3   Design Process of Financial Ontology

In the literature many different approaches to design of an ontology can be found (a broad review of the issue is presented in: [12]). There are many methods describing the methods of creating ontology for information systems. These are, inter alia: Cyc, KBSI, TOVE, EMA, HOLSAPPLE, HCONE, System KACTUS, SENSUS, UPON, METHAONTOLOGIA, On-To-Knowledge method (a wide review of the issue is presented in: [13, 14]). But so far there is no single approach accepted by all.

Based on the analysis of existing methodologies and our research, a method of creating an ontology of financial indicators has been proposed. In this method, the following stages are distinguished (see also: [1, 6, 15, 16]):

1. Definition of the goals, scope, and constraints of the created ontology. While creating an ontology, assumptions about the created model of knowledge that will apply during its building have to be provided. That requires an answer to the question: *what will the created ontology be used for?* The result of this stage is a definition of the scope of developed ontology and its required level of detail.
2. Conceptualization of the ontology. Independently of the field that is to be modeled by using an ontological approach, it is the most important stage in creating a model based on ontology (see inter alia [17, p. 2036]). It includes the identification of all concepts, definition of classes and their hierarchic structures, modeling relations, identification of instances, specification of axioms, and rules of reasoning. The result of this stage is the ontology's model of the defined area of financial knowledge.
3. Verification of the ontology's correctness by experts. In this stage, the constructed ontology is verified by experts who did not participate in the process of conceptualization. Verification is carried out in two steps. The first concerns a formal verification of the specified ontology (e.g. incorrect relations are indicated) with the use of a given editor. The second step is carried out by experts from the given field and concerns content verification, which includes verification of the correctness of topics' definitions, correctness of taxonomic topics, and correctness of relational dependences between topics. In the proposed method of financial knowledge, the verification and the validation were separated in accordance with the approach used in software engineering (see [18]). The result of this stage is the verified ontology.

4. Encoding the ontology concerns the knowledge description, using a formal language or an editor of ontology. Two basic stages of encoding of ontology are: (1) entering all topics and creating a taxonomy of these topics, and (2) entering all other types of relations between topics. The result of this stage is the encoded ontology.

5. Validation and evaluation of the built ontology. In this stage, the encoded ontology is checked against the needs of the managers. Validation is carried out in three areas. Firstly, validation of usefulness and correctness of the created ontology is provided by experts (managers) who will potentially use it. Secondly, evaluation of the application with a created ontology is carried out by managers. Finally, the validation of predefined use cases is carried out. That requires an answer to the question: *will the created ontology be useful for the managers who will use it?* The result of this stage is validated ontology of financial knowledge.

Figure 2 shows the design process of an ontology of financial knowledge. The presented method is characterized by iterative design.

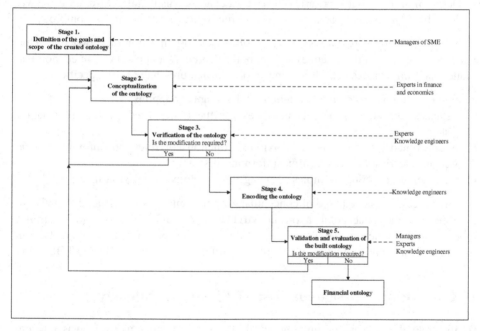

Fig. 2. Design process for an ontology of financial knowledge. source: own elaboration.

The important stage in the described process is the conceptualization of financial indicators. This is carried out by an expert, or in collaboration with an expert, responsible for creating the model of knowledge (see inter alia [17, p. 2036]). In the literature [13, 14]) the following phases in the conceptualization of the ontology of financial knowledge are shown (see also: [6]):

a. Identification and definition of all topics. A topic, representing any concept, is "a syntactic construct that corresponds to the expression of a real-world in a computer system" [10, p. 60]. A topics' list is determined by experts in a given domain of economic knowledge. These topics include, beside their names, also their synonyms and descriptions.

b. Creating a taxonomy of topics. Specification of taxonomic relations between distinguished topics and defining classes and subclasses. In general, these relationships describe the topics generalization. The description of a taxonomy can be presented in graphic or tabular form. An interesting approach to creating a taxonomy is proposed in METHONTOLOGIA (see i.e. [13]).

c. Definition of all other types of relations between topics, notably the basic relationships aggregate of (Aggregate – Member), was defined. Moreover, within each ontology, additional relations can be defined.

d. The list of all the individual relationships existing in the ontology. The list includes: the name of the relationship, source topic, and target topic.

e. Description of functions and rules. This description contains: name, input, output, initial and final conditions, and definition of operations.

f. Description of usage scenarios. Usage scenarios, also called use case views, describe demonstration analyses of economic topics occurring in this ontology.

Building an ontology always denotes analysis and organization of knowledge. That work has required multi-domain expertise, both theoretical and practical, in economics, finance, and informatics. The following important features have been specified:

- type of relations: to define taxonomic and semantic relations;
- instances: the sources of data instances for the topics used by the information system;
- axioms/functions/rules: to define axioms, functions or rules, so ontology can be used in inferring knowledge from information system;
- use cases; to describe examples of using the ontology in decision making.

The process presented here of conceptualizing the ontology of financial knowledge is closest to the conceptualization in METHONTOLOGY. Except for a similar approach to the conceptualization of the ontology, our proposed method of creating an ontology of financial knowledge is completely different from the METHONTOLOGY.

4 Case Study – Design and Use of Financial Ontology

To illustrate the process of ontology design a case of sales analysis was chosen. Assume that the company's efficiency is evaluated using the Return on Sales (ROS) indicator. This measure is helpful to management by providing insight into the profit structure of sales. The manager knows that the increase of ROS indicates that the company is growing more efficiently, while the decrease of ROS signals financial troubles. Managers also use the ROS indicator to identify market opportunities and areas where they could increase the volume of sales.

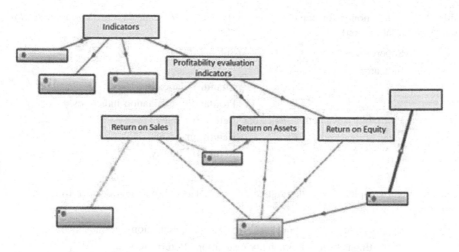

Fig. 3. Space of profitability indicators (source: own elaboration).

Table 1. The example of topics list (source: own elaboration).

Name	Synonym	Description
Return on sales	ROS	A ratio widely used to evaluate a company's operational efficiency. ROS is also known as a firm's "operating profit margin. It is computed using the formula: Net_profit/Revenues_from_sales
		Recommendation: Compare a company's ROS over time to look for trends, and compare it to other companies in the same sector.

The design of the financial ontology related to the ROS indicator can be done as follows:

1. Identification and definition of all topics. Figure 3 shows the start of identification and definition of the domain of profitability evaluation indicators. Table 1 presents the example of the description of the topics list.
2. Creating a taxonomy of topics. Table 2 presents the taxonomy for topic *Indicators* and topic *Profitability evaluation indicators.*
3. Definition of all other types of relations between topics. In this ontology, the basic relationship *aggregate of (Aggregate – Member)* is defined. Moreover, additional relations are defined, for example: *potential growth, proportional positive/negative change, is the sum, is the quotient, engagement.*
4. The list of all the user defined relationships existing in the ontology. The description of a taxonomy can be presented in graphic or tabular form. Table 3 presents the example of the description of the relationships. Figure 4 shows the definition of the domain of profitability evaluation indicators. In this figure there are two types of lines between topics: (1) the solid line represents a relation *Subclass – of* and (2) the dashed line represents the experts' defined relations.

Table 2. The taxonomy for topic *Indicators* and topic *Profitability evaluation indicators* (Source: own elaboration).

Superclass	Subclass
Indicators	Debt indicators
	Liquidity indicators
	Profitability evaluation indicators
Profitability evaluation indicators	Return on Sales
	Return on Assets
	Return on Equity

Table 3. The example of the description of the relationships: *engagement* (Source: own elaboration).

Name	Synonym	Description
Engagement	Profitability evaluation	Return on Sale
Engagement	Profitability evaluation	Return on Assets
Engagement	Profitability evaluation	Return on Equity

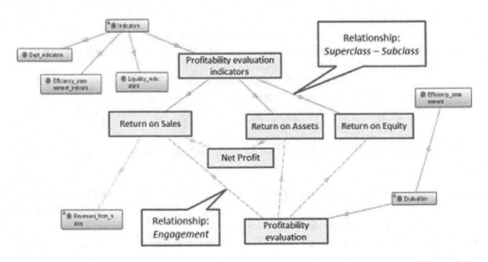

Fig. 4. The domain definition of profitability evaluation indicators (source: own elaboration).

5. Description of functions and rules. The definition describes how to compute and interpret their values. This description can contain: name, input, output, initial and final pre-conditions, and definition of formula (see also: [9]). The following description specifies the example of the indicator *Return on Sales*:

Name:
   Indicator Return on Sales (ROS)

Input:
   Result of Net profit (NP)
   type: value extracted from Balance Sheet
   Revenues from sales (RS)
   type: number, value extracted from Balance Sheet

Output:
   Return on Sales

Description/formula:
   ROS = NP/ RS

Final conditions:
   if (ROS < value_1)
      Interpretation_1
   else if (value_1 > ROS < value_2)
      Interpretation_2
   else if ....
      ....
   else if (ROS > value_n)
      Interpretation_n

6. Description of usage scenarios. One of the important questions is: *what is the performance of sales management?*
   a. The most common way is to look at the sales reports. From the BI system the manager receives the values of the Revenues on Sales in 2013 and 2014 (Fig. 5).
   b. To better understand the situation of the company, he searches in the ontology the concept of Profitability evaluation indicators. One of the available indicators is Return on Sales.
   c. The semantic network shows that the Return on Sales indicator depends on two values: Net profit and Revenues from Sales.
      if (ROS <= 0.10)
         Poor financial situation
      else if (0.10 > ROS <= 0.30)
      Good financial situation
      else
      Very good financial situation
   d. After having computed the ROS for each year, in the ontology he finds the following interpretation of ROS:
   e. Applying the rule the results are as follows:

   For 2013 year : *Poor financial situation, because ROS = 0,08*
   For 2014 year : *Good financial situation, because ROS = 0,11*

Although *Net profit* is lower in 2014 than in 2013, the company achieved a better *Return on Sales*.

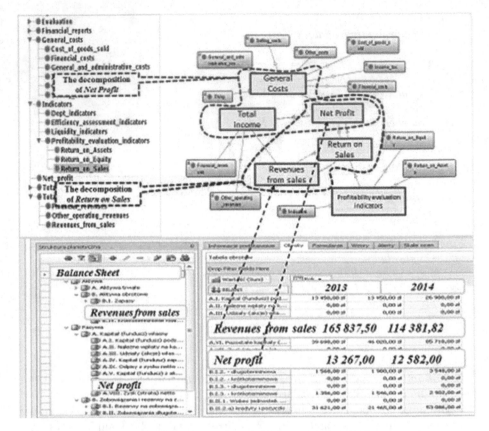

Fig. 5. Ontology and of balance reports extracted from the TETA BI system (source: own elaboration).

f. Using the ontology (Fig. 6) the manager can obtain more information as to which indicators and economic data have an impact on the values of Revenues from sales. This gives the manager the opportunity to search data sources taking into account not only structural dependences, but also the semantic context.

Business data contain a lot of hidden relationships and dependencies that make their understanding and usage difficult. To interpret the values of financial indicators correctly, many measures and ratios need to be examined that either directly or indirectly influence the final result. Explicit visualization not only makes the interpretation of indicators easier, but it also contributes to finding explanations of current values of indicators.

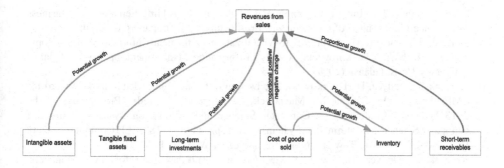

Legend:
- potential growth, i.e. growth of value of first indicator should be accompanied by increasing values of second indicator (green lines),
- proportional growth, i.e. growth of value of first indicator should be accompanied by proportional increasing value of second indicator (blue line),
- proportional positive/negative change, i.e. growth or decrease of value of first indicator causes proportional respectively increase or decrease of second indicator (red line).

Fig. 6. Domain definition of *Revenues from sales* (source: own elaboration).

5 Conclusion

The use of a financial ontology seems to be a promising extension for Business Intelligence systems. It not only improves the efficiency of analysis, but also increases the capacity of understanding of financial data. This paper presents the approach to the ontology of the financial knowledge design process. The stages of ontology design were described and illustrated using the Business Intelligence system.

The research on using the presented approach of creating a financial ontology, despite its initial character, is challenging. Many extensions and applications of this work are possible, notably on content understanding, semantic search, interface adaptation. Current work is directed toward the development of smart navigation throughout the very large field of ontological concepts, and the method of financial ontology updating by adding new concepts either through a SME manager or data mining algorithms.

References

1. Korczak, J., Dudycz, H., Dyczkowski, M.: Specification of financial knowledge – case of intelligent dashboard for managers. Bus. Inf. Wrocław Univ. Econ. Res. Pap. **2**(28), 56–76 (2013)
2. Nelson, G.S.: Business Intelligence 2.0: Are we there yet? SAS Global Forum 2010 (2010). http://support.sas.com/resources/papers/proceedings10/040-2010.pdf
3. Raden, N.: Business Intelligence 2.0: Simpler, More Accessible, Inevitable, 01 February 2007. http://www.informationweek.com/news/software/bi/197002610

4. Sell, D., Cabral, L., Motta, E., Domingue, J., Pacheco, R.: Adding Semantics to Business Intelligence (2008). http://dip.semanticweb.org/documents/WebSpaperOUV2.pdf
5. Korczak, J., Dudycz, H.: Approach to visualization of financial information using topic maps. In: Kubiak, B.F., Korowicki, A. (eds.) Information Management, pp. 86–97. Gdańsk University Press, Gdańsk (2009)
6. Korczak, J., Dudycz, H., Dyczkowski, M.: Design of financial knowledge in dashboard for SME managers. In: Ganzha, M., Maciaszek, L., Paprzycki, M. (eds.) Proceedings of the 2013 Federated Conference on Computer Science and Information Systems. Annals of Computer Science and Information Systems, vol. 1, pp. 1111–1118. IEEE Computer Society Press, AlamitosPolskie Towarzystwo Informatyczne, Warsaw, Los (2013)
7. Korczak, J., Dudycz, H., Dyczkowski, M.: Intelligent dashboard for SME managers, architecture and functions. In: Ganzha, M., Maciaszek, L., Paprzycki, M. (eds.) Proceedings of the Federated Conference on Computer Science and Information Systems FedCSIS 2012, pp. 1003–1007, Polskie Towarzystwo Informatyczne. IEEE Computer Society Press, Warsaw, Los Alamitos (2012)
8. Wise, L.: The Emerging Importance of Data Visualization, part 1, 29 October 2008. http://www.dashboardinsight.com/articles/business-performance-management/the-emerging-importance-of-data-visualization-part-1.aspx
9. Smolnik, S., Erdmann, I.: Visual navigation of distributed knowledge structures in groupware – base organizational memories. Bus. Process Manage. J. **9**(3), 261–280 (2003)
10. Grant, B.L., Soto, M.: Topic maps, RDF graphs, and ontologies visualization. In: Geroimenko, V., Chen, C. (eds.) Visualizing the Semantic Web, XML-based Internet and information visualization, 2nd edn, pp. 59–79. Springer, London (2010)
11. Wienhofen, L.W.M.: Using graphically represented ontologies for searching content on the semantic web. In: Geroimenko, V., Chen, C. (eds.) Visualizing the semantic web, XML-based Internet and information visualization, 2nd edn, pp. 137–153. Springer, London (2010)
12. Smith, B.: Ontology and Information Systems (2010). http://ontology.buffalo.edu/ontology%28PIC%29.pdf
13. Gomez-Perez, A., Corcho, O., Fernandez-Lopez, M.: Ontological Engineering: with Examples from the Areas of Knowledge Management, e-Commerce and the Semantic Web. Springer, London (2004)
14. Noy, F.N., McGuinness, D. L.: Ontology Development 101: A Guide to Creating Your First Ontology (2005). http://www.ksl.stanford.edu/people/dlm/papers/ontology101/ontology101-noy-mcguinness.html
15. Dudycz, H.: The topic map as a visual representation of economic knowledge (in polish). Wydawnictwo Uniwersytetu Ekonomicznego we Wrocławiu, Wrocław (2013)
16. Dudycz, H.: Approach to the conceptualization of an ontology of an early warning system. In: Jałowiecki, P., Łukasiewicz, P., Orłowski, A. (eds.) Information Systems in Management XI, Data Bases, Distant Learning, and Web Solutions Technologies, pp. 29–39 (2011)
17. Almeida, M.B., Barbosa, R.R.: Ontologies in knowledge management support: a case study. J. Am. Soc. Inf. Sci. Technol. **10**(60), 2032–2047 (2009)
18. Sommerville, I.: Software Engineering, 9th edn. Addison-Wesley, Harlow (2010)

Construction and Restructuring of the Knowledge Repository of Website Evaluation Methods

Paweł Ziemba[1]([⊠]), Jarosław Wątróbski[2], Jarosław Jankowski[2],
and Waldemar Wolski[3]

[1] The Jacob of Paradyż University of Applied Sciences in Gorzów Wielkopolski,
Teatralna 25, 66-400 Gorzów Wielkopolski, Poland
pziemba@pwsz.pl
[2] West Pomeranian University of Technology,
Żołnierska 49, 71-210 Szczecin, Poland
{jwatrobski, jjankowski}@wi.zut.edu.pl
[3] University of Szczecin, Mickiewicza 64, 71-101 Szczecin, Poland
wwolski@wneiz.pl

Abstract. Many methods can be employed to evaluate the quality of websites. Although the methods can be used for different purposes and require various assessment approaches it is challenging to select a proper method adequate to the needs. The research presented in the article is focused on building a repository of knowledge about the methods for assessing the quality of a website. The repository in the form of ontologies covers a variety of quality assessment methods and makes their proper selection possible. The proposed approach was verified with major methods and the resulting ontology may act as a repository of domain knowledge.

Keywords: Ontology construction · Ontology integration · Ontology restructuring · Website quality evaluation methods · Principal component analysis

1 Introduction

For companies using commercial websites, the quality of their sites may have a main influence on sale [1]. Poor website quality and poor user experience may be responsible for losses in the number of present customers [1], potential sales, and repeated visits [2]. Consequently, in order to increase profits from e-commerce or online advertising, website owners ought to guarantee only the highest quality experience and services.

The quality of a website can be understood as an attribute determining how well it meets users' demands [3]. One needs to point out that the quality is defined by a model consisting of characteristics and features/criteria describing its different components [4]. In the literature, there are many methods which are used to evaluate the quality of Internet websites. The most formalized methods are: eQual [5], Ahn [6], SiteQual [7], Web Portal Site Quality [8] and Website Evaluation Questionnaire [9]. The methods are commonly used in both academic work [10] and business practice [11].

© Springer International Publishing Switzerland 2016
E. Ziemba (Ed.): FedCSIS 2015, LNBIP 243, pp. 29–52, 2016.
DOI: 10.1007/978-3-319-30528-8_3

By examining various methods some similarity between them was observed: they employ similar characteristics and criteria (models) of quality assessment; the assessment of sites is based on a Likert scale; they also use questionnaires as a source of gaining opinion. Different methods are often based on the same scientific theories and source references, hence the reason for these similarities.

Literature analysis as well as the analysis of fields of practical use of methods and models for the assessment of website quality indicate a research gap. No IT solution, which would make the implementation of the methods possible, and no repository of knowledge were found. The ontological form will provide access to the knowledge about individual assessment methods and paves the way for the computer processing of this knowledge. It is also vital to make the integration of heterogeneous data [12] from a range of assessment methods possible. Consequently, it will also be feasible to evaluate websites through a variety of methods included in the ontology as well as compare individual results of that assessment on one reference plane.

In this original approach, the issue of building such a repository is split into three subproblems which successively concern (1) the construction of the source ontologies, reflecting specific methods for quality assessment; (2) the integration of constructed source ontologies in the target ontology constituting a repository; (3) the restructuring of the ontology which is the result of the integration process and gaining the final form of the repository of knowledge. The concept presented in this article along with the research results are an extension of the approach proposed in [13]. The proposed approach of constructing a repository of knowledge is graphically represented in Fig. 1.

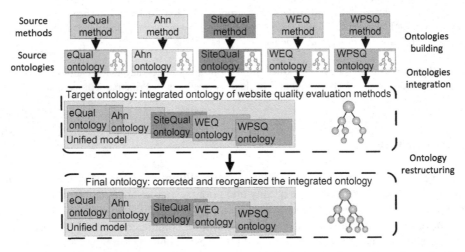

Fig. 1. Proposed approach to build a repository of knowledge by integration of ontologies

This article presents guidelines on how to design an ontology reflecting different quality assessment methods and their integration in the repository of knowledge. Next, on the basis of these assumptions an integration algorithm was formulated. The algorithm was used to integrate and restructure five methods in the repository.

2 Literature Review

The possibility of constructing a repository of knowledge on the methods and models for assessing the quality of Internet services in the form of ontologies confirms its definition, as the term "ontology" in computer science is defined as a "formal specification of conceptualization which allows capturing field knowledge" [14]. The application of ontology will pave the way for constructing notional models explaining the structures of criteria of individual assessment methods and will also make it possible to share and use these structures many times. The analysis of the literature demonstrates that ontologies are employed in the systems and methods of quality assessment. For instance, [15] shows a quality ontology that formalizes the knowledge vital for evaluating the quality of e-government websites. In contrast, [16] proposes the use of an ontology in the quality assessment method of tourist information websites.

There are many methodologies, used in the construction of ontology, which are different in terms of degree of formalization, destination and detail [17, 18]. The most formal and detailed methodologies are Methontology [18] and NeOn [19]. NeOn formalizes the problem of ontology specification to a great extent, whereas Methontology defines the process of conceptualization in detail. In the two methodologies there is also a notion of ontology restructuring. It means correcting and reorganizing the knowledge contained in the conceptual model [18, 20]. In the NeOn methodology, restructuring is presented as one of construction scenarios of an ontology network [19]. However, in the context of Methontology the notion of restructuring functions as a step of ontology re-engineering. Whereas, the re-engineering process can be seen as an extension to Methontology [18]. The restructuring activity contains two phases, that is, analysis and synthesis. In the analysis phase one needs to evaluate ontology in terms of correctness of concept hierarchy, completeness, consistency, conciseness as well as syntactic correctness. The synthesis phase is to correct ontology and to substantiate introduced changes with examples [18, 20].

As far as the integration of ontologies is concerned, it ought to be noted that the concept of integration is not clearly defined in different works. In [21] there are three types of ontology integration: integration and reusing, integration of ontologies into applications, and integration by merging. Integration and reusing is focused on the construction of a new ontology by using existing ontologies. Merging is defined as the unification of multiple ontologies from a given field into a new ontology. Merged ontologies might vary, among other things, in appearance and function, including taxonomy of concepts, a method of implementation, etc. Conflicts arising from these differences ought to be resolved while merging ontologies [21]. Reference [22] stated that ontology created by such a merger should capture all the knowledge contained in the original ontologies. As a result, one new ontology may come into existence which reflects source ontologies or a so-called bridge ontology can be built. The bridge ontology contains the imported ontologies and the relationships between them. Reference [23] defines integrating and merging operations as equivalent. They contain the creation of a new ontology from two or more existing ontologies with overlapping parts. On the other hand, [24] points out that merging refers to joining two same-field ontologies, whereas integration refers to joining two ontologies coming from different fields. What is more, references [22, 24] define the terms as similar to integration, i.e. alignment and mapping. Alignment is an introductory process by which it is possible to integrate an ontology in a widely understandable way. It is a process of discovering similarities between ontologies. These similarities may take place between the concepts, their instances, or similarities of the structure of aligned ontologies [25, 26]. Nonetheless, mapping refers to representing the relationships existing between ontologies. As a consequence, a specification of the semantics' coverage of one ontology by another or, to put it simply, a map describing mutual relationships taking place between the elements of mapped ontologies is received. Relationships between ontologies are kept separately from the ontology and are not their part. Therefore, mapping does not introduce changes in any of the ontologies. Mapping allows receiving a result somewhat similar to bridge ontology. Yet, in bridge ontology, as opposed to mapping, source ontologies and connections between them are stored in one entity. On the basis of the aforementioned definitions a map of their dependences was prepared. The map also includes achievable forms of output data. Figure 2 depicts the map.

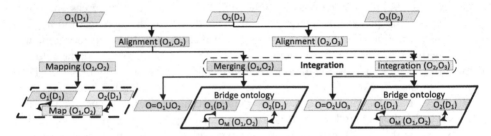

Fig. 2. Map of dependencies between aligning, reproducing, merging and integrating ontologies

3   Research Methodology

3.1   Assumptions Related to the Construction and Integration of Ontologies

In order to maximally simplify integration, it is vital to construct appropriate source ontologies reflecting various website quality assessment methods. Therefore, the design of source ontologies is influenced by the structure of the quality models contained in the assessment methods and the necessity of taking them into consideration in their future integration. As it was shown in Paragraph 1, every evaluation methods is based upon the quality model composed of characteristics and features/criteria presenting its various components. Each of the source ontologies ought to reflect the quality model, which can be represented by a general structure; as illustrated in Fig. 3. As for the structure of the ontology generated by integration, it is assumed that the target (integrated) ontology ought to contain a unified model, which includes all the characteristics and evaluation criteria, and simultaneously the ontology must contain quality models derived from different methods. The ability to determine the source method of a given criterion enables the integration in a knowledge base of heterogeneous data descending from a variety of assessment. The inclusion, in the ontology, of a unified model allows using the ontology as a knowledge repository about evaluation criteria. As a consequence, the ancestor of each criterion should simultaneously be: a model from which the criterion is derived and a unified model comprising characteristics of individual methods. Moreover, if certain criteria are found in many different models of assessment contained in the ontology, then it will have more than two direct ancestors. This issue is illustrated in Fig. 4.

Fig. 3. General quality model

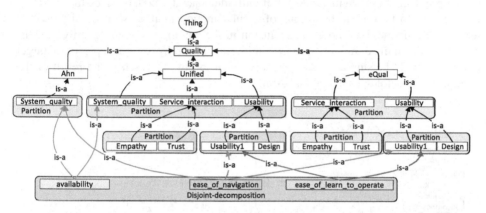

Fig. 4. Issue of criteria membership for the evaluation models included in the target ontology

Figure 4 depicts part of the quality characteristics contained in Ahn and eQual methods. Furthermore, Fig. 4 also includes a hypothetical model, which is a consequence of the unification of the ontologies of these methods. Three further instances of criteria are included, of which "availability" comes from the Ahn method, "ease_of_learn_to_operate" is derived from the eQual method, and "ease_of_navigation" occurs in both methods. Taking into consideration that a unified model for the assessment is to contain the union of assessment models included in the methods eQual and Ahn, it should also include the criteria found in these models. Thus, ancestors of the criterion of "availability" ought to be characteristics included in the Ahn model and a unified model. The criterion "ease_of_learn_to_operate" should be in the form of ancestral characteristics of the eQual model and the unified model. By contrast, the ancestors of the criterion "ease_of_navigation" should be the characteristics of each of the three models. Nonetheless, such a link between criteria with multiple characteristics by means of subsumption relations should not take place, as this would mean redundancy. A redundant occurrence of a subsumption relationship is in turn seen as an error in the integration methods formulated in [23, 27–29].

The problem discussed above can be solved with the use of the idea of construction ontology adopted by the authors. At the stage of the source ontology specification, it was found that the constructed ontology criteria would be separated from the characteristics. This is coherent with the representation of open and closed world assumptions in the ontology [30]. Every quality model contained in the individual assessment models is a closed model, which means that it is complete, and no new characteristic can be added to it. The quality evaluation criteria are an open portion of the world, which means that there may be supplementary criteria that are not yet included in the ontology. As a consequence, the part of ontology reflecting quality models was used to partition taxonomic relationships between concepts taking place at the same level of hierarchy. By contrast, disjoint-decomposition taxonomic relationship was among the criteria used, as these criteria describe the different parts' quality, although there may be other criteria for depicting the quality. This solution allows, in a way, criteria to be independent of quality models. This independence, in turn, is a solution to the presented problem of criteria membership of individual quality models, since that makes it unnecessary to tie criteria by means of a subsumption relation with quality characteristics. Furthermore, it allows for inclusion in the ontology of many quality models, including the unified model. Consequently, the hierarchy of concepts of a target ontology should be similar to structure presented in Fig. 5, which is the result of the integration of ontologies eQual and Ahn.

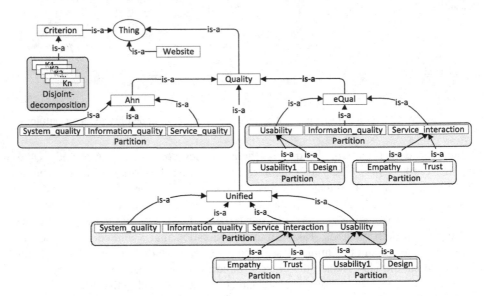

Fig. 5. Hypothetical effect of eQual and Ahn integration in the target ontology

Figure 5 depicts a hypothetical ontology with three quality models eQual, Ahn and model obtained as a result of their unification. Moreover, in the illustrated ontology, regardless of the quality models the criteria belonging to these models were incorporated. To obtain a similar structure as that shown in Fig. 5, a compromise between a fully integrated ontology and a so-called bridge ontology was chosen [22]. The target ontology should contain a fully unified quality model, including the characteristics derived from the source ontologies, along with the methods of assessment, for which the source ontologies were built. Additional models, such as eQual and Ahn comprising quality characteristics, ought to be included in the target ontology in the form of components, which can be simply named as external. This will avoid any inconsistencies, where the same quality characteristics will take place in the different models; for instance, the characteristics of "Information_quality" appearing in the eQual and Ahn models. As a consequence of the full integration, only one such characteristic appears in the resulting ontology, and it would be included in the unified model and the eQual and Ahn models. This would include criteria that belonged to both the eQual and Ahn model. As a result, in each of these models, a union of information quality criteria existed. These models would not be as consistent with their actual structure, as defined in the relevant methods of quality assessment. The solution to this problem, which allows for the incorporation of quality models (e.g. eQual and Ahn) as "external", but simultaneously makes it possible to include them in the target ontology, is to apply for them other IRI identifiers than for a unified ontology.

3.2   Relationship Between Criteria and Characteristics of Quality

Separating the criteria from the quality characteristics concept hierarchies of source ontologies requires that the reasoner infers membership criteria for the characteristics of the subsumption relation linking them. For this purpose, the criteria ought to be linked to characteristics using the appropriate relationship, as presented in Fig. 6.

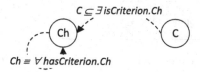

Fig. 6. Proper configuration of relation "isCriterion" and "hasCriterion"

The diagram depicted in Fig. 6 contains concepts Ch and C, where Ch represents any quality characteristics, and C defines any criterion. By analyzing Fig. 6, one can see that the relation "hasCriterion" with a universal quantifier is established as a necessary and sufficient condition ($\equiv$) Ch concept, which is also the domain and scope of this relationship. The relationship "isCriterion" with an existential quantifier is a necessary condition ($\subseteq$) criterion C, for which coverage is a quality characteristic Ch. This solution can be understood as follows: (a) there are certain criteria in the C group that belong to the characteristics of the Ch group ("C isCriterion some Ch"), (b) the characteristics of Ch are only those criteria that belong to the characteristic ("Ch hasCriterion only Ch"). This configuration of the relationship between "isCriterion" and "hasCriterion" allows the reasoner to explore membership criteria to the characteristics and describe this kind of membership as comprising specific criteria in the relevant characteristics. Presented in the form indicated, the relationship is very crucial, as our study showed that a different configuration could lead to erroneous conclusions inferred by the reasoner. An example of such a configuration error in the indicated relationships is depicted in Fig. 7.

Fig. 7. Incorrect configuration of relation "isCriterion" and "hasCriterion"

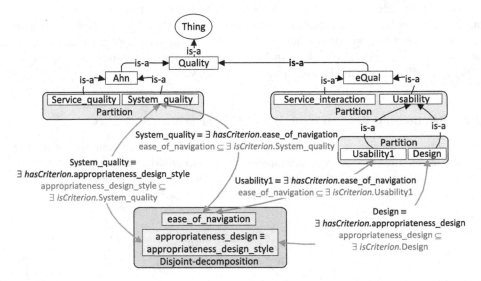

Fig. 8. Relationships between criterion and characteristics which raise the inconsistency inference

Figure 7 presents a configuration in which the relationship "has Criterion" is marked as a necessary and sufficient condition (≡) with an existential quantifier, and the scope of this relationship is a criterion C. This formulation relationship "hasCriterion" could cause an inconsistent ontology at the level of the relationship. This will be explained on the basis of the example provided in Fig. 8. In addition, in the explanation a description of the reasoning process, saved with the use of descriptive logic in expressions (1)–(12), will be used.

$$\text{Usability} \equiv \text{Design} \sqcup \text{Usability1} \tag{1}$$

$$\text{Design} \equiv \neg\text{Usability1} \tag{2}$$

$$\text{Design} \equiv \exists\text{hasCriterion.appropriateness\_design} \tag{3}$$

$$\text{Usability1} \equiv \exists\text{hasCriterion.ease\_of\_navigation} \tag{4}$$

$$\text{System\_quality} \equiv \exists\text{hasCriterion.ease\_of\_navigation} \tag{5}$$

$$\text{System\_quality} \equiv \\ \exists\text{hasCriterion.appropriateness\_design\_style} \tag{6}$$

$$\text{appropriateness\_design} \equiv \\ \text{appropriateness\_design\_style} \tag{7}$$

$$\text{from (4) and (5)} \qquad \text{Usability1} \equiv \text{System\_quality} \tag{8}$$

$$\text{from (7)} \qquad \exists\text{hasCriterion.appropriateness\_design} \equiv \\ \exists\text{hasCriterion.appropriateness\_design\_style} \tag{9}$$

$$\text{from (9), (3) and (6)} \qquad \text{Design} \equiv \text{System\_quality} \tag{10}$$

$$\text{from (8) and (10)} \qquad \text{Design} \equiv \text{System\_quality} \equiv \text{Usability1} \tag{11}$$

$$\text{from (2) and (11)} \qquad ((\text{Design} \equiv \text{Usability1}) \wedge (\text{Design} \equiv \neg\text{Usability1})) \equiv \bot \tag{12}$$

Figure 8 shows a portion of the target ontology, which is a hypothetical result of the integration of eQual and Ahn. The contents of Fig. 8 include the quality characteristics eQual, i.e. "Design" and "Usability1", which make up the partition (i.e. they are disjoint and fully fill the space of the eQual concept), which describes the axioms (1) and (2). In addition, Fig. 8 contains the concepts "ease_of_navigation", "appropriateness_design" and "appropriateness_design_style", which are some of the criteria. The criterion "ease_of_navigation" is used in the Ahn method in the characteristics "System_quality" and the eQual method in the characteristics "Usability1". The criterion "appropriateness_design" occurs in the characteristics of the "Design" eQual method and an "appropriateness_design_style" functions in the characteristics "System_quality" of the Ahn method. In addition, the concepts "appropriateness_design" and "appropriateness_design_style" were considered to be equivalent to (7). Therefore, the concepts relating to design in an integrated ontology will be linked to the relationship "isCriterion" both with the concept "System_quality" as well as "Design". The concept "ease_of_navigation" in an integrated ontology will be linked to the relationship "isCriterion", the concepts "Usability1" and "System_quality". Assuming that:

- in the concepts "Design" and "System_quality," as necessary and sufficient conditions, relations "hasCriterion some appropriateness_design" and "hasCriterion some appropriateness_design_style" (expressions (3) and (6)) would be included,

- in the concepts "Usability1" and "System_quality", as necessary and sufficient conditions, the relationships "hasCriterion some ease_of_navigation" (expressions (4) and (5)) would be covered,

during the integration of ontology, inconsistency would arise. The inconsistency is related to the reasoner's activity and relationships "hasCriterion" which are defined as the necessary and sufficient conditions. If, for example the concept "System_quality" has the necessary and sufficient condition "hasCriterion some ease_of_navigation", then it shall be deemed by the reasoner to be equivalent to other concepts having the same condition. Therefore, it will be deemed to be equivalent to the concept "Usability1" (8). On the other hand, based on a necessary and sufficient condition, "hasCriterion some appropriateness_design_style" shall be deemed equivalent to the concept "Design", which has an equivalent condition "hasCriterion some appropriateness_design" (9) and (10) – here all the time, the subject is the concept "System_quality." The situation will appear when the concept "System_quality" is equivalent to the concepts "Usability1" and "Design" (11). Accordingly, the reasoner also recognizes that these concepts are equivalent (12). It is an important fact that the concepts "Usability1" and "Design" create a partition, so that they are mutually exclusive and cannot be considered equivalent to (12). This raises the inference inconsistency.

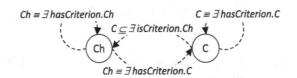

Fig. 9. Result of applying a reflective relations hasCriterion

Another example of an incorrect configuration of the relationship between the characteristics and quality criteria is depicted in Fig. 9.

In this example, the relation "hasCriterion" is given the reflexive property, what allows the reasoner to discover criteria's membership to quality characteristics. In addition, both the domain and range of "hasCriterion" and "isCriterion" were defined. However, owing to the operations the conclusions introduced by the reasoner do not retain the defined taxonomy of concepts. It was presented with the use of descriptive logic in expressions (13)–(19). The dependencies, which were presented in (13), between the concepts result from the concept taxonomy determined while conceptualizing. Furthermore, the dependency between the relation "hasCriterion" in the form of an existential quantifier and the concept "eQual" results from the fact that in a group of concepts "C" the relation functions as a necessary and sufficient condition ($\equiv$). It means that it is set as equivalent to concepts contained in the concept "eQual", therefore, similarly to these concepts, it is contained in the concept "eQual." An expression (14) means that: if a certain concept is related, as a subject, by means of the relation "hasCriterion," to any other concept (a T-class object), then it belongs to the class "eQual." An expression (15) says that any concept is contained in a class whose concepts are reflexively connected to the relation "hasCriterion." In that case, if in the expression (14) an object characterized by a reflective relation (e.g. any criterion) is substituted for any object (a T-class object), then a dependency (16) will be obtained. On the basis of expressions (13) and (16) one can deduce dependencies (17) which are corresponding with the definition of concept equivalence contained in a formula (18). Therefore, the concepts "eQual" and "Thing" are equivalent (19). The taxonomy, included in an expression (13), of the concepts is not kept.

$$\exists hasCriterion.C \subseteq eQual \subseteq Quality \subseteq T \tag{13}$$

$$\exists hasCriterion.T \subseteq eQual \tag{14}$$

$$T \subseteq \exists hasCriterion.Self \tag{15}$$

$$\text{from (14) and (15)} \qquad T \subseteq \exists hasCriterion.Self \subseteq eQual \tag{16}$$

$$\text{from (13) and (16)} \qquad (eQual \subseteq T) \wedge (T \subseteq eQual) \tag{17}$$

$$A \equiv B \Leftrightarrow (A \subseteq B) \wedge (B \subseteq A) \tag{18}$$

$$\text{from (17) and (18)} \qquad eQual \equiv T \tag{19}$$

The provided examples of inconsistency do not occur in a target ontology because of the fact that the relations "hasCriterion" and "isCriterion" between the concepts of characteristics and quality criteria were defined in the way presented in Fig. 6. During integration there may be other inconsistencies that must be addressed on a regular basis. This will be discussed using the example of concepts called "Criterion" coming from the ontology eQual and SiteQual. In view of the fact that the method eQual a grading scale covers a range of values from 1 to 7, a restriction "hasEvaluationValue only integer [>=1, <=7]" should be imposed on the concept "Criterion" in the ontology eQual. Meanwhile, in the SiteQual method the evaluation of criteria includes the values from 1 to 9, so that the concept of "Criterion" in the ontology describing this method will be limited to "hasEvaluationValue only integer [>=1, <=9]". While the integration of ontologies these concepts should be unified, the question arises: "What range of values should include restricting the concept "Criterion" in a unified model of the target ontology?". In order to solve the conflicts mentioned, we decided to adopt a solution from the PROMPT algorithm. It occurs when one ontology is considered to be the preferred one and conflicts of this type are resolved in its favor [31]. During the integration, a target ontology unifying source ontologies will be the preferred one. Therefore, the order of the integrated source ontologies will have a partial effect on the resulting form, a unified model of the target ontology.

Based on these observations, conclusions and guidelines, the source ontologies were built, reflecting the website evaluation quality methods. These ontologies, in the form of primary evidence, and inferred by the reasoner, are presented in: eQual [32], Ahn [33] SiteQual [34] Website Evaluation Questionnaire [35] and Web Portal Site

Quality [36]. More of the construction process of source ontologies is described in [37]. Based on the literature analysis presented earlier, feedback and observations, we formulated the integration algorithm that was then applied in the process of ontology integration of website quality evaluation methods.

3.3 Source Ontologies Integration Algorithm in the Target Ontology

The developed ontology integration algorithm is closely related to refactoring and ontology merging support tools offered by the Protégé editor [38]. These tools make it much easier to carry out the integration process. The integration algorithm is divided into three parts.

Part I is performed only once as part of the integration process. It concerns the preparation for the integration and the integration of the first source ontology. In this part, by using a tool "Merge ontologies" included in the Protégé editor, in an empty target ontology a first source ontology is inserted. It is vital to give proper IRI identifiers to concepts stemming from a source ontology and being a part of a source ontology in the target ontology. This action will preserve the quality model of the source ontology in the target ontology.

Part II includes the integration of the criteria and the placement, in the target ontology, of the individual models of evaluation coming from the integrated ontology, so also from the methods that are reflected by the different source ontologies. As a result of this part of the algorithm, another source ontology will be placed into the target ontology (another website evaluation quality model and their criteria). This part has a similar course to the first part of the algorithm, thus, here, the target ontology is not empty, but contains source ontologies which were integrated before.

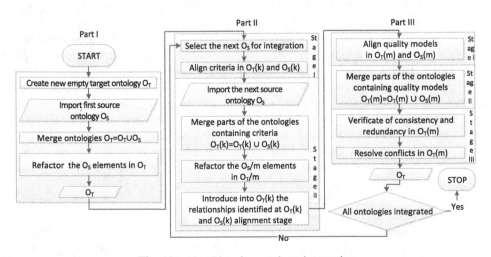

Fig. 10. Algorithm for ontology integration

Part III deals with the construction of a unified quality model in the target ontology. An important part of this part of the algorithm is a construction of a new quality model comprising quality characteristics contained in the source and target ontologies. In this part one also needs to carry out a verification of consistency and absence of redundancy and to resolve conflicts in the target ontology. A detailed integration algorithm was presented in [13]. A block diagram of the integration algorithm is shown in Fig. 10.

4 Research Findings

The ontology integration was conducted according to the algorithm presented above. Firstly, in the empty target ontology the source ontology eQual was integrated. Next, in the target ontology, which already contained the ontology eQual, the source ontology Ahn was integrated. In order to do that an alignment of concepts representing criteria in these ontologies was carried out. In this step links were identified between the target ontology and the source ontology Ahn. Selected samples of the links detected are shown in Table 1.

Table 1. Selected samples of aligning the concepts of criteria in the target ontology containing the eQual model and source ontology Ahn

Relation type	Target ontology (containing eQual)		Source ontology (Ahn)	
	Characteristic	Criterion/Concept	Characteristic	Criterion/Concept
Equivalence	Usability1	Ease of navigation	System quality	Ease of navigation
Equivalence	Design	Appropriateness design	System quality	Appropriateness design style
Equivalence	Empathy	Personalization	Service quality	Adaptation to the user's needs

Based on the identified relationship between the criteria set out in Table 1, the next stage of integration was carried out. In this framework the following things were achieved: importing the Ahn source ontology to the target ontology, ontology merging with the use of the tool "Merge ontologies", the change values of IRI identifiers for

Table 2. Aligning the concepts of a quality model in the target ontology containing the eQual model and source ontology Ahn

Relation type	Target ontology (containing eQual)		Source ontology (Ahn)	
	Parent concept	Characteristic	Parent concept	Characteristic
Equivalence	Quality	Information quality	Quality	Information quality
Reverse subsumption	Quality	Service interaction	Quality	Service quality

concepts/criteria in the Ahn ontology, linking respective pairs of concepts with equivalent relationships. Therefore, the target ontology, which is a unified ontology eQual and Ahn at the level of criteria, was achieved.

Then the concepts representing the characteristics of quality models Ahn and eQual were aligned, as shown in Table 2. The relationships between the characteristics were determined in the way presented in Table 2 so that the criteria included in a particular characteristic were tied to it at the same level of hierarchy.

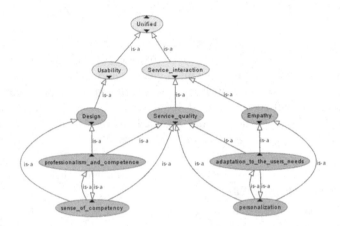

Fig. 11. Redundancy of relationships in the target ontology containing the source ontologies eQual and Ahn

The last step was to check the consistency and lack of redundancy in an integrated ontology. Such redundancy appeared as a result of the reasoner, in the case of the criteria from the target and source ontology having the same name or having been recognized as equivalent, and belonging to two different characteristics included in the unified model. In each of these cases, there was a redundancy of subsumption relationship between the criteria and characteristics of the unified model. Selected examples of such redundancy are presented in Fig. 11.

For example, a couple of equivalent concepts "personalisation" and "adaptation_to_the_user's_needs" belongs to the characteristics of the "Service_quality" and "Empathy". On the other hand, the subcharacteristics are included in the single characteristic "Service_interaction". So here there is a redundancy within one characteristic. This redundancy resulted from the fact that the criterion "personalisation" in the ontology eQual being part of the category of "Empathy" and the criterion "adaptation_to_the_user's_needs" in the Ahn ontology being one of the characteristics "Service_quality". As a result of the recognition of these criteria as being equal to each other, they take the relationship between them and the characteristics to which they belong. This type of redundancy relationship is resolved in accordance with the assumptions described in Sect. 3 of the article, i.e. for the benefit of the target ontology, retaining relationships which derived from it, and removing relationships coming from the source ontology (in this case from the ontology Ahn). An ontology integrating the models eQual and Ahn and including the quality model unifying the two methods were presented in the elementary form and in the deduced form in [39].

Subsequent iterations of the integration process of individual source ontologies with the target ontology proceeded analogously to the integration presented above. To the target ontology were systematically attached previously built ontologies: SiteQual, Website Evaluation Questionnaire and Web Portal Site Quality [40]. Therefore, the ontology [40] contains five source ontologies. A unified quality model, consisting of five basic models, in the form deduced by the reasoner, is also presented in [40].

The analysis of the ontology presented in [40] allows observing that a unified quality model included in an ontology is to some extent chaotic. The chaos is reflected in the fact that some criteria, which seem to concern similar website elements, are included in different characteristics which are not related to each other. For instance, a criterion "information_objectivity" is included in a characteristic "Accuracy", although, as it seems, it should be part of a characteristic "Information_quality". Moreover, some characteristics contain only one or no criterion (for example "Comprehension" or "Completeness"). Examples of this chaotic structure of a unified quality model, contained in an ontology, are presented in Fig. 12.

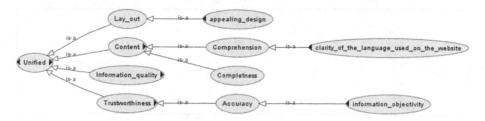

Fig. 12. Examples of quality characteristics not containing any criteria or containing only one criterion

Because of the presented disadvantages of the obtained unified quality model, it was necessary to modify it to receive more organized structure. In the diagram presented in Fig. 1, this stage was named as an ontology restructuring. Therefore, a factor analysis was used, or more specifically a principal component analysis (PCA). Its application makes it possible to analyse a set of variables with reference to its correlations, to isolate groups of mutually independent variables (or least dependent on each other) and to determine their structure [41]. The research into the structure of assessment criteria belonging to a unified quality model was carried out in the Statistica program. For this an exploratory factor analysis module was used and the PCA method was employed to isolate factors. The maximum number of isolated factors was set to 67 so as not to impose the possible maximum number of elements. The applied limitation of the isolated factor number was the Kaiser normalisation according to which only the elements, whose eigenvalues were >1, were isolated. Additionally, while isolating the factors a normalized Varimax rotation was applied. The data which were analyzed were 133 questionnaires. Those polled determined in the questionnaires which individual quality criteria are essential. The use of this type of questionnaires in the factor analysis is

Table 3. Factor loadings obtained by individual criteria

Group	Criterion	1	2	3	4	5	6	7	8	9	10	11	12	13	14	15	16
1	K1									0.70							
	K2	0.23								0.83							
	K3	0.27								0.66		0.22					
	K4			0.42		0.25				0.51							
	K23	0.24			0.36					0.40						0.37	
	K25							0.38		0.54				0.24			
	K50	0.21							0.24	0.43		0.45				0.21	0.22
	K54	0.36		0.25	0.26					0.35		0.35				0.30	
	K60		0.23			0.43				0.39						0.26	0.41
2	K5			0.78													
	K6	0.26	0.28	0.64								0.27		0.21			
	K7	0.49		0.38				0.30				0.21					
	K8	0.32		0.58		0.29	0.23					0.23					
3	K37	0.35						0.31	0.23				0.33			0.29	0.29
	K55	0.26								0.32			0.44		0.21		0.31
	K63				0.45								0.50				0.35
	K65						0.22						0.74				
4	K36						0.20			0.71							
	K62			0.22		0.22				0.68		0.23					
5	K39				0.58	0.36			0.29			0.20		0.23			
	K56					0.53						0.35	0.30			0.26	0.27
	K57					0.59					0.22	0.34					
	K58				0.22	0.60								0.35			
	K59					0.73							0.30				
6	K9	0.72								0.25							0.24
	K10	0.73								0.27		0.22					
	K43	0.43				0.24						0.28					0.30
	K47	0.48		0.20		0.27				0.35			0.37				
	K48	0.58			0.28				0.27			0.26			0.21		
7	K15	0.35							0.39				0.48		0.27		
	K27	0.41								0.29			0.49				0.22
	K40	0.28			0.21				0.22	0.20			0.54	0.24			
	K46	0.39			0.21				0.22				0.58				
	K49	0.32								0.33			0.39	0.28		0.32	0.25
	K51				0.24					0.21			0.55	0.26			0.36
	K52	0.35		0.26		0.39						0.29	0.45				
	K53	0.31				0.32				0.22			0.48		0.31		0.26
	K64				0.24	0.27							0.34	0.44	0.33		
8	K11	0.35														0.69	
	K12	0.28										0.28			0.21	0.75	
	K13	0.36									0.29	0.27	0.26			0.40	
	K14	0.20		0.23		0.22	0.25	0.28		0.24		0.33				0.42	
	K28							0.37						0.27		0.28	0.32
9	K17				0.73												
	K18				0.49						0.27	0.30	0.31				
	K24	0.34		0.27	0.44					0.23			0.22		0.28		
	K33			0.23	0.40				0.26			0.33	0.26	0.27	0.33	0.26	
	K34			0.32	0.40	0.20						0.29			0.33	0.38	
	K42			0.22	0.32			0.27	0.27	0.22					0.20		0.28
10	K19		0.23		0.27				0.62		0.21						
	K20		0.35			0.28	0.26		0.49	0.27							
	K29								0.36		0.36		0.33		0.32	0.24	0.29
	K30								0.76			0.21					
11	K38				0.26			0.29	0.28					0.28	0.56		
	K41			0.22	0.31				0.38			0.29			0.48		0.27
	K67					0.22									0.73	0.22	
12	K22							0.20							0.70		
	K26			0.22		0.22		0.40							0.53		0.22
	K31									0.34	0.23	0.24			0.57		
13	K16	0.31		0.29	0.32			0.49	0.21					0.26	0.21		
	K35	0.26	0.23					0.45			0.26			0.29	0.24	0.21	0.26
14	K21		0.78	0.24													
	K44										0.22	0.71	0.24				
	K45				0.26							0.62	0.21			0.24	
	K61			0.21		0.27			0.25			0.20	0.56				
	K66					0.21				0.30				0.63			
	K32	0.62											0.27				

supported by the observation that users evaluate the significance of criteria comprising similar quality areas in a similar way. For instance, they similarly evaluate the weight of adequacy and relevance of information presented in a website, yet they evaluate the weight of criteria concerning a website's attractive appearance in a slightly different manner. However, when using weights of individual criteria in the analysis, one can often notice the effect of reaching high values of factor loadings for the same factors by different and semantically unrelated criteria. Therefore, the results of the factor analysis were not arbitrarily applied, but they constituted only a certain form of assistance when reorganizing the criterion structure of a unified quality model. The result of applying the factor analysis was a set of 16 main components, all of which explains at least 1 % of all variations; in total they explain over 72 % of changeability. The results of the factor analysis, in the form of the value of factor loadings obtained by individual criteria, are presented in Table 3. Names of criteria are shown in Appendix A.

In the results, presented in Table 3, one can observe some patterns describing criterion membership to individual groups. They are not unique patterns, but in connection with a semantic analysis they could be used to group criteria. As a result of the factor analysis 14 such groups of criteria were singled out. However, some groups, in authors' opinion, concern similar quality elements. First five groups seem to refer to a website's usability, other three groups of criteria comprise the quality of information and information navigation and other five groups deal with services delivered by websites. The last fourteenth group contains criteria not assigned, as a result of the factor analysis, to any of the previous groups or criteria which were, in authors' view, incorrectly assigned. Here, incorrect assignment indicates a high factor loading of a criterion k with relation to a factor comprising other criteria not related semantically to k. An example of this kind of incorrect assignment can be a high value of loading of

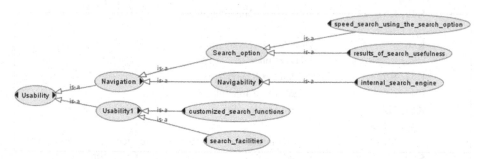

Fig. 13. Location of criteria related to the mechanism of searching information in a website in a unified quality model contained in an integrated ontology

Factor 11 for Criterion K45 ("user_friendliness"), since Factor 11 is related to criteria related to the quality of information. Nonetheless, as a result of a factor analysis, groups of criteria were singled out, which were predominantly correct. An example of that is Group 5, which comprises criteria related to the mechanism of searching information in a website. In the structure of a unified quality model, contained in an

Table 4. Chosen cases of newly defined connections of criteria with quality characteristics

Group	Criterion	Position in the structure of a unified quality model	
		Previous	New
1	K1, K2, K3, K4, K60	Usability -> Usability1	Usability -> Usability1
	K23, K25	System quality	
	K50	Usability -> Navigation -> Structure	
	K54	Content -> Comprehension	
2	K5, K6, K7, K8	Usability -> Design	Usability -> Design
3	K37	Usability -> Tangibility	Usability -> Design
	K55	Lay out	
	K63, K65	Adequacy of information	
4	K36	Usability -> Tangibility	Usability -> Usability1
	K62	Usefulness of content	
5	K39	Usability -> Navigation -> Navigability	Usability -> Search option
	K56, K57	Usability -> Navigation -> Search option	
	K58, K59	Usability -> Usability1	
6	K9, K10	Information quality	Information quality
	K43	Trustworthiness -> Accuracy	
	K47, K48	Usability -> Navigation -> Hyperlinks	
7	K15, K27, K40, K49	Information quality	Information quality
	K49, K51	Usability -> Navigation -> Structure	
	K46	Usability -> Navigation -> Hyperlinks	
	K52, K53	Content -> Relevance	
	K64	Adequacy of information	
8	K11, K12, K13, K14, K28	Information quality	Information quality
9	K17, K18	Service interaction -> Trust	Service quality -> Interaction
	K24	System quality	
	K33	Service interaction -> Service quality	
	K34	Service interaction -> Empathy	
	K42	Usability -> Relevant representation	
10	K19, K20	Service interaction -> Empathy	Service quality -> Trust and empathy

(Continued)

Table 4. (*Continued*)

Group	Criterion	Position in the structure of a unified quality model	
		Previous	New
	K29, K30	Service interaction -> Service quality	
11	K38	Usability -> Navigation -> Navigability	Service quality -> Interaction
	K41	Usability -> Relevant representation	
	K67	Interaction	
12	K22	Service interaction -> Trust	Service quality -> Trust and empathy
	K26	System quality	
	K31	Reliability	
13	K16	Service interaction -> Trust	Service quality -> Trust and empathy
	K35	Service interaction -> Empathy	
14	K21	Service interaction -> Empathy	Service quality -> Trust and empathy
	K44	Trustworthiness -> Security	
	K45	Usability -> Navigation -> Ease of use	Usability -> Usability1
	K61	Usefulness of content	
	K66	Accessibility	Usability -> Design
	K32	Service interaction -> Empathy	

integrated ontology, these criteria were located in different characteristics, what is presented in Fig. 13. However, the use of factor analysis demonstrates that the criteria should occur within one characteristic.

On the basis of the data obtained with the use of factor analysis, the structure of the unified quality model was reorganized by reassigning criteria to certain characteristics. Apart for the factor analysis, also, a semantic analysis was applied to avoid making incorrect connections of characteristics with criteria. When in doubtful situations, the most appropriate, in authors' opinion, characteristic describing a given criterion was chosen. The result of the reorganisation of the criterion structure is presented in Table 4 which contains already existing and newly defined connections of criteria with quality characteristics.

In Table 4 the situation of Criterion K49 may be ambiguous, since it is related to its membership, in the previous unified quality model, to two different characteristics, that is "Structure" and "Information_quality". The membership to the characteristic "Structure" was because of the fact that in the ontology WEQ from which comes Criterion K49, it belonged to this characteristic. Moreover, in the course of integration the subsumtion between this criterion and a characteristic "sufficient _information_-contents_where_expected" was determined. Next, the feature belongs to a

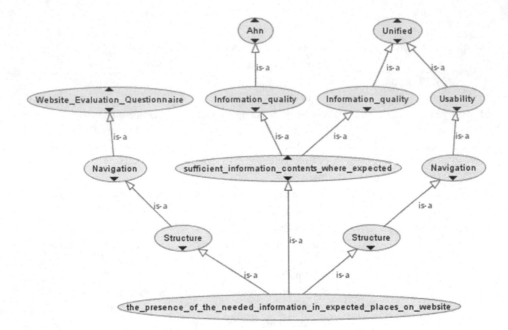

Fig. 14. Membership of Criterion K49 simultaneously to two quality characteristics

characteristic "Information_quality" because of the structure of the ontology Ahn. Therefore, there is a situation presented in Fig. 14. However, thanks to using the factor analysis, this element of the unified quality model was corrected by assigning Criterion K49 to the characteristic " Information_quality" to which a superior criterion for K49 belongs as well. The final ontology containing a unified quality model after it was reorganized was presented in [42] in the form deduced by the reasoner.

5 Conclusion

Even a cursory analysis of [40] shows a very high level of complexity in this built ontology. At the same time, it can be concluded that the construction of such an extensive ontology, as a result of the integration of the source ontologies, is much less complex than its construction process from scratch, even with the use of formalized methodologies of ontology construction. Thanks to the presented approach, the problem of ontology construction unifying quality assessment methods was decomposed into a few minor problems involving the construction of the source ontologies which then were integrated. This resulted in an ontology containing quality models used in the various methods and a model that unifies the different methods. Since the model unifying individual methods was characterized by certain chaos, it was reorganized with the use of the factor analysis. As a result of the performed restructuring, quality criteria were assigned to appropriate characteristics. Consequently, a complete knowledge repository on evaluation methods of the quality of websites and assessment criteria of the methods was obtained [42]. It is worth noting that in all of the integrated methods a total of 115 criteria were used. In the integrated ontology, 94 criteria are listed, due to the fact that part of the criteria are repeated in the various methods. However, when one takes into account the fact that some criteria are equivalent to those of others, one can consider that there are 67 different quality criteria in the integrated ontology. Therefore, we managed to limit the number of applied ontology criteria by almost 40 %. The resulting ontology presented in [42] can act as a repository of domain knowledge, due to the fact that it includes a number of methods and models that evaluate the quality of websites. It may also allow for the integration of heterogeneous data from a variety of assessment methods, and thus assessment websites through a variety of methods defined in the ontology, so that the individual results of the assessment can be compared in a the same terminology and a reference plane. The constructed repository of knowledge, together with presented in [43] the assessment criteria selection procedure could be at the core of the expert system of website quality assessment, which should be the direction of further research. In addition, further work should include the development of ontology about the possibility of environmental data records of ontology users.

Appendix: Names of Particular Criteria

Criterion	Concept name	Criterion	Concept name
K1	ease_of_learn_to_operate	K35	courteous_manner_of_deal_with_customers
K2	clear_and_understandable_interaction	K36	providing_latest_technology
K3	ease_of_navigation	K37	visual_appealing_of_all_components
K4	ease_of_use	K38	location_in_search_engines
K5	attractiveness_appearance	K39	internal_search_engine
K6	appropriateness_design	K40	sufficient_information_contents
K7	sense_of_competency	K41	value-added_experience
K8	positive_experience	K42	consistent_and_standardized_representation
K9	information_accuracy	K43	information_objectivity
K10	information_believability	K44	privacy_of_personal_information
K11	information_timeliness	K45	user_friendliness
K12	information_relevance	K46	directing_to_needed_information
K13	ease_of_understand_of_information	K47	immediate_pointing_of_the_needed_information
K14	right_level_of_detail_of_information	K48	hyperlinks_lead_to_the_expected_information
K15	appropriate_format_of_information	K49	the_presence_of_the_needed_information_in_ expected_places_on_website
K16	reputation	K50	clear_website_structure
K17	transactions_safety	K51	convenient_set-up_to_help_find_the_information_ searched
K18	security_of_personal_information	K52	information_helpfulness
K19	personalization	K53	information_usefulness
K20	sense_of_community	K54	clarity_of_the_language_used_on_the_website
K21	communication_with_organization	K55	appealing_design
K22	confident_about_delivery_goods_ and_services_on_time	K56	speed_search_using_the_search_option
K23	transaction_processing_time	K57	results_of_search_usefulness
K24	availability	K58	customized_search_functions

(*Continued*)

(*Continued*)

Criterion	Concept name	Criterion	Concept name
K25	relevant_functionality	K59	search_facilities
K26	error-free_transactions	K60	security_features_adequacy
K27	information_completness	K61	tips_on_products_or_services
K28	site-specyfic_information	K62	content_uniqueness
K29	instills_confidence	K63	complete_description_of_the_product_or_service
K30	follow-up_service_to_users	K64	information_comprehensiveness_relative_to_other_ portals
K31	dependability_of_service_requests	K65	detailed_contact_information
K32	distractions_minimalization	K66	page loading_speed
K33	anticipation_and_responding_to_user_needs	K67	message_board_forum
K34	customer_interests		

References

1. Kim, S., Stoel, L.: Dimensional hierarchy of retail website quality. Inf. Manag. **41**(5), 619–633 (2004)
2. Hwang, J., Yoon, Y.S., Park, N.H.: Structural effects of cognitive and affective responses to web advertisements, website and brand attitudes, and purchase intentions: the case of casual-dining restaurants. Int. J. Hospitality Manag. **30**, 897–907 (2011)
3. Jankowski, J.: Integration of collective knowledge in FUZZY models supporting web design process. In: Jędrzejowicz, P., Nguyen, N.T., Hoang, K. (eds.) ICCCI 2011, Part II. LNCS, vol. 6923, pp. 395–404. Springer, Heidelberg (2011)
4. ISO/IEC 25010:2010(E), Systems and software engineering — Systems and software Quality Requirements and Evaluation (SQuaRE) — System and software quality models
5. Barnes, S.J., Vidgen, R.: Data triangulation and web quality metrics: a case study in e-government. Inf. Manag. **43**(6), 767–777 (2006)
6. Ahn, T., Ryu, S., Han, I.: The impact of Web quality and playfulness on user acceptance of online retailing. Inf. Manag. **44**(3), 263–275 (2007)
7. Webb, H.W., Webb, L.A.: SiteQual: an integrated measure of Web site quality. J. Enterp. Inf. Manag. **17**(6), 430–440 (2004)
8. Yang, Z., Cai, S., Zhou, Z., Zhou, N.: Development and validation of an instrument to measure user perceived service quality of information presenting Web Portals. Inf. Manag. **42**(4), 575–589 (2005)
9. Elling, S., Lentz, L., de Jong, M., van den Bergh, H.: Measuring the quality of governmental websites in a controlled versus an online setting with the 'Website Evaluation Questionnaire'. Gov. Inf. Q. **29**(3), 383–393 (2012)
10. Sorum, H., Andersen, K.N., Clemmensen, T.: Website quality in government: exploring the webmaster's perception and explanation of website quality. Transforming Gov. People Process Policy **7**(3), 322–341 (2013)
11. Kaya, T.: Multi-attribute evaluation of website quality in e-business using an integrated Fuzzy AHPTOPSIS methodology. Int. J. Comput. Intell. Syst. **3**(3), 301–314 (2010)
12. Cruz, I.F., Xiao, H.: Ontology driven data integration in heterogeneous networks. In: Tolk, A., Jain, L.C. (eds.) Complex Systems in Knowledge-based Environments: Theory, Models and Applications. SCI, vol. 168, pp. 75–98. Springer, Heidelberg (2009)

13. Ziemba, P., Jankowski, J., Wątróbski, J., Wolski, W., Becker, J.: Integration of domain ontologies in the repository of website evaluation methods. In: Proceedings of the Federated Conference on Computer Science and Information Systems, pp. 1585–1595 (2015)

14. Gruber, T.R.: A translation approach to portable ontology specifications. Knowl. Acquis. **5** (2), 199–220 (1993)

15. Magoutas, B., Halaris, C., Mentzas, G.: An ontology for the multi-perspective evaluation of quality in e-government services. In: Wimmer, M.A., Scholl, J., Grönlund, Å. (eds.) EGOV. LNCS, vol. 4656, pp. 318–329. Springer, Heidelberg (2007)

16. Mich, L., Franch, M.: Instantiating Web Sites quality models: an ontologies driven approach. In: CAISE 2005 Workshop on Web Oriented Software Technologies (2005)

17. Casellas, N.: Legal Ontology Engineering: Methodologies, Modelling Trends, and the Ontology of Professional Judicial Knowledge. Springer, Dordrecht (2011)

18. Gomez-Perez, A., Fernandez-Lopez, M., Corcho, O.: Methodologies and methods for building ontologies. In: Gomez-Perez, A., Fernandez-Lopez, M., Corcho, O. (eds.) Ontological Engineering, With Examples from the Areas of Knowledge Management, e-Commerce and the Semantic Web, pp. 107–197. Springer, London (2004)

19. Villazon-Terrazas, B., Ramirez, J., Suarez-Figueroa, M.C., Gomez-Perez, A.: A network of ontology networks for building e-employment advanced systems. Expert Syst. Appl. **38**(11), 13612–13624 (2011)

20. Suarez-Figueroa, M.C.: NeOn Methodology for Building Ontology Networks: Specification, Scheduling and Reuse (2010)

21. Pinto, H., Gomez-Perez, A., Martins, J.: Some issues on ontology integration. In: Proceedings of IJCA I999 Workshop on Ontologies and Problem Solving Methods (1999)

22. de Bruijn, J., Ehrig, M., Feier, C., Martin-Recuerda, F., Scharffe, F., Weiten, M.: Ontology mediation, merging, and aligning. In: Davies, J., Studer, R., Warren, P. (eds.) Semantic Web Technologies: Trends and Research in Ontology-Based Systems, pp. 95–113. Wiley, Chichester (2006)

23. Klein, M.: Combining and relating ontologies: an analysis of problems and solutions. In: IJCAI Workshop on Ontologies and Information Sharing, pp. 53–62 (2001)

24. Lin, F., Sandkuhl, K.: A new expanding tree ontology matching method. In: Meersman, R., Tari, Z. (eds.) OTM-WS 2007, Part II. LNCS, vol. 4806, pp. 1329–1337. Springer, Heidelberg (2007)

25. Nezhadi, A.H., Shadgar, B., Osareh, A.: Ontology alignment using machine learning techniques. Int. J. Comput. Sci. Inf. Technol. **3**(2), 139–150 (2011)

26. Ichise, R.: Machine learning approach for ontology mapping using multiple concept similarity measures. In: Proceedings of the Seventh IEEE/ACIS International Conference on Computer and Information Science, pp. 340–346. IEEE (2008)

27. Zhang, J., Lv, Y.: An approach of refining the merged ontology. In: Proceedings of the 9th IEEE International Conference on Fuzzy Systems and Knowledge Discovery, pp. 802–806 (2012)

28. Taboada, M., Martinez, D., Mira, J.: Experiences in reusing knowledge sources using Protege and PROMPT. Int. J. Hum.-Comput. Stud. **62**, 597–618 (2005)

29. Gaeta, M., Orciuoli, F., Ritrovato, P.: Advanced ontology management system for personalised e-Learning. Knowl.-Based Syst. **22**(4), 292–301 (2009)

30. Knorr, M., Alferes, J.J., Hitzler, P.: Local closed world reasoning with description logics under the well-founded semantics. Artif. Intell. **175**(9–10), 1528–1554 (2011)

31. Noy, N.F., Musen, M.A.: The PROMPT suite: interactive tools for ontology merging and mapping. Int. J. Hum.-Comput. Stud. **59**(6), 983–1024 (2003)
32. http://tinyurl.com/WQM-eQual-example-inst, http://tinyurl.com/WQM-eQual-inferred-example-ins
33. http://tinyurl.com/WQM-Ahn, http://tinyurl.com/WQM-Ahn-inferred
34. http://tinyurl.com/WQM-SiteQual, http://tinyurl.com/WQM-SiteQual-inferred
35. http://tinyurl.com/WQM-WEQ, http://tinyurl.com/WQM-WEQ-inferred
36. http://tinyurl.com/WQM-WPSQ, http://tinyurl.com/WQM-WPSQ-inferred
37. Ziemba, P., Jankowski, J., Watróbski, J., Becker, J.: Knowledge management in website quality evaluation domain. In: Núñez, M., et al. (eds.) ICCCI 2015. LNCS, vol. 9330, pp. 75–85. Springer, Heidelberg (2015). doi:10.1007/978-3-319-24306-1_8
38. http://protege.stanford.edu/
39. http://tinyurl.com/ont-integration1, http://tinyurl.com/ont-integration1-inferred
40. http://tinyurl.com/ont-integration, http://tinyurl.com/ont-integration-inferred
41. Everitt, B., Hothorn, T.: An Introduction to Applied Multivariate Analysis with R. Springer, New York (2011)
42. http://tinyurl.com/ont-restructured-inferred
43. Ziemba, P., Piwowarski, M., Jankowski, J., Wątróbski, J.: Method of criteria selection and weights calculation in the process of web projects evaluation. In: Hwang, D., Jung, J.J., Nguyen, N.-T. (eds.) ICCCI 2014. LNCS, vol. 8733, pp. 684–693. Springer, Heidelberg (2014)

Information Technology for Business and Public Organizations

Risk Factors Relationships for Information Systems Projects – Insight from Polish Public Organizations

Ewa Ziemba[✉] and Iwona Kolasa

Faculty of Finance and Insurance, University of Economics in Katowice,
1 Maja 50, 40-287 Katowice, Poland
{ewa.ziemba,iwona.kolasa}@ue.katowice.pl

Abstract. The aims of this study are to identify risk factors affecting information system (IS) projects in public organizations in Poland and find contextual interactions among these factors. This study is based on a critical review of literature, practical collaboration, case studies, logical deduction, and experts' judgments. In order to explore relationships between identified factors, Interpretive Structural Modeling methodology was used. The study results show eleven risk factors affecting IS projects in public organizations, namely (1) Top management support, (2) Manage processes in organization, (3) Involve IS end-users, (4) Manage information system development process, (5) Make system requirement analysis, (6) Manage project plan, (7) Manage, monitor and evaluate project, (8) Manage project team, (9) Manage team experience, (10) Manage team communication and (11) Manage public sector procedures and processes. Based on the relationships between them, the linkage, dependent and independent factors are identified.

Keywords: Risk factors · Information systems · IS project · Public organizations · Risk management · Interpretive Structural Modeling · ISM approach

1 Introduction

Information systems (IS) projects are always connected to a substantial risk. Risk are those things and future uncertain events that may derail an IS project and keep it from a successful completion. For example, a considerable number of IS projects still use more resources than planned, take longer to complete and provide less quality and functionality than expected [1, 2]. The questions are, what are risk factors for IS projects and how to manage risk in IS projects? Among some most common risk factors for IS projects are: unrealistic goals, inaccurate estimation of necessary resources, badly defined requirements, poor presentation of a project status, and unmanaged risk [3, 4]. It has been identified that a poor risk management (RM) of IS projects often leads to failure in IS projects both in public and business organizations [5].

Although some managers claim that they manage risk in their projects, there is evidence that they do not manage it systematically [6]. This shows that public and

© Springer International Publishing Switzerland 2016
E. Ziemba (Ed.): FedCSIS 2015, LNBIP 243, pp. 55–76, 2016.
DOI: 10.1007/978-3-319-30528-8_4

business organizations should improve not only their ability to identify risk, but also manage the risk associated with projects [7].

The existing studies mostly examine risk factors for IS projects in business organizations [8–10]. There are only few studies concerning risk factors for IS projects in public organizations [11, 12]. This portrays the need for studying risk factors influencing the success of IS projects in public organizations. Therefore, conducting research among Polish public organizations should contribute to greater understanding of risk factors affecting IS projects and should help fill the gap in the existing body of knowledge.

This paper focuses on analyzing risk factors affecting IS projects in public organizations in Poland. Its aims are to: (1) indicate risk factors influencing IS projects in public organizations in Poland and (2) find relationships among indicated risk factors.

The paper is structured as follows. Section 1 is an introduction to the subject. Based on the literature review, Sect. 2 indicates risk factors affecting IS projects and a framework of risk factors is proposed. Section 3 describes a research methodology. Section 4 presents the research findings on risk factors affecting two IS projects in Polish public organizations. Then, the risk factors presented in the literature are enhanced and their proposed framework is widened. Moreover, the contextual relationships among identified risk factors are presented. Section 5 provides the study's contributions and limitations, implications for the findings, and the stream of future works.

2 Literature Review

2.1 IS Projects Success and Its Risk Factors

Is there a relationship between risk factors and project success? This question has already been considered relevant by people from both academic and practitioners' communities for a long time, especially in the area of IS, where projects have a long history of failing [13–16]. What exactly is defined as a risk? A risk is the occurrence of any event that has consequences for, or an impact on the success of an IS project [17]. Many authors define that all projects involve a risk of some sort [18]. There is no project without a risk. Risk management (RM), therefore, is one of the main issues of a project. Its positive impact on planning, decision making, avoiding bad events, and giving a proper response to a risky situation is remarkable [19]. RM is an art for identifying the treats, assessing and controlling them by applying the most effective manner of mitigating them [20].

The success of IS projects is traditionally measured by time, budget and requirements criteria. Many researchers define a project success in terms of compliance with time limits, cost limits and meeting requirements [21]. RM has a significant impact on projects success [22]. It helps to identify and manage risk, and thereby prevent IS projects from getting off the track. RM involves identifying the potential risk, measuring, monitoring and controlling it in an organization to meet its strategies and objectives, and leads to decrease the undesired effects in project life cycles.

There is a general consensus that effective planning and implementation of a RM methodology both positively affect the success rate of any project [23–26]. There are several methodologies of project RM that represent the course of actions required to manage risk during IS projects [27]. However, the main point is to identify the exact risk factors for IS projects [28].

After a literature review covering papers published after 2010, we identified five studies referred to risk factors affecting IS projects in business organizations. These studies are summarized in Table 1.

Table 1. Research on risk factors affecting IS projects (Source: [41, p. 1576])

Publication	Research methods	Research result
S. Liu, L. Wang (2014)	Survey, 26 respondents (IS managers)	Identified 27 risk factors
S. Sundararajan, M. Bhasi, P. K. Vijayaraghavan (2014)	1 case study	Identified 20 risk factors
C. Lopez, J.L. Salmeron (2012)	Interview, 12 respondents (IS/IT projects experts); risk evaluation using IPA method	Identified 46 risk factors
L.Jun, W. Qiuzhen, M. Qingguo (2011)	Survey, 93 respondents; the influence between risk factors were measured	Identified 7 risk factors
P.K. Dey, B.T. Clegg, D. J. Bennett (2010)	1 case study	Identified 41 risk factors

Based on the literature findings, there have been identified ten risk factors (RF), namely (1) Top management support; (2) Manage processes in organization; (3) Involve IS end-users; (4) Manage information system development process; (5) Make business requirement analysis; (6) Manage project plan; (7) Manage, monitor and evaluate project; (8) Manage project team; (9) Manage team experience; (10) Manage team communication. Each of risk factors is clearly defined by particular risk factors constructs. The framework of risk factors and their constructs are proposed in Table 2.

2.2 Risk Factors Affecting IS Projects in Public Organizations

In the literature, only very few of researchers conducted studies of identifying risk in public organizations. Patanakul [11] examined large-scale IS projects in the public sector and defined the risk factors such as:

Table 2. Framework of risk factors affecting IS projects (Source: [41, p. 1577])

Risk factors	Risk factor constructs	Source
RF1 Top management support	01 Lack of top management commitment to project	[28, 29, 31]
	02 Top managers make important IT decisions without consulting the others	[28, 31]
	03 Unrealistic projects outcomes	[29, 32]
	04 Excessive project size	[28, 30]
	05 Change in ownership or senior management during development process	[29]
	06 Time too short/too long	[28]
	07 Unrealistic schedule	[28]
RF2 Manage processes in organization	08 Resources shifted away from project because of changes in organizational priorities	[28, 29]
	09 Major effect of project implementation on organizational structure	[29, 32]
	10 Mismatch between organization's culture and required business process changes needed for IS	[29]
	11 Changes in organizational priorities	[28]
	12 Continuous changes in organizational environment	[28]
RF3 Involve IS end-users	13 Lack of user participation	[28–32]
	14 Users resistant to change	[28, 29, 31]
	15 Target users are unfamiliar with technology and require additional training	[28–30]
	16 Users with negative attitudes toward project	[29, 31]
	17 User is not committed to project	[28, 29]
	18 Users constantly request further changes	[28]
	19 Conflicts between users departments	[28]
RF4 Manage information system development process	20 High level of technical complexity	[28–31]
	21 Immature technology	[28, 29, 31, 32]
	22 New technology and use of technology that were not adapted in prior projects	[28, 29, 31]
	23 Lack of effective development methodology	[29, 31, 32]
	24 Large number of links to other system required	[28, 29]
	25 Inadequate system documentation; incomplete or non-existent	[28, 31, 32]
	26 Lack of proper tests	[28, 31]
	27 Lack of integration between systems	[28, 31]

(Continued)

Table 2. (*Continued*)

Risk factors	Risk factor constructs	Source
RF5 Make system requirement analysis	28 Continually changing scope and system requirements	[28, 29, 31]
	29 Unclear or incomplete system requirements	[28, 29, 32]
	30 System requirements not adequately identified	[28, 29, 31]
	31 Conflicting system requirements	[29]
	32 Failure to manage end-user expectations	[28]
	33 Lack of frozen requirements	[28]
RF6 Manage project plan	34 Poor project planning	[28–31]
	35 Inadequate estimation of required resources	[29, 31, 32]
	36 Critical activities are not identified	[28]
RF7 Manage, monitor and evaluate project	37 Project progress not monitored closely enough	[28–32]
	38 Lack of an effective project management methodology	[28, 29, 31, 32]
	39 Ineffective communication	[28, 29, 31, 32]
	40 Inexperienced project manager	[28, 29]
	41 Project manager lacks required skills	[28]
RF8 Manage project team	42 Lack of knowledge management	[32]
	43 Frequent turnover within development team	[28, 29, 31, 32]
	44 Team members are unmotivated	[28, 31, 32]
	45 Inadequate composition of project team	[28, 31]
	46 Improper definition of roles and responsibilities	[28, 32]
RF9 Manage team experience	47 Team members lack of specialized skills required by project	[28–31]
	48 Inadequately trained development team members	[29, 31]
	49 Team members are unfamiliar with technology	[28]
RF10 Manage team communication	50 Conflict and no cooperation between team members	[28]
	51 Team members are in many localizations	[32]
	52 Inadequate team size	[32]

- system design and implementation;
- problems in requirement identification;
- project management and governance;
- problems in managing project risk;
- problems in project monitoring, control and managing changes;
- problems in project governance; and
- contract management.

Aritua, Smith, and Bower [12] ran research on risk factors in public sector in the UK. The researchers focused on public organizations' projects in general, not in the context of IS projects. According to them, the following risk factors can be distinguished for the public sector:

- linking strategy and projects;
- markets and demand changes;
- difficulties in project delivery;
- health and safety risks;
- reputation risks;
- skills shortage and resources;
- fraud;
- cash flow and funding problems;
- sustainability and environmental legislation;
- challenges of procurement;
- competition for contractors;
- disastrous events and terrorism;
- stakeholder expectation management; and
- change in government policy.

Analyzing the above risk factors, it can be noticed, that some of them are the same as those defined in the framework presented in Table 2. However the risk factors, namely: contract management, challenges of procurement, and change in government policy are not included among the risk factors defined for business organizations.

3   Research Methodology

3.1   Research Goals

The aims of this research were to identify risk factors affecting IS projects in public organizations and find contextual interactions among those identified factors. The following research questions were posed:

1. What are the risk factors affecting IS projects?
2. What are the risk factors affecting IS projects in public organizations?
3. Are there any significant relationships between risk factors affecting IS projects in public organizations?

3.2 Research Procedure

Research methods included a critical review of literature, case studies, practical collaboration, semi-structured interviews, logical deduction supported by the experts' judgments. The following steps were taken in the research process.

The first step. A review of the literature was conducted to identify risk factors for IS projects. The empirical evidence was searched aimed at peer-reviewed journal publications from 2010 to 2015. The process was supported by the use of electronic tools for the search and selection of publications. The search included journals indexed in bibliographic databases, i.e. Ebsco, ProQuest, Science Direct. The search was conducted using a relevant set of keywords and phrases such as "software project" or "information technology project" and "risk management" or "risk factors", and "project success" included in paper abstracts in all possible permutations and combinations (taking into consideration the logical AND, and OR as appropriate). A search was done on the appearance of any combination of these terms, with a result of 933 hits. All hits of four pages or less were excluded and narrowed to reviewed academic journals in English. Then, a second selection was made by evaluating the abstracts of the publications selected in the first round. In the second round, it was necessary to make sure that the publications included all three topics: software/IT project, project success, and project risk management. The search process resulted in a total of 13 journal publications, published between 2010 and 2015. From those 13 publications only five identified risks factors.

The second step. A risk factors framework for IS projects was created on the basis of literature findings and authors practical collaboration with IT companies dealing with IS projects for business and public organizations.

The third step. Using the case study approach, the risk factors affecting IS projects in public organizations in Poland were defined. Moreover, semi-structured interviews with end-users of IS and project team members were conducted as well as shareable documentations related to IS projects management were analyzed during the study. Data was obtained from documents and records such as a statement of work, project plan, risk management plan, minutes of meetings, review meetings, reports, project overview presentations and project closure reports. This study was conducted in 2010 and 2013. It concerned two IS projects in Polish public organizations. The IS projects included development and implementation of integrated IS. Based on the findings, the framework of risk factors affecting IS projects was enhanced by adding risk factors strictly related to public administration.

The fourth step. The contextual relationships among risk factors affecting IS projects in public organizations were defined. In order to define these relationships, the Interpretive Structural Modeling (ISM) methodology was used.

3.3 ISM Methodology

ISM is a methodology for identifying and summarizing relationships among specific items, which define an issue or problem [33]. ISM allows to explore the relationships between risk factors and determine their level. The ISM process transforms a set of different directly and indirectly related elements into a comprehensive model [33].

In the ISM methodology, decision regarding interdependences among the variables is based on the expert judgments, hence it is interpretive in nature [34]. The ISM methodology is interpretive from the fact that the judgment of the group decides whether and how the variables are related. ISM is primarily intended as a group learning process, but it can also be used individually [35]. ISM has been applied in many domains related to management [36–38]. The ISM methodology allows to transform the undecided and inadequately expressed models into observable and distinct models [39]. The following steps involved in the ISM methodology are [33, 36, 39, 40]:

1. Identification of factors. The risk factors are defined using a literature review and case studies.
2. Contextual relationship. A contextual relationship is indicated among each risk factor (identified in step 1) with respect to which the pairs of factors would be examined. The contextual relationship is shown in the form of a matrix called the structural self-interaction matrix (SSIM).
3. Initial reachability matrix. SSIM is converted into a binary matrix, called the initial reachability matrix.
4. Transitivity check. The initial reachability matrix developed from SSIM is checked for transitivity. The transitivity of the contextual relationship is a basic assumption made in ISM. It states that if variable A is related to B and B is related to C, then A is necessarily related to C. As a result the final reachability matrix is created.
5. Levels partitions. The final reachability matrix obtained in step 4 is converted into the canonical matrix format by arranging the elements according to their levels.
6. Digraph and ISM model. The digraph is drawn and the transitive links are removed based on the relationships given in the above final reachability matrix. The digraph is converted into the ISM model by replacing nodes of the factors with statements.
7. MICMAC analysis. Based on analyzing the driving and dependence powers of factors, the key risk factors are defined.

4 Research Findings

4.1 Case Studies of IS Projects in Polish Public Organizations

Public organizations in Poland, due to territorial scope of their operations are divided into public organizations at the state level embracing the whole Poland, and public organizations at the local level embracing districts and counties. The described case studies of IS projects refer to the state level, where project management took place and the local levels, where IS was implemented.

Two similar projects, one successful and one not, will be used to present the application of risk factors affecting IS projects [33]. Information about a project was gathered by participation in those projects and conducting series of semi-structured interviews. Data was obtained from documents and records such as a statement of work, project plan, risk management plan, minutes of meetings, review meetings, reports, project overview presentations and project closure reports.

Table 3 shows that those two projects were similar in terms of scope and size, although the outcomes of the projects were different. Project A ended only as a partial success. Finally, IS was implemented but it was not fully used by the end-users after 12 months. The completion of project A was also significantly delayed. Project B was fully successful. IS was implemented and it is fully used by its end-users.

Project A was carried by a public organization at the state level. The aim of the project was to improve and automate government processes, and to implement an integrated information system, i.e. Enterprise Resource Planning (ERP) system in sixteen public organizations at the local level. The ERP system used to this point of time was out of date. The results of change were to centralize management of the organizational structure of all sixteen public organizations and automation of supporting government processes for finance and accounting, human resources management, payroll management, inventory management, and fixed assets management. The expected benefits of the project were to eliminate unnecessary documentation, systemize document circulation, ensure a smooth flow of information, and make information accessible (which is relevant, timely to appropriate users and in an appropriate form). A specifically set up project team of the central public organization was responsible for the implementation of the ERP system. The project team was composed of people from the departments of the central public organization, such as: accounting, human resources, payroll, fixed assets and inventory management, and from the IT department. Moreover, the project team was supported by the members of IT company, in particular business analysts, systems analysts, and project team leaders.

Table 3. Project A and project B – comparison of basic features (Source: [41, p. 1579]).

Features	Project A	Project B
Project type	Information system	Information system
Sector	Public organizations	Public organizations
Initial schedule	12 months	18 months
Budget	Realistic	Realistic
Success criteria	On time, within budget, successful installation of ERP system	On time, within budget, successful installation of web-based information system
IS software	Custom made	Custom made
Customers	Public organization employees	General public, public organizations employees
No of end-users	400	35 000
Project management methodology	PRINCE2 (only few basic documents where created)	PRINCE2 (full documentation needed was created)
Risk management	No (no risk registry provided)	Yes (risk registry provided)
Project result after 12 months	Software was implemented but not fully used after 12 months	Software was implemented and fully used after 12 months

Although project A was managed using PRINCE2 methodology, only few documents were created. Despite creating a risk procedure, the risk was never escalated to a steering committee. The risk registry was fulfilled at the beginning of the project, but was not updated during the project. The project team was not properly instructed about necessity of risk reporting. The basic risk management approach was missing. The risk was not properly managed. Often the risk was not identified but happened as an issue.

Project B was also carried out by a public organization. The aim of the project was to implement IS for supporting processes of service provision for citizens. As a result of the project the following types of IS were implemented: integration platform, business intelligence, enterprise portal, web based information portal and mobile terminal software. The project was undertaken as a consequence of the diagnosed problems arising from the lack of IT system integration. The lack of integration made it impossible to have quick access to information indispensable for effective functioning and monitoring of operations of public organizations and caused an ineffective flow of information between the public organizations and the cooperating institutions. The lack of system cooperation compounded the difficulties in monitoring funds allocation and expenditure, and the difficulties in monitoring the use of funds by the individual public organizations.

Project B was managed using PRINCE2 methodology, where all necessary documents essential for effective project management were created. The project team was formally established. Particular people were permanently assigned to particular parts of the project. Their scope of responsibilities was explicitly defined. The project team consisted of an IT specialist group and a government group made up of specialists who were the main users of the system. Risk management was conducted concurrent with the project implementation. The end-users participated in a series of conferences where a clearly defined project goal and successively accomplished tasks were presented. Moreover, they actively participated in analysis meetings where they defined the system requirements. The project had a coherently worked-out schedule that also included a business team meeting schedule. The business team was kept informed about the project progress and participated in the final IS testing.

4.2 Risk Factors Affecting IS Projects in Polish Public Organizations

In project A, the risk was not identified and managed. Whereas, RM was applied to project B in a methodologically correct manner. It can be stated that in case of project A, 27 risk factors did not occur, although 25 risk factors occurred and they were not managed [41]. The lack of RM could have contributed to the failure of the IS project. Finally, IS was created and implemented with a significant delay. In case of project B, 38 risk factors did not occur, and 14 risk factors occurred and they were managed [41]. Project B was completed on the schedule. It can be assumed that RM played a significant role in the IS project success.

However, there were several other risk factors which were not included in the framework of risk factors affecting IS projects in business organizations presented in Table 2. They were [41]:

- **Changing government processes during project implementation.** Changes in government processes during the project always generate the need to change the IS requirements. The changes of IS requirements are one of the most frequent reasons of IS project failures. The change of requirements influences the scope of the project and its functionalities and can extend the project duration.
- **Changing and inconsistent legal regulatory framework.** Changes to the rule of law which take place during the project can affect and often affect IS requirements. As it was mentioned above, the change to the requirements influence the scope of the project and its functionality and can extend the project duration. Unfortunately, the changes to Polish legal system are frequent. It is partially connected with the fact that recently the Polish economy has gone through the transition from a central planned economy to a market economy and it had to adjust and is still adjusting the legal system to the market economy.
- **Challenges of procurement procedure.** There are several factors which must be met in a procurement procedure. One criterion of offer evaluation must be a price. Other criteria may be freely chosen depending on the object of the contract, e.g. quality, technical merit, functionality, usability. Typically, a tender is chosen using the price criterion. In Poland, the cheapest offer is often chosen. As a result the ratio of price to quality is not always maintained.
- **Financial capability of project contractor.** The payment for the contractor for the works done within the IS project framework takes place after the final IS technical acceptance. In practice it may take from few to several months. During this time the contractor has to cover the running costs from own resources. This creates the risk of losing financial liquidity if the contractor does not have appropriate financial backing.
- **Managing contract.** An effectively managed contract can impact on a timely completion of IS project. However, it is extremely difficult to predict all conditions that may occur during the contract realization process. There is a need for long term planning and considering, e.g. identifying all current and future systems that must be integrated. There is a high risk that some minor requirements might be omitted in the contract. The contract cannot be significantly changed during the project, as it is one of the procurement procedures.

The risk framework need to be completed by eleventh risk factor, i.e. RF11 (Manage public sector procedures and processes), which includes five risk factor constructs presented in Table 4.

Table 4. Typical risk factor and its constructs affecting IS projects in public organizations – follow up the risk factors framework presented in Table 2.

Risk factor	Risk factor constructs
R11 Manage public sector procedures and processes	53 Changing government processes during project implementation
	54 Changing and inconsistent legal regulatory framework
	55 Challenges of procurement procedure
	56 Financial capability of project contractor
	57 Managing contract

4.3   The Interrelationships Between Risk Factors

Identifying and understanding risk factors are crucial for successful implementation of IS in organizations. However, it is also important to find and understand the relationships between risk factors because the occurrence of one risk can increase the occurrence of other risk factors. In addition, there is a need to examine the depth of relationships between risk factors.

Contextual Relationship. In this study the contextual relationship was done with the help of expert consultation. The opinion of experts was used to identify the nature of contextual relationship among risk factors. As a result, the structural self-interaction matrix (SSIM) was created. It is presented in Table 5.

Table 5. Structural self-interaction matrix of risk factors.

Group of risks factors	RF11	RF10	RF9	RF8	RF7	RF6	RF5	RF4	RF3	RF2
RF1 Top management support	X	O	O	O	A	A	O	V	X	X
RF2 Manage processes in organization	X	O	O	O	A	A	O	V	X	X
RF3 Involve IS end-users	X	V	V	A	A	A	A	V	X	
RF4 Manage information system development process	A	O	O	O	O	A	A	X		
RF5 Make system requirement analysis	V	O	O	A	A	A	X			
RF6 Manage project plan	V	V	V	V	V	X				
RF7 Manage, monitor and evaluate project	V	V	O	V	X					
RF8 Manage project team	O	V	V	X						
RF9 Manage team experience	O	V	X							
RF10 Manage team communication	A	X								
RF11 Manage public sector procedures and processes	X									

SSIM shows that one factor helps to ameliorate another factor. Based on this, contextual relationships between the selected factors were developed. For analyzing the relationships between factors, the following symbols were utilized to indicate the direction of interaction between two risk factors (i and j):

- V – risk factor i will help to achieve risk factor j;
- A – risk factor j will help to achieve risk factor i;
- X – risk factor i and j will help to achieve each other; and
- O – risk factor i and j are unrelated.

Initial Reachability Matrix. SSIM was converted into a binary matrix called the reachability matrix. In this matrix, symbols V, A, X, O are substituted by 1 and 0 as per the following rules:

- If the (i, j) entry in the SSIM is V, the (i, j) entry in the reachability matrix becomes 1 and the (j, i) entry becomes 0;
- If the (i, j) entry in the SSIM is A, then (i, j) entry in the reachability matrix becomes 0 and the (j, i) entry becomes 1;
- If the (i, j) entry in the SSIM is X, the (i, j) entry in the reachability matrix becomes 1 and the (j, i) entry also becomes 1; and
- If the (i, j) entry in the SSIM is O, the (i, j) entry in the reachability matrix becomes 0 and the (j, i) entry also becomes 0.

Following this rule, the initial reachability matrix was created, as show in Table 6. It incorporates the transitive relations between the risk factors. The driving and dependence power of each risk factor is calculated. The driving power of a particular factor refers to the total number of factors influenced by this factor. On the other hand, the dependence power refers to the total number of factors affecting this factor. In other words, the driving power of a particular risk is the total number of risks factors (including itself) which may help activate it. The dependence power is the total number of risks factors which may help achieve it.

Transitivity Check. The final reachability matrix is formed from the initial reachability matrix. It incorporates the transitive relations among factors. The basic assumption is made in ISM. It states that if factor 1 is related to 2, and factor 2 is related to 3, then factor 1 is necessarily related to 3. The final reachability matrix of risk factors affecting IS project in public organizations is shown in Table 7.

Level Partitions. The reachability set for an individual risk factor comprises of the risk factor and the other risk factors which it may assist to reach. The reachability set consists of the risk factor itself and the other risk factors that it may impact, whereas the antecedent set consists of the risk factor itself and the other risks factor that may impact it. If the reachability set and the intersection set for a given risk factors are the same, then that risk factor is considered to be in level 1st and is assigned as the utmost position in the ISM hierarchy. Once the top-level factor is identified, it is removed from consideration. Then, the same process is repeated to find out the factors in the next level. This process is continued until the level of each factor is found. These levels allow to build a digraph and an ISM model [33]. The partitioning results are shown in Table 8. Seven levels were identified from level partitioning.

Digraph and ISM Model. The structural hierarchical model of the various risk factors was constructed based on the final reachability matrix (Table 7) and the final level partitioning of risk factors (Table 8). It is shown in Fig. 1.

Table 6. Initial reachability matrix of risk factors.

Risk Factors	RF11	RF10	9	RF8	RF7	RF6	RF5	RF4	RF3	RF2	RF1	Driving power
RF1 Top management support	1	0	0	0	0	0	0	1	1	1	1	5
RF2 Manage processes in organization	1	0	0	0	0	0	0	1	1	1	1	5
RF3 Involve IS end-users	1	1	1	0	0	0	0	1	1	1	1	7
RF4 Manage information system development process	0	0	0	0	0	0	0	1	0	0	0	1
RF5 Make system requirement analysis	1	0	0	0	0	0	1	1	1	0	0	4
RF6 Manage project plan	1	1	1	1	1	1	1	1	1	1	1	11
RF7 Manage, monitor and evaluate project	1	1	0	1	1	0	1	0	1	1	1	8
RF8 Manage project team	0	1	1	1	0	0	1	0	1	0	0	5
RF9 Manage team experience	0	1	1	0	0	0	0	0	0	0	0	2
RF10 Manage team communication	0	1	0	0	0	0	0	0	0	0	0	1
RF11 Manage public sector procedures and processes	1	1	0	0	0	0	0	1	1	1	1	6
Dependence power	7	7	4	3	2	1	4	7	8	6	6	

RF6 (Manage project plan) leads to RF7 (Manage, monitor and evaluate project), then leads to RF8 (Manage project team). RF8 leads to RF5 (Make system requirement analysis) and simultaneously RF5 leads to RF3 (Involve IS end-users), and RF11 (Manage public sector procedures and processes). RF7 leads to RF1 (Top management

Table 7. Final reachability matrix of risk factors.

Risk factors	RF1	RF2	RF3	RF4	RF5	RF6	RF7	RF8	RF9	RF10	RF11	Driving power
RF1 Top management support	1	1	1	1	0	0	0	0	1ᵃ	1ᵃ	1	7
RF2 Manage processes in organization	1	1	1	1	0	0	0	0	1ᵃ	1ᵃ	1	7
RF3 Involve IS end-users	1	1	1	1	0	0	0	0	1	1	1	7
RF4 Manage information system development process	0	0	0	1	0	0	0	0	0	0	0	1
RF5 Make system requirement analysis	1ᵃ	1ᵃ	1	1	1	0	0	0	1ᵃ	1ᵃ	1	8
RF6 Manage project plan	1	1	1	1	1	1	1	1	1	1	1	11
RF7 Manage, monitor and evaluate project	1	1	1	1ᵃ	1	0	1	1	1ᵃ	1	1	10
RF8 Manage project team	1ᵃ	1ᵃ	1	1ᵃ	1	0	0	1	1	1	1ᵃ	9
RF9 Manage team experience	0	0	0	0	0	0	0	0	1	1	0	2
RF10 Manage team communication	0	0	0	0	0	0	0	0	0	1	0	1
RF11 Manage public sector procedures and processes	1	1	1	1	0	0	0	0	1ᵃ	1	1	7
Dependence power	**8**	**8**	**8**	**9**	**4**	**1**	**2**	**3**	**9**	**10**	**8**	

ᵃMarks explain the transitivity relationships between factors

support) and RF2 (Manage processes in organization). The four risk factors: RF1, RF2, RF3, RF11 lead to RF4 (Manage information system development). RF3 leads to RF9 (Manage team experience) and next RF9 leads to RF10 (Manage team communication). RF3 and RF11 also lead to RF10.

RF6 (Manage project plan) has been identified as the most driving risk factors in Table 7. That is why RF6 is presented at the bottom of the ISM model. The most dependent factor shown in Table 7 is RF10 (Manage team communication). Right behind RF10, the most dependent factors are RF4 (Manage information system development process) and RF9 (Manage team experience). The factors with the strongest dependence power are placed at the top of the ISM model.

MIMAC Analysis. The objective of the cross-impact matrix multiplication (MIC-MAC) analysis is to analyze the driving power and the dependence power of risk factors [33]. The risk factors are classified into four categories: autonomous, linkage, dependent and independent factors. **The autonomous factors** have weak driving power and weak dependence power. They have few links, which may be very strong. **The linkage factors** have strong driving power and strong dependence power. These factors are unstable in the fact that any action on these factors will have an effect on others and also a feedback effect on themselves. **The dependent factors** have weak driving power but strong dependence power. **The independent factors** have strong

Table 8. Level partitioning results of risk factors.

Risk factors	Reachability set	Antecedent set intersect	Intersection set	Level
RF1 Top management support	1,2,3,4,9,10,11	1,2,3,5,6,7,8,11	1,2,3,11	**III**
RF2 Manage processes in organization	1,2,3,4,9,10,11	1,2,3,5,6,7,8,11	1,2,3,11	**III**
RF3 Involve IS end-users	1,2,3,4,9,10,11	1,2,3,5,6,7,8,11	1,2,3,11	**III**
RF4 Manage information system development process	4	1,2,3,4,5,6,7,8,11	4	**I**
RF5 Make system requirement analysis	1,2,3,4,5,9,10,11	5,6,7,8	5	**IV**
RF6 Manage project plan	1,2,3,4,5,6,7,8,9,10,11	6	6	**VII**
RF7 Manage, monitor and evaluate project	1,2,3,4,5,7,8,9,10,11	6,7	7	**VI**
RF8 Manage project team	1,2,3,4,5,8,9,10,11	6,7,8	8	**V**
RF9 Manage team experience	9,10	1,2,3,5,6,7,8,9,11	9	**II**
RF10 Manage team communication	10	1,2,3,5,6,7,8,9,10,11	10	**I**
RF11 Manage public sector procedures and processes	1,2,3,4,9,10,11	1,2,3,5,6,7,8,11	1,2,3,11	**III**

driving power but weak dependence power. Factors with a very strong driving power are called the 'key factors'.

The MICMAC analysis diagram is presented on Fig. 2. The driving and dependence power of each of the risk factors are calculated based on Table 7.

There can be observed that risk factors with a very strong driving power called the 'key factors' fall into the cluster III and IV as independent and linkage factors.

The independent factors are RF6 (Manage project plan), RF7 (Manage, monitor and evaluate project), RF8 (Manage project team), RF5 (Make system requirement analysis). These factors have high impact on other factors, although they are not strongly dependent on other factors.

The linkage factors are RF1 (Top management support), RF2 (Manage processes in organization), RF3 (Involve IS end users) and RF11 (Manage public sector procedures and processes). These linkage factors are linking between independent and dependent factors and coming in the middle of the ISM based hierarchical model.

The risk factors identified as the dependent factors are: RF9 (Manage team experience), RF4 (Manage information system development), and RF10 (Manage team communication). The dependent factors are coming at the top of the ISM based hierarchical model and these are desired to be constantly monitored in the IS projects.

None of the factors was defined as an autonomous factor.

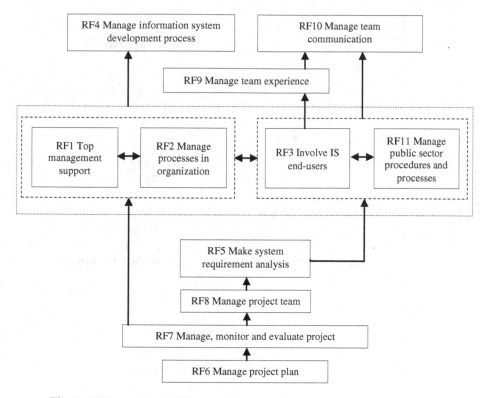

Fig. 1. ISM model of risk factors affecting IS projects in public organizations.

ISM Findings. ISM gives a realistic picture of the risk factors relationships. The ISM model allows to find key risk factors of IS project in public organizations, i.e.: RF6 (Manage project plan), RF7 (Manage, monitor and evaluate project), RF8 (Manage project team), RF5 (Make system requirement analysis), RF1 (Top management support), RF2 (Manage processes in organization), RF3 (Involve IS end-users) and (RF11 Manage public sector procedures and processes). The clue is that RF11 (Manage public sector procedures and processes) has significant influence on other risk factors, especially shown in the ISM model presented in Fig. 2. Moreover, RF11 is a linkage factor. This means that risk occurred in factors RF6, RF7, RF8, RF5, RF1, RF2 and RF3 can increase the probability of RF11 risk occurrence.

The driving-dependence diagram shown in Fig. 2 provides valuable insight into the relative importance and interdependencies among risk factors:

1. From the ISM model, it is observed that RF6 (Manage project plan) is placed at the bottom level of the hierarchy, which results from its highest driving power The second highest driving power is RF7 (Manage monitor and evaluate project). Therefore, the management should place high priority on tackling these factors which have a high driving power.

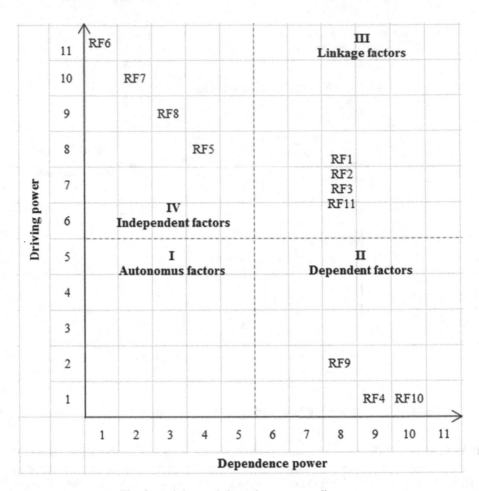

Fig. 2. Driving and dependence power diagram.

2. There are no autonomous factors on the driving dependence diagram. This means that all of the identified factors have influence on managing the risk in organization.
3. There are few dependent factors: RF9 (Manage team experience), RF10 (Manage team communication), and RF4 (Manage information system development).

5   Conclusion

5.1   Research Contribution

Identifying and understanding risk factors are crucial for the success of IS projects in public organizations. The paper enhances the framework of risk factors identified in the literature and proposes the comprehensive risk factors framework for IS projects in public organizations.

This study contributes to the extant research on risk factors affecting IS projects in two ways. Firstly, the risk factors for IS projects in public organization are analyzed and presented. Secondly, relationships among the indicated risk factors are examined.

There are eleven risk factors affecting IS projects in public organizations, namely (1) Top management support; (2) Manage processes in organization; (3) Involve IS end-users; (4) Manage information system development process; (5) Make system requirement analysis; (6) Manage project plan; (7) Manage, monitor and evaluate project; (8) Manage project team; (9) Manage team experience; (10) Manage team communication (11) Manage public sector procedures and processes.

The most significant risk factor is RF6 (Manage project plan). It means that when RF6 occurs, there is high probability that other risks will materialize.

5.2 Implications for Research and Practice

This study has implications for researchers. Firstly, researchers may develop, verify and improve the methodology of examining risk factors affecting IS projects in public organizations. Secondly, they can implement the proposed methodology to identify risk factors affecting IS projects in other countries. Thirdly, researchers may evaluate and enhance the ISM model of risk factors affecting IS projects in public organizations.

The findings of this study also have important implications for practitioners. In this research, public organizations could find knowledge related to the risk factors impacting successful IS projects. Especially, this research can be useful for the Central and Eastern European countries. This is because the countries are similar. Their similarity concerns their analogous geopolitical situation, their joint history, traditions, culture, and values. In addition, the similarity reflects in building democratic state structures and a free-market economy, participating in the European integration process, the levels of information systems implementation in public organizations. Moreover, they have to resolve the same problems and overcome the same political, economic, social, technological obstacles in their transition from traditional public organizations to organizations based on information systems.

5.3 Limitations and Future Research

As with many other studies, this study has its limitations. The main is that it is only based on two case studies in Poland. Caution should be taken when generalizing these findings. The issues of risk factors for IS projects in public organizations, therefore, should be explored in greater depth. There is a need to examine other case studies, and verify and enhance the risk factors framework. This will be considered as a future work. Also, the ISM model has its own limitations. Firstly, the model is highly dependent on the judgments of the experts. Secondly, although the ISM model provides an understanding of the relations between the risk factors, but it fails to quantify and test the influence of each risk factors constructs. This will be considered as a future work. Despite of the limitation, some generalization of the results is still possible.

Acknowledgement. This research has been supported by a grant entitled "Transformation of business and public administration by information technology and information systems" from the University of Economics in Katowice, Poland, 2014–2016.

References

1. Barros, M.O., Werner, C.M.L., Travassos, G.H.: Supporting risks in software project management. J. Syst. Softw. **70**(1–2), 21–35 (2004)
2. Nelson, R.R.: IT project management: infamous failure, classic mistakes, and best practices. MIS Q. Executive **6**(2), 67–78 (2007)
3. Charette, R.N.: Why software fails. IEEE Spectr. **42**(9), 42–49 (2005)
4. Bock, K., Trück, S.: Assessing uncertainty and risk in public sector investment projects. Technol. Invest. **2**, 105–123 (2011)
5. Zhou, L., Vasconcelos, A., Nunes, M.: Supporting decision making in risk management through an evidence-based information systems project risk checklist. Inf. Manag. Comput. Secur. **16**(2), 166–186 (2008)
6. Dey, P.K., Kinch, J., Ogunlana, S.O.: Managing risk in software development projects: a case study. Ind. Manag. Data Syst. **107**(2), 284–303 (2007)
7. Jiang, J.J., Klein, G., Discenza, R.: Information system success as impacted by risks and development strategies. IEEE Trans. Eng. Manag. **48**(1), 46–55 (2001)
8. Jani, A.: Escalation of commitment in troubled IT projects: influence of project risk factors and self-efficacy on the perception of risk and the commitment to a failing project. Int. J. Project Manag. **29**, 934–945 (2011)
9. Keil, M., Wallace, L., Turk, D., Dixon-Randall, G., Nulden, U.: An investigation of risk perception and risk propensity on the decision to continue a software development project. J. Syst. Softw. **53**(2), 145–157 (2000)
10. Tesch, D., Kloppenborg, T.J., Frolick, M.N.: IT project risk factors: the project management professional's perspective. J. Comput. Inf. Syst. **47**(4), 61–69 (2007)
11. Patanakul, P.: Managing large-scale IS/IT projects in the public sector: problems and causes leading to poor performance. J. High Technol. Manag. Res. **25**, 21–35 (2007)
12. Aritua, B., Smith, N.J., Bower, D.: What risks are common to or amplified in programmes: evidence from UK public sector infrastructure schemes. Int. J. Project Manag. **29**, 303–312 (2011)
13. Whittaker, B.: What went wrong? unsuccessful information technology projects. Inf. Manag. Comput. Secur. **7**(1), 23–30 (1999)
14. Baccarini, D., Salm, G., Love, P.E.D.: Management of risks in information technology projects. Ind. Manag. Data Syst. **104**(4), 286–295 (2004)
15. Wateridge, J.: IT projects: a basis for success. Int. J. Project Manag. **13**(3), 169–172 (1995)
16. Yildiz, M.: E-government research: Reviewing the literature, limitations, and ways forward. Gov. Inf. Q. **24**(3), 646–665 (2007)
17. Kliem, R., Ludin, I.: Reducing Project Risk. Gower Publishing Limited, Aldershot (2000)
18. Cadle, J., Yeate, D.: Project Management for Information Systems. Financial Times/Prentice-Hall, Harlow (2001)
19. Zwikael, O., Pathak, R.D., Singh, G., Ahmed, S.: The moderating effect of risk on the relationship between planning and success. Int. J. Project Manag. **32**, 435–441 (2014)

20. McGaughey Jr., R., Snyder, C., Carr, H.H.: Implementing information technology for competitive advantage: risk management issues. Inf. Manag. 26(5), 273–280 (1994)
21. Jugdev, K., Perkins, D., Fortune, J., White, D., Walker, D.: An exploratory study of project success with tools, software and methods. Int. J. Manag. Projects Bus. 6(3), 534–551 (2013)
22. Rabechini Junior., R., Monteiro de Carvalho, M.: Understanding the impact of project risk management on project performance: an empirical study. J. Technol. Manag. Innov. 8, 64–78 (2013)
23. Raz, T., Michael, E.: Use and benefit of tools for project risk management. Int. J. Project Manag. 19(1), 9–17 (2001)
24. Nalewaik, A.: Risk management for pharmaceutical project schedules. AACE Int. Trans. 7, 71–75 (2005)
25. Das, T.K., Teng, B.S.: Managing risks in strategic alliances. Acad. Manag. Executive 13(4), 50–62 (1999)
26. Cook, P.: Formalized risk management: vital tool for project- and business-success. Cost Eng. 47(8), 12–13 (2005)
27. Holzmann, V., Spiegler, I.: Developing risk breakdown structure for information technology organizations. Int. J. Project Manag. 29, 537–546 (2011)
28. Keil, M., Cule, P., Lyytinen, K., Schmidt, R.: A framework for identifying software project risks. Commun. ACM 41(11), 76–83 (1998)
29. López, J.C., Salmeron, L.: Risks response strategies for supporting practitioners decision-making in software projects. Procedia Technol. 5, 437–444 (2012)
30. Liu, S., Wang, L.: Understanding the impact of risks on performance in internal and outsourced information technology projects: the role of strategic importance. Int. J. Project Manag. 32, 1494–1510 (2014)
31. Jun, L., Qiuzhen, W., Qingguo, M.: The effects of project uncertainty and risk management on IS development project performance: a vendor perspective. Int. J. Project Manag. 29, 923–933 (2011)
32. Dey, P.K., Clegg, B.T., Bennett, D.J.: Managing enterprise resource planning projects. Bus. Process Manag. J. 16(2), 282–296 (2010)
33. Attri, R., Dev, N., Sharma, V.: Interpretive Structural Modelling (ISM) approach: an overview. Res. J. Manag. Sci. 2(2), 3–8 (2013)
34. Mishra, R.P., Kodali, R.B., Gupta, G., Mundra, N.: Development of a framework for implementation of world-class maintenance systems using Interpretive Structural Modeling approach. Procedia CIRP 26, 424–429 (2015)
35. Barve, A., Kanda, A., Shankar, R.: Analysis of interaction among the barriers of third party logistics. Int. J. Agile Syst. Manag. 2(1), 109–129 (2007)
36. Luthra, S., Garg, D., Haleem, A.: An analysis of interactions among critical success factors to implement green supply chain management towards sustainability: an Indian perspective. Resour. Policy 46, 37–50 (2014). http://dx.doi.org/10.1016/j.resourpol.2014.12.006i
37. Yadav, D.K., Barve, A.: Analysis of critical success factors of humanitarian supply chain: an application of Interpretive Structural Modeling. Int. J. Disaster Risk Reduct. 12, 213–225 (2015)
38. Venkatesh, V.G., Rathi, S., Patwa, S.: Analysis on supply chain risks in Indian apparel retail chains and proposal of risk prioritization model using Interpretive Structural modeling. J. Retail. Consum. Serv. 26, 153–167 (2015)
39. Sage, A.: Interpretive Structural Modeling: Methodology for Large Scale Systems. McGraw-Hill, New York (1977)

40. Govindan, K., Palaniappan, M., Zhu, Q., Kannan, D.: Analysis of third party reverse logistics provider using Interpretive Structural Modeling. Int. J. Product. Econ. **140**, 204–211 (2012)
41. Ziemba, E., Kolasa, I.: Risk factors framework for information systems projects in public organizations – insight from Poland. In: Proceedings of the IEEE Conference, vol. 5, pp. 1575–1583 (2015)

Moral Hazard in IT Project Completion.
An Analysis of Supplier and Client Behavior
in Polish and German Enterprises

Bartosz Wachnik[✉]

Faculty of Production Engineering,
Institute of Organization of Production Systems,
Warsaw University of Technology, Narbutta 86, 02-524 Warsaw, Poland
bartek@wachnik.eu

Abstract. Implementing management support information systems with the use of outsourcing is the prevalent method of completing this type of project. Agency theory is one of the significant categories of theories used in the analysis of IT outsourcing. Literature studies indicate a research gap concerning the phenomenon of moral hazard in IT projects consisting in the implementation of management support information systems. The scope of this article is to present research results on the phenomenon of moral hazard amongst Polish and German clients and suppliers of MIS. The author used the case study method. The research results may be interesting for theoreticians of business informatics and for practitioners completing IT projects both in enterprises and government agencies.

Keywords: Moral hazard · IT project · MIS

1 Introduction

According to J. Lee [1], IT outsourcing means managing a company's IT infrastructure through administration mechanisms exercised in cooperation with external organizations. A particularly interesting area of IT outsourcing is the purchase of implementation services as part of the completion of IT projects consisting in management information system implementation. The issue of outsourcing in this type of project is clearly visible in the majority of companies and it requires further research by theoreticians of business informatics. Internationally, issues linked to IT outsourcing have been the subject of research by business informatics theoreticians for many years. J. Dibbern [2] analyzed 84 articles on IT outsourcing published between 1992 and 2000. 10 categories of theories used to analyze the question of IT outsourcing were identified, which were then divided into three groups: strategies, economy and

© Springer International Publishing Switzerland 2016
E. Ziemba (Ed.): FedCSIS 2015, LNBIP 243, pp. 77–90, 2016.
DOI: 10.1007/978-3-319-30528-8_5

social-organizational groups. Agency theory was ranked third in terms of the number of publications[1], which shows that it is frequently used in research on IT outsourcing.

Agency theory stems from the need to explain the behavior of participants in relations client-contractor, where both parties have different goals. The risk is known as agency problem, relations – as contract, and the parties of the relation – as principal and agent. Agency theory addresses the phenomenon of dependency, where the principal delegates tasks to the agent. Agency problem is considered in two aspects [3]. First, it refers to the contradictory goals of both parties, which result in different expectations dependent on classifying the risk priority differently – the so-called risk preferences, linked to the agent's activities carried out on the principals' orders. Both sides of the relation try to minimize the risk. Different goals may result from opportunism, where both sides enforce the realization of their own goals over common goals. The second problem refers to the mechanism which influences specific behaviors of the agent, according to the principal's expectations [4]. The unit which constitutes the basis of theory analysis is the contract defining the rules of cooperation between the principal and the agent. Important concepts introduced by the theory are: moral hazard, adverse selection and programmability. According to the research carried out by Dembe and Boden [5], the term "moral hazard" dates back to the 18th century and was widely used by British insurance companies until the end of the 19th century. The early usage of the term has negative connotations, linked to fraud or other immoral behavior – usually on the insuree's part. Renewed scientific interest in the phenomenon of moral hazard appeared amongst economists in the 1960s, and it was not applied to instances of fraud or immoral behavior. The term would be used to describe ineffectiveness, which could appear in case of bad risk management, rather than in the context of ethics.

We need to stress here that the agency theory, alongside institutionalism, the theory of contracts and the theory of transaction costs, constitutes a component of the new institutional economics [6], which is based on the idea of institution understood in three categories: *A.* social, defining the norms of human relations, *B.* legal, regulating the creation, duration and termination of legal relationship between legal entities and *C.* organizational, regulating the functioning of formal organizations, safeguarding certain norms.

J.M. Buchanan [7] confirmed that a new contractarian paradigm of a new institutional economics is forming, which he described by saying that "economics comes closer to being a 'science of contract' than a 'science of choice' [...] The maximizer must be replaced by the arbitrator, the outsider who tries to work out compromises among conflicting claims." This statement, as well as the concept of treating an enterprise as a cluster of contracts and making the project's success dependent upon the quality of contracts, fully confirm the rationale of the new institutional economics as a central element creating a model of IT services in the form of outsourcing.

---

[1] The ranking of theories applied to research of IT outsourcing with the use of 84 articles conducted by J. Dibbern, T. Goles, R. Hirscheim and B. Jayatilaka [2]. Theory of transaction costs—16, Strategic management theory—14, Agency theory—10, Group of resource allocation theories—9, Group of social exchange theories—7, Game theory—4, Theory of power group—2, Diffusion of innovations theory—2, Other theories, e.g. of knowledge management, risk management, psychological contract—13.

The scope of the article is to present research results concerning the incidence of moral hazard in IT project completion as part of outsourcing. The subject of research are two groups of enterprises and their behavior:

Clients (principals)—enterprises in Poland and Germany which implemented MIS on the basis of outsourcing.

Suppliers (agents)—enterprises in Poland and Germany which completed MIS implementations for their clients.

In the article, the author focuses on projects consisting in the implementation of management support information systems (MIS), i.e. ERP and BI. The article stems from an attempt to identify the conditions influencing the effectiveness of completing a given group of IT projects based on outsourcing. According to the author, the factors influencing the effectiveness of IT project completion have been changing over the years and their character has become increasingly nuanced. This results from many factors, i.e. the rapidly changing technology, the evolution of project completion methods, the fast-growing saturation of IT system markets, the hypercompetition amongst suppliers, the behaviors and practices of clients and suppliers during the process of sale or project completion.

According to the author, researching the problem of outsourcing in IT projects is important, where the results will be beneficial both for theoreticians of business informatics and practitioners working in companies and government agendas. The article belongs to a cycle of the author's articles written to present the results of research on IT project completion as part of outsourcing [8–10].

2 Literature Review

According to Y. Lichtenstein [11], agency theory describes the methods of completing IT projects during the whole life cycle of a project, i.e. as part of the following three stages:

Stage 1—Organization and completion of a tender aimed at selecting a MIS and a company to implement it.

Stage 2—IT project completion.

Stage 3—Information system operation on the basis of an SLA contract.

Agency theory presents the contract for the service of implementation of a management support information system between the supplier and the customer as a relation between an agent and a principal. During the first stage of a project's life, an outsourcing agreement for the provision of IT system implementation services is established, and later on a Service Level Agreement is negotiated. Y. Lichtenstein [11] indicates that in case of negotiating IT project agreements, and later their implementation, an incompatibility of both parties' interests occurs. The client's goal and interest is the completion of an IT project within the planned time frame and budget, considering the Total Cost of Ownership (TCO) and meeting all the organizational and technological requirements designed for the project. The supplier's goal and interest lies in achieving a planned income in the whole life cycle of the project, meeting the planned quality of completed work. Table 1 presents the contradictions between the

Table 1. Goals and interests of both transaction parties (Source: own study)

Client's goals and interests	Supplier's goals and interests
Fulfilling business goals	Completing the project according to the
Fulfilling technological goals	planned quality
Completing the project within the time frame	Maximizing the project's profitability in its
Completing the project within the planned	entire life cycle, i.e. implementation and
budget	usage
Minimizing the total cost of software	Obtaining reference information after the
ownership (TCO)	completion of the project, which will allow
Achieving functional and technological	the supplier to sell services to other projects
solutions creating a temporary competitive	
edge	

client's and supplier's interest in case of completing an IT project consisting in the MIS implementation.

The author's research [8, 10] indicates that a high level of information asymmetry between the agent-supplier and principal-client in an IT implementation project means that both parties may be prone to an abuse of trust (moral hazard) at all stages of the project life cycle. The level of information asymmetry between the agent and the principal is dynamic and changes both in individual stages of project life and in individual project tasks of the implementation project, i.e. in stage 2. Literature study shows that information asymmetry researchers focus mainly on the client's perspective; as a result moral hazard on the supplier's side becomes the most important area of research, marginalizing this phenomenon on the client's side. The author's intention is to attempt to diagnose and understand the phenomenon of moral hazard both on the side of the supplier and the client.

Describing the phenomenon of moral hazard on both sides, it is worth quoting the opinion of Y. Lichtenstein [11] points out that a high level of information asymmetry between the supplier-agent and the client-principal means that at every stage of the project's life cycle, the supplier-agent may be prone to the abuse of trust: moral hazard, which results directly from the high level of information asymmetry concerning both the ERP, CRM, DMS and BI-class software as such, and the method of implementing the project. Especially in the case of projects completed on the basis of a fixed budget, the supplier-agent may have a strong motivation to push the cost below the planned budget, which can have an influence on the quality of services[2].

The supplier-agent possesses all the information about their current activities and all their plans linked to project completion, while the client-principal has only a limited knowledge in this area. Knowledge concerning the completion of IT projects consisting

---

[2] The research was carried out in 2013. It covered 500 enterprises where 895 IT projects consisting in the implementation of ERP, CRM, BI, DMS, BI and E-learning-class MIS were completed. The chosen enterprises were based in Mazovia and Lesser Poland and the research was conducted among enterprises employing less than 400 people. Research results showed that in the MIS market in Poland, the structure of agreement types is as follows: 68 %—fixed price contract, 27 %—time and material contract, 5 %—cost-reimbursable contracts.

in the implementation of management support information systems is increasingly robust and dynamically changing, which means that the client-principal is not able to effectively negotiate a favorable contract, and then supervise this type of project on their own. Analogically, the supplier-agent may not be able to obtain and define their client's functional requirements. Due to the fact that both parties' interests are not equal, they may be prompted to take inappropriate action, i.e. abuse trust (moral hazard), in a situation where they are not controlled because their knowledge and experience limit the possibilities of effective control. Potentially morally hazardous behavior of one of the parties is aimed at securing their own goals and individual interests, which may result from opportunism. To sum up, the result of trust abuse by the supplier-agent or the client-principal in the project's whole life cycle may be the occurrence of one, or a combination of several organizational complications impacting the effectiveness of an IT project, i.e.:

1. Interrupting the project or terminating the implementation agreement by one of the parties.
2. Lack of complete or partial fulfillment of project goals.
3. Unjustified exceeding of the budget in the completion of the second stage, as well as the third stage, the so-called Total Cost of Ownership.
4. Unjustified exceeding of the planned time frame for the completion of the second stage.

An important organizational aspect of the contract between the supplier-agent and the client-principal is an attempt to construct a mechanism which would effectively eliminate the possibility of trust abuse in the second and third stage of the project life cycle, also including transaction costs at each stage. Designing such a mechanism may turn out to be costly and difficult to complete [4]. The author's research results will allow us to indicate and describe selected attempts to abuse trust by the client-principal and supplier-agent in IT projects consisting in the implementation of MIS (ERP and BI).

3   Research Methodology

In his research, the author has used the case study method. The subjects of research are characterized in Table 2.

Table 2. Research subjects characteristic (Source: own study)

	Poland	Germany
Suppliers	Two enterprises implementing ERP and BI systems	Two enterprises implementing ERP and BI systems
Clients	Two enterprises that implemented ERP and BI systems based on the outsourcing strategy	Two enterprises that implemented ERP and BI systems based on the outsourcing strategy

The goal of the case study is developing the agency theory, and especially a better understanding of the notion of moral hazard in management support information systems. The author analyzes the case study, as it allows us to develop the existing theory and provide explanations of phenomena unrecognized before, such as moral hazard in IT projects. The focus is on analyzing the phenomenon of moral hazard both on the side of the client-principal and the supplier-agent during the whole life cycle of an IT project in an enterprise, i.e. from the bidding stage to the usage of MIS. The choice of research method: case study, is motivated chiefly by two circumstances [12]:

- The early stage of knowledge development in the given research area, i.e. agency theory in a specific group of IT projects.
- Lack of recognition of moral hazard in real conditions.

As part of the multiple case study analysis, the author poses the following research question: In what behaviors does moral hazard in the relation between the principal (client) and the agent (supplier) manifest itself in case of IT projects consisting in the implementation of MIS based on outsourcing?

The choice of studied cases was carried out through purposive sampling. According to B. Flyvbjerg [13], there are five main criteria of case selection. Table 3 presents the criteria along with their characteristics in the context of conducted research.

Table 3. Five main criteria of case selection (Source: [13])

Criterion	Information on the fulfillment of the criteria
Data availability	Guaranteed
Distinctiveness of the case, clearly illustrating studied patterns	Projects that ended in partial failure, but not interrupted during the implementation
Variation in the analyzed cases	Variation in the analyzed cases is expressed in the selection of: – IT projects consisting in the implementation of MIS systems, i.e. ERP and BI – Client profile and supplier profile – The results of project implementation
Critical character of the phenomenon allowing to formulate a general statement	The incidence of moral hazard between the agent (supplier) and the principal (client) during the whole life cycle of project implementation influences the results of project implementation from the client's perspective.
Metaphor allowing to point the researcher's attention towards a specific course of the studied phenomenon	Aiming to analyze the phenomenon of moral hazard in the entire project life cycle, the author selected cases that could be studied in all the stages: bidding, agreement negotiations, implementation and information system usage.

4 Research Findings

Respondents in the client group were board members and company owners responsible for operational enterprise management, especially MIS implementations. Table 4 presents the results of case study research amongst the clients.

Table 4. Results of case study research amongst clients (Source: own study)

	Poland		Germany	
Client	Company CP1	Company CP2	Company CD1	Company CD2
Supplier	Company VP1	Company VP2	Company VD1	Company VD2
Supplier (agent) profile	Software re-seller	Software re-seller	Software re-seller	Software re-seller
Sold system class	ERP	BI	BI	ERP
Implementation results	Profitability of stage 2 close to the planned profitability	Profitability of stage 2 30 %–40 % lower than the planned profitability	Profitability of stage 2 close to the planned profitability	Profitability of stage 2 20 %–30 % lower than the planned profitability.
	The supplier obtained a client reference	The supplier did not obtain a client reference	The supplier obtained a client reference	The supplier did not obtain a client reference
Implementation services agreement type	Fixed budget	Fixed budget	Fixed budget	Fixed budget
How does moral hazard manifest itself in the client's actions during project completion?	1. A desire to increase the project's functional scope compared to the originally established scope and fixed budget, e.g. performing additional programming changes enriching the standard	1. A desire to make the supplier responsible for a part of project work that according to the original agreement was supposed to be carried out by the client, e.g. designing system documentation	1. A desire to increase the functional scope of the implementation project, compared to the originally established scope and fixed budget, e.g. performing additional reports and analyses, without	1. A desire to increase the number of trained system users, despite originally declaring a lower number

(*Continued*)

Table 4. (*Continued*)

Poland		Germany	
system configuration without additional remuneration for the supplier		additional remuneration for the supplier	
2. A desire to treat mistakes of the system end users in stage 3, i.e. usage as mistakes resulting from wrong system configuration in stage 2	2. Client's attempt to postpone the acceptance of the tasks completed during the project, without a rational justification, in order to delay the payment		2. Client's attempt to postpone the acceptance of the tasks completed during the project, without a rational justification, in order to delay the payment

Respondents in the supplier group included board members and company owners responsible for selling implementation services and completing the projects for the clients. Table 5 presents results of case study research amongst the suppliers.

Table 5. Results of case study research amongst suppliers (Source: own study)

	Poland		German	
Client	Company CP1	Company CP2	Company CD1	Company CD2
Supplier	Company VP1	Company VP2	Company VD1	Company VD2
Supplier (agent) profile	Software re-seller	Software re-seller	Software re-seller	Software re-seller
Sold system class	ERP	BI	BI	ERP
Implementation results	Profitability of stage 2 close to the planned profitability	Profitability of stage 2 30 %–40 % lower than the planned profitability	Profitability of stage 2 close to the planned profitability	Profitability of stage 2 20 %–30 % lower than the planned profitability
	The supplier obtained a client reference	The supplier did not obtain a client reference	The supplier obtained a client reference	The supplier did not obtain a client reference
Implementation services agreement type	Fixed budget	Fixed budget	Fixed budget	Fixed budget
How does the supplier's	1. In stage 1, the stage 2 budget was calculated	1. Consciously giving the client	1. Consciously giving the client	1. Consciously giving the client general

(*Continued*)

Table 5. (*Continued*)

	Poland		German	
moral hazard manifest itself during project completion?	by the supplier based on a much lower hourly rate for the consultant than maintenance services in stage 3, completed on the basis of an SLA agreement. The difference in rates equaled 40 %	general meta-information concerning the services and software license in stage 1 in order to prevent them from being able to define precisely the TCO of the purchased IT system	general meta-information concerning the services and software license in stage 1 in order to prevent them from being able to define precisely the TCO of the purchased IT system	meta-information concerning the services and software license in stage 1 in order to prevent them from being able to define precisely the TCO of the purchased IT system
	2. Consciously giving the client general meta-information in stage 1 in order to prevent them from being able to define precisely the TCO of the purchased IT system	2. Engaging people with a low level of qualifications and little professional experience in the area of IT system implementation on the supplier's side	2. Decreasing the engagement of the supplier's consultants in some of the implementation tasks, e.g. the completion of acceptance tests and system tuning, compared to the obligations included in the offer/agreement covering the workload of this task	2. Engaging people with a low level of qualifications and little professional experience in the area of IT system implementation on the supplier's side
	3. Decreasing the engagement of the supplier's consultant in some of the implementation tasks, e.g. the completion of acceptance tests and system tuning, compared to the obligations included in the offer/agreement covering the workload of this task	3. Poor quality of knowledge transfer performed by the seller, both in terms of system configuration and usage by the end users, aimed at creating a competence gap on the client's side	3. Poor quality of knowledge transfer performed by the seller, both in terms of system configuration and usage by the end users, aimed at creating a competence gap on the client's side	3. Decreasing the engagement of the supplier's consultants in some of the implementation tasks, e.g. the completion of acceptance tests and system tuning, compared to the obligations included in the offer/agreement covering the workload of this task
	4. The supplier's consultant-programmer programs the system to decrease the workload in the stage 2 completion, e.g. entering constants instead of variables in the code, eliminating the possibility to perform configuration of the given function in stage 3 easily and without a big workload			4. The supplier's consultant-programmer programs the system to decrease the workload in the stage 2 completion, e.g. entering constants instead of variables in the code, eliminating the possibility to perform configuration of the given function in stage 3 easily and without a big workload

The subject of analysis were ERP and BI-class MIS implementations completed as part of an agreement based on a fixed budget. All the analyzed implementations, both in Poland and in Germany, ended in partial failure, i.e. at least one of the conditions was not fulfilled:

- Completing the project according to the budget planned in stage 1.
- Completing the project according to the schedule planned in stage 1.
- Completing the project goals.

We need to stress that despite a partial failure, none of the projects was interrupted during its completion. The author's analysis consisted in diagnosing the behaviors where moral hazard resulting from the opportunism[3] predominantly occurred and where a high level of information asymmetry between them manifested itself in IT projects. During the research, the author identified the following behaviors of suppliers providing services linked to ERP and BI system implementations both in Poland and Germany, where moral hazard occurred in all the stages of project life cycle.

Behavior 1. An attempt to minimize the supplier's cost of completing stage 2 and 3 of the project by:

- Engaging specialists with low competences and little experience, which is linked to their lower salary.
- Lowering the actual workload of consultants working on specific tasks in the project in comparison to the workload declared in the agreement regulating the outsourcing of implementation services.

Behavior 2. An attempt to sell implementation services concerning stage 2 at a lowered price, which will allow them to win the tender in the conditions of hyper-competition in the market. The supplier's intention is to compensate for the possible losses in stage 2 with profits in stage 3.

Behavior 3. An attempt to intentionally complete chosen types of project tasks in stage 2 poorly, e.g. acceptance tests, training and project documentation in order to create a competence gap concerning system configuration amongst client's application users and make it impossible for them to introduce changes to the configuration independently, e.g. in stage 3, which will increase the number of client's orders from the supplier.

Behavior 4. The supplier's strategy of only passing general meta-information in stage 1 to the client concerning project completion in stage 2, the license scope, the implementation methodology, the consultants' competences and the completion of post-implementation services in stage 3. This means the client is not able to define the TCO of the implemented MIS in the whole project life cycle.

During the research, the author identified the following behaviors amongst the clients of ERP and BI system implementations both in Poland and in Germany, where moral hazard resulting from opportunism occurred in all the stages of system life cycle.

---

[3] *Polish Language Dictionary* (Warszawa: PWN, 1996), defines opportunism as concentrating on one's personal interest while ignoring common goals and generally assumed codes of behavior.

Behavior 1. In stage 1, client passing only meta-information concerning functional requirements for the implemented system. A lack of precise definition of the implementation's functional scope results in an attempt to increase the project's functional scope, compared to the meta-scope agreed on earlier based on the meta-information obtained both in stage 2, as well as in case of some tasks in stage 3, without additional remuneration for the supplier.

Behavior 2. Client's attempt to intentionally treat the actual mistakes of end users of MIS in stage 3 as mistakes resulting from the supplier's mistakes in configuring system in stage 2, hence justifying their desire to obtain compensation from the supplier.

Behavior 3. Client's attempt to intentionally postpone sharing the results of acceptance tests in stage 2 in order to delay their payment for the tasks completed by the supplier.

To sum up, in their entire life cycles, the analyzed projects did not end in full project success, however we need to stress that the projects were not interrupted and abandoned. Two main results of project complications were observed, i.e. exceeding the budget both in stage 2 and 3, and exceeding the time frame without justification while completing stage 2. In each case, both in projects completed in Poland and Germany, the clients engaged external consultants, who in the first two stages of the project played the part of the "client's advocates", indicating the dangers linked to the supplier's behavior and the possible consequences of their materialization. Another role of the external consultants was suggesting counter-actions to the client, in order to minimize the danger of the project ending in a total failure. Most probably, it was the engagement of these external consultants that led to the projects' partial success and prevented them from failing completely. The respondents from the client's and supplier's side clearly indicated that the behavior on both sides, where the moral hazard occurred, was one of the sources of project complications.

Amongst the researched IT projects in Polish and German companies, four types of behavior were identified where moral hazard on the side of the supplier-agent occurred. An in-depth analytical workshop with representatives of the supplier-agent's side have shown that their intention was to achieve and guarantee their planned profitability and obtaining a client reference. It is noteworthy that neither of the suppliers managed to achieve their planned profitability in stage 2, although all the suppliers admitted that the project completion was profitable. It is interesting that none of the suppliers managed to obtain a reference from their clients supporting their handling of the implementation project as a proof of their company's skills and competence.

Amongst the researched IT projects in Polish and German companies, three types of behavior were identified where moral hazard on the side of the client-principal occurred. An in-depth analytical workshop with representatives of the client-principal's side have shown that their intention was for their company to achieve a business value allowing to build a temporary competitive edge at the lowest possible cost.

We need to stress that the respondents from the client's and the supplier's side pointed out that moral hazard at each stage of the IT project leads to a deep crisis of trust and decreases the chances of a successful project completion. The mutual loss of trust influences the increase of transaction costs [14], especially the cost of monitoring the agreement implementation, the adjustment cost and the cost of terminating the agreement by the client, which can on its own lead to a complete failure of the project.

In the analyzed cases, increasing client's and supplier's transaction costs was visible mostly in the increasing workload of the stage 1 and project tasks. Table 6 presents the results of in-depth workshops with representatives from the client's side and supplier's side along with their suggestions that they would like to pass on to the future client's and supplier's project managers, in order to minimize the occurrence of moral hazard in future projects.

Table 6. Project manager suggestions – client and supplier side (Source: own study)

Suggestions for client's project managers	Suggestions for supplier's project managers

– Engaging external consultants as the client's "advocates", supporting the client in the completion of stage 1 and 2
– Designing an implementation agreement that could help eliminate those of the supplier's behaviors where moral hazard manifested
– Professional preparation for project completion by the client's project group employees:
  - Defining precisely (ex-ante) functional requirements for the system
  - Defining precisely (ex-ante) the direct and indirect project benefits.
  - Defining precisely (ex-ante) supplier requirements
  - Defining precisely (ex-ante) IT system requirements
	– Passing on important information concerning the software licensing rules, both those beneficial for the client and not, which will allow to define the TCO of the purchased license
	– Passing on important information concerning the organization of the IT system implementation project
	– Passing on important information concerning the IT system sold in stage 1 and implemented in stage 2
	– Transferring full and complete information concerning the IT system, which will allow to define the TCO
	– Designing an implementation agreement that could help eliminate those of the supplier's behaviors where moral hazard manifested
	– Professional preparation for project completion by the supplier's project group employees

5   Conclusion

In the MIS market, what dictates the decision behind information purchase is the buyer's subjective belief that the product that they do not know can meet their specific needs and that its price reflects its usage value. The difference between a material product and an information product lies in the fact that in case of a material product the potential buyer may demand the type of product information that they find indispensable to making a transaction decision. In case of an information product, this is not possible. In the stage 1, the buyer has to do with certain meta-information, usually hard to verify, which may present a simplified image of the purchased product, while in stage 2 the supplier often gets general meta- information from the client, which constitutes verbalized system requirements. According to the author, the "pig in a poke" syndrome occurs in the MIS market and is noticeable both amongst the suppliers and the recipients [15]. The author's research indicates that IT implementation projects are characterized by a high information asymmetry between the supplier and the client as part of the agreement [16].

The respondents stressed that the agreements of software licensing purchase, service purchase and Service Level Agreement are not simple and even in the current economic structure there are very few specialized lawyers who, combining their legal and MIS knowledge, could secure the company's interests. During in-depth analytical workshops, the respondents indicated that many lawyers designed the agreements trying to eliminate morally hazardous behavior, struggling between two extreme approaches, i.e. case-specific agreement, which was supposed to foresee and eliminate the majority of dangers resulting from cooperation in stage 2 and 3, and a simplified agreement regulating only the basic aspects of the cooperation. In case of case-specific agreements, transaction costs increase dramatically[4]. The presented research results expose the main behaviors of suppliers and clients, where moral hazard resulting from opportunism and a high level of information asymmetry between the client (principal) and the supplier (agent) occurs in IT projects. All types of behavior typical to moral hazard increased the risk of effective IT project completion and transaction costs, for example through the loss of mutual trust. An analysis of research results shows that very similar morally hazardous behaviors can be observed both amongst the suppliers and the clients of IT projects in Poland and Germany. It is worth noting the respondents' opinion that the level of trust is higher between German companies than between Polish companies. The difference of trust levels influences transaction costs and the duration of period when the project is defined and the details of the agreement negotiated – both of them in stage 1. In case of projects completed in Poland, the above actions took 7 months during an ERP implementation and 6 months in case of a BI implementation. In Germany-based projects, the above actions took 3 months in case of an ERP implementation and 2.5 months during a BI implementation. It needs to be stressed that the above mentioned periods of time do not cover the purchase/sale process, which include supplier and system presentations, as well as the final selection of the supplier.

The new institutional economics treats enterprises as a cluster of contracts and it makes the success of the projects dependent on the quality of agreements. We need to underline that the institutional economics focuses not only on analyzing the available choices and making those choices, but also on solving conflicts as part of the enterprise's stream of contracts. Considering the current and projected saturation of the market with MIS, we need to stress that a cluster of contracts regulating IT outsourcing constitutes one of the most important agreement groups in a large group of enterprises. The author believes that the subject of reducing the occurrence of moral hazard, both amongst the suppliers and the clients, during purchase/sale transactions of technologically advanced products currently constitutes a very important problem, which should be touched upon both by academic theoreticians and practitioners.

---

[4] In one of the analyzed cases in Poland, the case-specific implementation services agreement for stage 2 was over 300 pages long, it was negotiated for 4 months, while the implementation project lasted 3 months and did not exceed 50 000 PLN (around 12 000 EUR).

References

1. Lee, J.N., Miranda, S.M., Kim, Y.M.: IT outsourcing strategies: universalistic, contingency, and configurational explanations of success. Inf. Syst. Res. **15**(2), 110–131 (2004)
2. Dibbern, J., Goles, T., Hirscheim, R., Jayatilaka, B.: Information systems outsourcing: a survey and analysis of the literature. Data Base Adv. Inf. Syst. **35**(4), 6–102 (2004)
3. Auksztol, J.: IT Outsourcing in Management, Theory and Practice (Outsourcing Informatyczny w Teorii i Praktyce Zarządzania), pp. 50–51. University of Gdańsk Press, Gdańsk (2008)
4. Eiscnhardt, K.M.: Agency theory: an assessment and review. Acad. Manag. Rev. **14**(1), 57–74 (1989)
5. Dembe, A.E., Boden, L.I.: Moral hazard: a question of morality? New Solutions **10**(3), 257–279 (2000)
6. Gruszecki, T.: Modern Enterprise Theories (Współczesne Teorie Przedsiębiorstwa), p. 193. PWN, Warsaw (2002)
7. Buchanan, J.M.: A contractarian paradigm for applying economic theory. Am. Econ. Rev. **65**(2), 225–230 (1975)
8. Wachnik, B.: Reducing information asymmetry in IT projects–action research results. Sci. J. (Zeszyty Naukowe) **188**, 237–249 (2014). University of Economics in Katowice Publisher, Katowice
9. Wachnik, B.: Information asymmetry in four IT projects: the client's perspective. A multiple case study. Inf. Syst. Manage. **2**, 155–168 (2015)
10. Wachnik, B.: An analysis of effectiveness factors in the completion of it projects - the supplier's perspective. Sc. J. (Zeszyty Naukowe) 234, 1–12 (2015). University of Economics in Katowice Publisher, Katowice
11. Lichtenstein, Y.: Puzzles in Software Development Contracting. Commun. ACM **47**(2), 61–65 (2004)
12. Yin, R.: Case Study Research: Design and Methods. Sage Publications, Thousand Oaks (1984)
13. Flyvbjerg, B.: Five misunderstandings about case-study research. In: Seale, C., Gobo, G., Gubrium, J.F., Silverman, D. (eds.) Qualitative Research Practice. Sage Publications, London, Thousand Oaks (2004)
14. Williamson, O.E.: Market and hierarchies: some elementary considerations. Am. Econ. Rev. **61**(2), 112–123 (1971)
15. Wachnik, B.: Information Asymmetry in the MIS Market (Asymetria Informacyjna na Rynku Systemów Informatycznych Wspierających Zarządzanie). In: Porębska-Miąc, T., Sroka, H. (eds.) Proceedings of the 27th Conference on Organization Support Systems 2013 (XXVII Konferencja Systemy Wspomagania Organizacji SWO 2013), pp. 272–286. University of Economics in Katowice Publisher, Katowice (2013)
16. Wachnik, B.: Reducing information asymmetry in IT projects. Bus. Inf. (Informatyka Ekonomiczna) **1**(31), 178–212 (2014). The Publishing House of the Wrocław University of Economics, Wrocław

Modelling of Software Agents in Knowledge-Based Organisations. Analysis of Proposed Research Tools

Mariusz Żytniewski[✉], Andrzej Sołtysik,
Anna Sołtysik-Piorunkiewicz, and Bartosz Kopka

Faculty of Informatics and Communication,
University of Economics in Katowice, 1 Maja 50, 40-287 Katowice, Poland
{mariusz.zytniewski,andrzej.soltysik,
anna.soltysik-piorunkiewicz,
bartosz.kopka}@ue.katowice.pl

Abstract. The development of the theory of multi-agent systems in the area of their use to support an organisation can be examined in the context of supporting the performance of business processes and knowledge management processes that take place in modern organisations, in particular knowledge-based organisations. Agent technologies created in this area can be considered in categories of software agent societies, where a multi-agent solution is supported by mechanisms for analysing behaviour of such a system. The aim of this paper is to analyse research methodology and scientific tools developed during the three last years by a team of researchers in the specified field. The paper presents theoretical issues connected with the use of knowledge management systems in organisations, partial results of interviews with developers of agent solutions in Poland, a proposal of a methodology for designing agent societies, elements of a developed prototype of an agent solution, findings of qualitative research in the area of usability of software agents and assessments of multi-agent systems supporting knowledge management.

Keywords: Software agent · Agent societies · Knowledge management · Knowledge-based organization · Usability

1 Introduction

Development of organization's theory for modern forms of management of the company's action results in that solutions need to adapt their structure and functionality to meet the specific needs of the organization. One example is to look at the management-oriented approach to knowledge, which is seen as an important organization's resource. Such knowledge, perceived in the literature as an overt or covert knowledge, is an essential part of business processes that such organizations implement. Solutions, which according to the authors have the indicated characteristics, are agent systems.

The development of a theory of agent systems as an element of knowledge supporting systems in organisations requires that new concepts are constructed in the form of methodologies, methods and models that support designing, construction and

© Springer International Publishing Switzerland 2016
E. Ziemba (Ed.): FedCSIS 2015, LNBIP 243, pp. 91–108, 2016.
DOI: 10.1007/978-3-319-30528-8_6

assessment of information systems of this type. Studies conducted over the last few years by a team of researchers enabled the development of a set of research tools to support the process of modelling software agent societies in knowledge-based organisations.

The studies conducted by the authors, initiated in 2012, on the modelling of a software agent society in organizations based on knowledge, were focused on the search for forms of use of software agents in the context of their use in modern organizations and determination whether these solutions, aided by semantic knowledge representation, contribute to the improvement of business processes. Due to their complexity, first an analysis of the literature in this area was conducted in order to arrange a society of agents in the registration system used in organizations [1–3]. Further, IT companies which offer agent-based solutions were asked to indicate their main problems with modelling and implementation [4, 5]. As a result, studies on currently used multi-agent platforms [6] and agent systems design methodologies [7] allowed the authors to propose a modelling methodology of a software agent society [8–10], its possible architecture [11, 12]. The second area of the studies was to develop a research method to assess the impact of software agents on participants of business processes. The studies presented in papers [13–15] enabled the development of a multi-stage research method to assess usability of software agents. The third element was the development of a trust and reputation model and indicators allowing trust and reputation to be assessed in an agent society. Results of these studies were presented in papers [10, 16–18]. The last element was the development of a method for examining a multi-agent system, which was used in the area of analysis of agent systems applied in e-health.

The elements of the specified research tools and results will be presented in this paper.

2 Knowledge Management in Organizations (Literature Review)

The concept of knowledge management (KM) was developed to discover tools and methodology of management of knowledge, which was described as one of classical factor of production with land, labour and capital by Drucker [19]. The term of knowledge management is one of the most promoted and integrated approach to identifying, capturing, evaluating, retrieving, and sharing all of an enterprise's information assets. These assets may include databases, documents, policies, procedures, and previously uncaptured expertise and experience in individual workers [20].

Knowledge management system (KMS) is dedicated to help an organization to meet its goals and to increase its effectiveness. The literature review shows that a number of different definitions of knowledge management system have been proposed in the literature, and debates about this concept have been expressed from a variety of perspectives and positions [21–23]. Also there are some models of life cycle knowledge management in organization [24, 25]. Information and communication technologies (ICT) may play an important role in effectuating the knowledge-based view of the organization to manage the knowledge it possesses [20, 24]. KMSs are technologies that support knowledge management in organizations, specifically, knowledge generation, codification, and transfer. Nowadays, modern ICT (interactive communication channels, agent oriented technologies, etc.) in a company due to the development of Web 2.0/3.0, i.e., social media, blogs, micro blogs, forums, wikis, and others, makes an impact in knowledge-based organization.

Knowledge-based organizations understand the importance of knowledge in the process of creating a competitive edge and focus on creating value added based on an effective use of knowledge [26]. ICT solutions focus on the aspect of supporting. Such organizations should support business processes that take place in them in the area of creating, processing and sharing a contextual knowledge about them. This results from the fact that knowledge-based organizations focus not only on business processes but also on knowledge management processes which should be treated in such organizations equivalently. Nowadays a knowledge management system is facilitated by Web-based ICTs. It is worth underlining, that the majority of companies use well known ICTs, for example: e-mails, online surveys, social networks, Internet forums, business blogs, comments posted on a producer website, business (specialized) portals, online price comparison [27–29].

One of the solutions, that can help such organizations, are software agent societies which can support the different stages of knowledge management systems life cycle [2, 30].

There are some models of life cycle knowledge management in organization. Some of the models refer to the first phase as knowledge creation, but Davenport and Prusak [24] use the term generate knowledge. The Turban's Knowledge Management Cycle [20] shows six steps of processes:

(1) Create knowledge; (2) Capture knowledge; (3) Refine knowledge; (4) Store knowledge; (5) Manage knowledge; (6) Disseminate knowledge.

The study shows the kind of models of agent supported organizations [1]:

- Information allocation model - an agent model refers to the way information flows between the organization and its environment, and additionally the influence of the information on the organization, using a software agent.
- The presence of authority's model - the participation of agents as the authorities in a decision making process relied on two features: modularity and decentralization.
- Organizational norms and culture model – an agent's behaviour depends on the organization's historical factors which are contained in the organization's norms and culture,
- Motivating model – the human factor can be subjected to various influences which in the case of the use of agent-based solutions come down to a certain decision imperative of an agent.

3 Methodological Aspects of Designing Software Agent Societies (Research Methodology)

Studies conducted by the authors allowed them to develop research tools in the form of a few coherent concepts which may contribute to the development of modelling of software agent societies in knowledge based organisations. They include a concept of methodology for modelling software agent societies, a trust and reputation model in a software agent society and a method for examining usability of software agents. The development of the specified solutions was preceded by a range of in-depth interviews with IT companies in Poland engaged in creation and implementation of agent solutions.

3.1 Software Agent Societies and Problems with Their Implementation

Agent solutions currently available on the market are used to support the interaction between the human being and the computer. Studies confirmed this trend. The solutions created by respondents should be considered in the vast majority in the context of supporting knowledge management systems. Most of them can be examined in their role of interface agents that communicate with the user in a way that is closest to natural communication [31], along with their most important functionality of active participation in business processes using their own database of codified knowledge linked with an organisation's information systems. Studies conducted by the authors allowed them to analyse and compare the approaches of different vendors of agent solutions designed to support the improvement of business processes in knowledge based organisations. Among the solutions offered to the market in the use of agent technologies in the sphere of supporting business processes in organizations managed by knowledge, the vast majority are so-called "virtual advisors" showing, in accordance with the adopted typology, lowest level of socialization [32, 33]. The studies enabled identification of the tools used by vendors of agent solutions at the stage of their development. The researchers' attention was focused mainly on methodologies for creating agent solutions. The developers of the solutions under examination stressed that their methodologies for building agent systems concentrated mainly on the architecture of these systems, and only to a small extent enabled modelling of the knowledge of a system. This results mainly from the lack of reliable solutions that use a methodological approach to modelling semantic mechanisms of knowledge representation for the purpose of agent structures. Respondents were mostly in favour of the use of popular agile methodologies, which are typically applied in the creation of traditional IT systems. They mostly based their works on good practices, identifying their own methodologies dedicated to agent solutions. None of the sets of tools used by the respondents included methodologies focused directly on creating software agent societies. The process of identifying methodologies requires, on the one hand, addressing the issues of methods for creating software, while on the other hand, taking into account the theory of knowledge engineering, which is required in the context of modelling agents' knowledge database. Apart from the problems concerning methodologies, the respondents indicated the necessity to find methods for assessing the impact of solutions they created on the operation of the organisation itself and its environment.

Despite the lack of universal designing methodologies dedicated to the process of creating agent solutions, the process of implementing an agent solution by different vendors is similar. In simple terms, we can assume that this process comprises four main stages.

The process begins with analysis and gathering of information from the user to be later used to formulate knowledge of an agent. The fundamental problem at this stage is lack of structuring and a large diversity of sources from which the information comes. Information is most often gathered by means of individual interviews or is obtained as a result of searching trough paper and electronic documents related to the user. The knowledge obtained as a result of processing received information is not always codified in a clear and comprehensible way, so it is often necessary to systematise it.

The second stage involves designing a model of obtained knowledge, systematising it and structuring into a form that is legible for an agent and allows it to identify a thread and provide the user with the right answers.

The next stage is the implementation of an agent system. The last stage usually involves testing of the system by the user and feedback about its functioning. Feedback from the customer makes it possible to assess whether the knowledge that has been fed to an agent is correct, complete, updated, whether the scope or substance of the knowledge has been somehow changed, and whether it is necessary to update the knowledge. Despite the lack of uniform formalised methodology and the use of own methodologies, companies rely on well-tried UML-based tools, which make it easier to model structures of databases, allow the structure of knowledge to be organised, relationships within the knowledge database to be described, and the architecture of agent systems to be designed. The range of agent solutions used in the process of creation is very wide. Apart from universal ones, such as: Enterprise architect, Power Designer, the respondents also mentioned such tools as: Eclipse, Semantic Works or Protege for building ontology. Companies also use CASE tools, which bring measurable benefits. Consistent use of such solutions at the company level guarantees maintainability of the system and good documentation of its architecture [34].

Despite the lack of official methodologies regulating the process of creating agent solutions, the respondents declared that the process of creating agent solutions in their companies was more or less in line with the model presented above. Undertaken actions are based on the common sense, are consistent and use necessary resources. In one case, the whole process of creating an agent solution was subject to corporate ISO procedures, which enabled the development of own methodology, that - though not consistent with any of the formally recommended methodologies - showed typical characteristics of agile methodologies. The solution used was fully formal (had documentation, its design contained established functions).

In the solutions examined, processes connected with knowledge acquisition were the most varied. As the respondents stressed, this resulted from the necessity to use individual methods and algorithms dedicated to specific customers and specific areas of application. The creation of such knowledge databases is very individualised. The implementation of knowledge databases that are based on ontologies is significantly hampered by the dynamics of changes in knowledge resources which occur in organisations. The volume of knowledge increases at such a fast pace that the time taken to update a knowledge database is longer than the period for which such knowledge is useful for the user. In such situations, a large repository of documents equipped with an advanced search engine is created instead of a traditional knowledge database. Knowledge acquisition is additionally hampered by insufficient level of knowledge possessed by organisations planning to implement agent solutions, by unique character of the knowledge used in knowledge databases of agent solutions, complete or partial lack of structuring of this knowledge, problems with its clear articulation or concerns over unauthorised use of acquired knowledge. Frequent problems are difficulties with appropriate categorisation and systematisation of knowledge as a result of which it can take form of elementary, unique portions of information (facts, threads...). However, the biggest problem during implementation is appropriate interpretation of a given piece of information and its use in the right context, which is caused by high ambiguity of an agent's statements. Creation and use of appropriate designing methodologies in the processes of creating agent solutions should make the gathering of knowledge from the different areas more efficient, and appropriate structuring, clear codification and adaptation to a specific model of knowledge - easier. The next stage should be to unify the notation of knowledge and to create a common format that can be exchanged between different solutions.

After implementation of the solution, manufacturers attach great importance to feedback from the customer, confirming the correctness of topicality and completeness of the knowledge that was introduced to an agent.

With the increasing number of implemented agent systems and their complexity merits, there is a natural need to systematize the knowledge concerning the activities undertaken and their standardization. The use of established methodologies in the implementation of solutions is not disputed by principle, but the very process of implementing the chosen methodology is not carried without complications. Among the fundamental problems that arise in the implementation of methodologies indicated by the respondents two groups were dominating:

The first group of objective problems, connected with the necessity to increase efforts to introduce and update adopted methodological solutions as well as methods and tools designed to implement these solutions, often result from the lack of flexibility and other imperfections of adopted methodologies, which entails the necessity to create appropriate organisational structure and operational procedures.

The second group includes problems that are very difficult to predict and subjectively related to specific individuals connected with the life cycle of a solution, such as: fear of change, loss of autonomy, being accustomed to the existing, not always fully formalised, way of working, sense of redundancy of seemingly unnecessary documents required when implementing the methodology; they reduce the possibility of practical use of methodologies in current projects, and consequently hamper the maintenance of the solution implemented.

Lack of developers' experience in working on complex systems, specificity and complexity of reputed methodologies used during implementation of projects involving complex, partially autonomous, structures of software agent societies - all these factors increase methodological problems encountered during implementation of individual solutions.

The studies focused on the aspect of modelling agent societies conducted by the authors allowed them to identify a range of problems faced by the developers of solutions available on the market. This created a chance to propose a methodology that will improve the development of societies of software agents. Specificity, variety and complexity of software agent societies designed to support organisational processes in an organisation managed by knowledge make it necessary to create a transparent and universal model based on respondents' long experience in creating similar solutions.

Conducted interviews indicated that currently created agent-based solutions offered by the companies relate to individual agent solutions. One of these aspects, that caused the lack of implementation in the area of multi-agent systems, was to identify the problems with the integration of knowledge abstracted within the agent system. Therefore, one of the research aspects was to develop proposals for taking up modelling methodology of software agent society in the context of highest level of agents' socialization, which will focus on the aspect of system's semantic knowledge codification methods and business processes organization. In order to develop such methodology, a number of multi-agent platforms [6] and methodologies [7] available in the literature and methods of agent design solutions [12] were tested.

3.2 Usability of Agent Systems

As part of the conducted qualitative research it was necessary to determine how software agent societies improve business processes in organizations based on knowledge. On the basis of the study, creators of agent solutions in Poland were diagnosed and a test method allowing for evaluation of the usability of agents in the context of human - computer interaction was proposed - AUKP - Agent Usefulness and Knowledge Propagation analysis method (Fig. 1).

During the tests of usability of software agents implemented in organizations, the analysis was conducted in the following stages [14]:

- Analysis of expectations and projected system usability. Aim: determine the expectations of the users in relation to the agent system and its functionality.

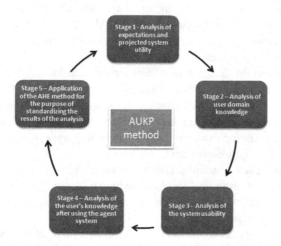

Fig. 1. Agent usability and knowledge propagation analysis method (*Source: own research*)

Proposed method: research survey analyzing the significance of the basic indicators of the system usability.

- Analysis of user domain knowledge. Aim: determine the user's base knowledge in terms of the domain aided by the agent system. Proposed method: survey of knowledge which the user obtains as a result of working with the agent system.
- Analysis of the system usability. Aim: determine the values of the specific indicators of the assessment of the system usability for the user and the organization. Proposed method: direct analysis of the agent system's operation.
- Analysis of the user's knowledge after using the agent system. Aim: to determine the user's knowledge in the field supported by the agent system after using the system. Proposed method: survey of knowledge obtained by the user as a result of working with the agent system (as in stage 1).
- Application of the AHP method for standardizing the results of the analysis. Aim: standardization of the results with regard to users' expectations for a comparative analysis of agent systems. Proposed method: application of the AHP method based on the results obtained in stage 1 and stage 3.

First, an analysis of previously conducted research on the human - computer interaction in the context of agent usability testing environments was performed. These studies have shown objectivity of examining the usability in terms of the agents' impact on the users. The assumptions concerning the developed method and the results of the conducted experiments are discussed in more detail in papers [15, 35, 36]. In these studies researchers assumed, that in accordance with the concept of usability, it is necessary to refer to the analysis of effectiveness, efficiency, satisfaction and propagation/dissemination of agent system's knowledge.

The aim of the above-mentioned research by the authors was to analyse agent solutions currently used on the Polish market using a proposed qualitative research method to evaluate usability and degree of knowledge distribution between the human being and the computer in terms of using agent systems. For this purpose, the process evaluation model for specified factors within the AUKP method was developed and 102 research experiments were carried out, the aim of which was to evaluate the operation of three software agents.

Agent A performed the function of a salesperson, and its task was to acquaint the user with the offer of products and functioning of the organisation. Agent B performed informational tasks; by substituting traditional hotline, it disseminated knowledge about social insurance, whereas Agent C supported the user in the area of the functioning of urban services for example through providing appropriate models of documents, directing to the right department, etc.

The experiment used multiple criteria, taking into account analysis of all pre-defined measures of usability, i.e. knowledge, usability, performance and satisfaction. It should be stressed that interface agents implementing various objectives and tasks were used in the experiment.

All tested software agents contributed to the improvement of the user's knowledge. The knowledge growth rate was above 0.7 for all agents. In the group of males and people over 25 years of age we observed a higher level of acquisition of the agent's knowledge. In the case of more simple tasks, people with lower education obtained better results. More complicated tasks were better performed by people with higher education. What's interesting, the research showed negative correlations between the level of computer skills of users and their satisfaction with working with agents. Such correlations were identified in the case of agents A and C [35]. This shows that agent solutions are better perceived by people with poor computer knowledge for whom contact with an agent is more of a form of cooperation with other users.

The results also confirmed [35, 36], that in the group of users and agents it can be indicated that the agent-based solutions contribute to the improvement of business processes in which they participate by improving customer satisfaction and propagation/dissemination of knowledge among users regarding the organization and the processes, in which the organization and the business process recipient participate.

All aggregate results shown here revealed, that in the case where it is possible to identify high efficiency of agents and their productivity, users indicated high levels of satisfaction and knowledge gain. What is characteristic, increased productivity of agents and their effectiveness influenced the increase in user's satisfaction and the amount of knowledge they acquired.

3.3 Modelling of Software Agent Societies

None of the methodologies analysed [7] fully define an organization's ontology or social relationships. Only three of them do this in a limited way, where designer is usually able to define only concepts of agent ontology. Also the mechanism of agent's interaction with the environment is not well realized by the methodologies analysed. Comparative analysis, at the stage of the assumptions related the to design of multi-agent system, indicated that the agent society, through the used methodology, will have limited functionality. The result of the study was to offer the methodology fully shown in the book "Agent technologies in knowledge-based organisations" [8].

This methodology was created as a combination of software agent society design good practice, ontologies design methods and BPMN notation used for the purpose of analyzing the requirements for the created agent society in the context of the organization it is supposed to support.

The proposed methodology consists of 8 stages, which include:

1. Analysis and development of business process
   1.1. Specification of organizations involved in the process and the posts performing the tasks.
   1.2. Determination of relationships inside the organization. At this stage, the relationship is defined within the organizational structure that supports the system. In the case of an organization, it is a structure linking the different departments and the process participants' positions.
   1.3. Defining the rules of starting and ending the process.
   1.4. Diagnosing the business process tasks.
   1.5. Diagnosing the business process events.
   1.6. Defining the conditions governing decision gates.

1.7. Determining the extent of an agent's support of a specific task (realization of tasks, assisting the task, none)

2. Identification of resources in an agent society
   2.1 Identification of inputs and outputs of the main task
   2.2 Identification of resources in the form of services or external data

3. Analysis of the roles and responsibilities of agent society
   3.1 Defining the tasks carried out in the agent society
   3.2 Defining the roles of agents in the system
   3.3 Diagnosing emergency situations (events)
   3.4 Defining the inputs and outputs based on events

4. Determining the hierarchical structure of the relationship inside the organization
   4.1 Reference of the organizational structure with the main tasks carried out by agents
   4.2 Determination of an organization's internal relationships within the agent society

5. Determination of the extent of agent societies' knowledge
   5.1 Identification of knowledge range of an agent society
   5.2 Identification of the resources provided by agent societies

6. Preliminary definition of agents' internal architecture
   6.1 Determining agent classes
   6.2 Assigning agent classes to roles
   6.3 Assigning agent classes to resources

7. Essential definition of the agents' internal architecture
   7.1 Agent knowledge specification
   7.2 Defining an agent's behaviour

8. Designing the interaction between agents

The proposed approach for an agent society modelling is considered in terms of the heterogeneous construction of agent societies and determines the combination of best practices for agent solutions modelling to support business processes within the organization's information systems. In particular, this methodology is dedicated for knowledge-based organizations through its focus on modelling of the organization's knowledge using semantic mechanisms of representation.

The proposed methodology has been developed upon the experience regarding the developed prototype of agent-based solutions supporting the operation of the organization and developed in the context of building solutions supporting the interaction of users within the business processes in which they participate [11].

The methodology proposed in the context of creating software agent societies was extended to include a model of analysing trust and reputation of agents.

3.4   Model of Trust and Reputation in a Society of Software Agents

Software agent societies in the aspect of a multi-agent system require the use of mechanisms for controlling the behaviour of agents in the system. In this area, the authors conducted literature studies and developed assumptions of a trust and reputation model in software agent societies. Results of these studies were presented in papers [10, 16, 17]. The aim of the model proposed by the authors was to show how it is possible in the case of autonomous software agents to control and analyse their behaviour in a society and to select agents for the implementation of specific tasks as part of business processes in which they participate. For that purpose, three areas of the model being created were distinguished in the studies:

- The area of an agent's own trust, which referred to analysis of own behaviour in the context of participation in business processes.
- The area of trust in actions of other agents in the society, connected with the assessment of the behaviour of agents remaining in the environment.
- The area of reputation in the society of software agents connected with sharing knowledge about the trust in agents in the society.

The areas defined and analysed in this way were divided according to a hierarchy resulting from a process view of the society under examination, which reflected the adopted methodology for designing such a society. The levels of the hierarchy analysed included:

- The level of the whole society.
- The level of a business process.
- The level of a task performed by an agent.
- The level of an action undertaken by an agent.

The research experiment conducted and described in paper [17] and the proposal of indicators showed a possibility of using such a solution in the area of building self-organising societies of software agents. The trust and reputation model proposed is still being developed. One of the areas in the development of the specified model is the use of AHP method for the purpose of assessing the operation of software agent societies [38].

3.5   The Research Model of Multi-agent Software in a Knowledge-Based Organization

There are different functionalities of knowledge management in this kind of agent supported knowledge-based organization, e.g. in business context [39], human capital management (HCM) context [31], health care context [40], etc.

In the context of HCM, we can see solutions consisting of task-specialised and cooperating software agents that form multi-agent systems (MAS), and within them there are specific societies of "HR agents" focused on the different HR processes taking place in an organisation [40, 41]. These systems support, in particular, processes connected with recruiting, creating and maintaining human capital in an organisation.

Multi-agent systems in HCM search for and process knowledge connected with employees' competence profiles, their development, career paths, the process of improving skills, trainings and self-improvement.

In the context of health care, MAS may play an important role in effectuating the knowledge-based view of the e-health organization by enhancing the capability to manage the knowledge it possesses [5, 32]: knowledge about the patient, knowledge of the presented medical problem, contextual knowledge about the course of the conversation in e-health, knowledge of the e-health organization.

The research model of multi-agent knowledge management system in healthcare is based on [43]: knowledge creation about the user, knowledge sharing of the presented problem, contextual knowledge about the course of the conversation during knowledge distribution, knowledge application in the organization.

There is a diversity of areas in medical industry and health care systems that could benefit from systems based on agent technology (especially MAS) [32, 33].

Nowadays, e-health area is one of the fastest growing sectors worldwide. It is worth mentioning, that healthcare units have to implement efficient knowledge management in order to provide high quality services and reduce unnecessary costs. Usage of computer science, Internet and other modern technologies give these opportunities. One of technologies of this kinds that could be helpful in healthcare is agent technology [43]. There are many examples of multi-agent systems (MAS) connected with healthcare [37], and human capital management. In healthcare, there are four main categories of MAS:

(1) Assistive Living Applications, (2) Diagnosis, (3) Physical Telemonitoring, (4) Smart-Hospital, Smart-Emergency Applications. In the second area, the most prevalent are applications based on interface agents that support communication and consulting processes. An equally important area supported by this type of solutions is the improvement of employees' skills, self-improvement and training processes designed to increase the value of human capital in an organisation. However, there are also theoretical and practical discussions highlighting the role of software agent societies in other HR processes. The main areas of such applications include: searching for employees, managing employees' competences at the stage of selection and management of career paths [40]. In these processes, it is necessary to use both societies of agents that acquire knowledge from an organisation's resources and societies of agents that search through a whole range of external sources containing information concerning candidates and trends on the labour market. The knowledge acquired in this way enables creation of knowledge databases, which are used to support HCM processes in an organisation. This model of knowledge processing is in line with Turban's classical model [20].

There is also an evaluation method of multi-agent software for knowledge management systems. The method of evaluation of multi-agent software (MAS) for knowledge management (KM) is based on some areas of knowledge management systems due to Turban's Knowledge Management Cycle [32]. The method of evaluation of MAS for e-health KM was based on four main phases of knowledge management cycle: (1) knowledge generation (acquisition, creation), (2) knowledge storage (capturing, refinement), (3) knowledge distribution (transfer, sharing) and (4) knowledge application (dissemination, utilization).

The findings show the critical factors of usage of a multi-agent system in healthcare in each phase of the knowledge management cycle, which are divided into four different categories [32]:

1. Content management tools: Tools that offer abilities to integrate, classify, and codify knowledge from various sources for e-health organization (knowledge of the health organization).
2. Knowledge sharing tools: Tools that support sharing knowledge between people or other agents in an e-health organization (knowledge about patients, etc.).
3. Knowledge search and retrieval systems: Systems that enable search and retrieval and have some knowledge discovery abilities (knowledge to solve the medical problem).
4. General KMS: Systems that propose an overall solution to a company's knowledge management needs (contextual knowledge about the course of the conversation).

4   Research Findings

The developed research tools for modelling software agent societies represents a set of tools that can be used to design and assess software agent societies.

The main characteristics of the proposed methodology for modelling software agent societies are: focus on business processes of an organisation (in the phase of defining system requirements), focus on processing an organisation's knowledge (both in the area of knowledge modelling and knowledge flows between the society of agents and an organisation's IT systems) and focus on the use of software agent societies in an organisation. The approach proposed herein offers the following advantages:

- Extending currently used standards for describing business processes to include sources of knowledge that supports the performance of users' tasks (in the context of the process, place and time).
- Enabling direct integration of organisational knowledge within any business processes taking place in an organisation within the scope of the process in which this knowledge should be used and the task that it supports.
- Automating processes of assessing the functioning of knowledge management systems in terms of their usefulness in supporting business processes.
- Generating new organisational knowledge at the interface of business processes and knowledge management.
- Using semantic mechanisms for knowledge description for easier integration of possessed knowledge with internal organisational knowledge.
- Operation independent from the used IT solutions and possibility of integration of any knowledge management systems and a process-oriented solution.

The use of 3.3 methodology enables the development of a model of an agent society that can be extended to include the proposed trust and reputation model.

The proposed trust and reputation model is dedicated to supporting the analysis of the behaviour of software agents in the context of their use to support operations of an organisation and refers to building autonomous, self-organising societies with mobility features. The main features of this model include:

- Focus on building a trust and reputation model based on a defined methodology for modelling agent societies.

- Focus on a specific multi-agent platform, i.e. JADE platform.
- Business orientation connected with the assessment of agents' actions in the context of performing business processes of an organisation.
- Hierarchic structure of the parameters of the trust and reputation model, which means that in the case when it is not possible to estimate the value of the model, the actions of an agent can be supported by more general indicators.
- Possibility of using this model in the context of building agents with mobility features, where information about agents' trust and reputation is shared among different agent societies.
- Possibility of using the proposed model in the context of security of a multi-agent system.

The model refers to agents' mutual impact on each other. In the context of using software agents as an element of a business process, it was necessary to develop a research method for assessing usability of software agents in the area of their use to support activities of an organisation. For that purpose, a range of proposed methods for examining the impact of agents on their environment were analysed, in particular in the area of HCI, and a research method was proposed that enabled classification of a range of indicators describing the operation of software agents and their impact on users. On this basis, qualitative research (in the form of experiments) was conducted to analyse the impact of software agents on participants of business processes. The characteristics of the research method proposed included:

- Focus of the analysis of agent usability for business processes of an organisation.
- Possibility of analysing efficiency, effectiveness, satisfaction and knowledge propagation in the context of agents' impact on participants of a business process.
- The development of a mathematical research model that can be further developed to include other indicators.

The research conducted on the Polish market by proposed AUKP method explicitly pointed out that from the perspective of the end user, agent systems that are part of an organization's information systems are considered useful by the users.

The experiments performed also allowed for some observations which were not a direct aim of the study: (1) errors resulting from human - agent communication, such as users' misspelling and the use of an agent incompatible with its purpose. (2) In addition, in users who have committed themselves to collaborating with an agent in this experiment, we observed a gradual increase in confidence and interest in this form of cooperation within the human – computer system. (3) Users' impression that they have obtained the necessary knowledge during the study has not been confirmed by the actual growth of knowledge in individual cases. This opens a field for further research. What's interesting, the research showed negative correlations between the level of computer skills of users and their satisfaction with working with agents, which leads to the conclusion that agent solutions are better perceived by people with poor computer knowledge for whom contact with an agent is more of a form of cooperation with other users.

Specialist applications of multi-agent systems, e.g. in the area of HCM or Health-care, enable free use of a wide offer of potential knowledge sources. Specific conditions of these areas of application often make it necessary to implement additional mechanisms. For instance, societies of agents that support recruitment processes allow competence profiles of candidates to be found quickly. However, the variety of information sources, methods for the analysis of candidates and the variety of candidate profiles found by the different agents inevitably lead to conflicts between agents within a society. If a knowledge model has been properly constructed, it is possible, thanks to the use of argumentation-based negotiation techniques, to prevent most conflicts. In cases when it is impossible to build appropriate rules or the knowledge contained in them is insufficient, a vertical architecture of multi-agent systems can be used, and in cases when the negotiation process between the agents has not produced a solution, the agent supervising the course of process will choose the solution to the problem on its own. The findings also show the critical factors of usage of multi-agent software in healthcare knowledge management system in four categories: knowledge of the health organization, knowledge about the patient, knowledge to solve the medical problem, contextual knowledge about the course of conversation in KMS. These factors are connected with abilities of a multi-agent system to integrate, classify, and codify knowledge from various sources for e-health organization, sharing knowledge between people or other agents in e-health organization, and other abilities of multi-agent system to solve the medical problem.

5 Conclusions

Modern organisations using knowledge management systems to support performed business processes require the use of dedicated IT solutions that support these activities. In particular, they require the development of methodologies, methods and models that support their development and evaluation. The paper presents research findings and proposed research tools developed over several years of research into modelling of software agent societies. In particular, it reveals the findings of qualitative research conducted in the form of interviews in Polish companies engaged in the creation of agent systems, presents elements of a designing methodology focused on supporting the modelling of software agent societies, indicates research method and findings of research into usability of agents and elements of a trust and reputation model, which can be applied in the process of supporting the operation of software agent societies.

The elements of the research tools presented herein enable the development and evaluation of agent systems in organisations, in particular in knowledge based organisations, in which organisational knowledge is one of the resources. Therefore, the elements of the proposed research tools mainly address the problem of modelling and analysis of knowledge that can exist in such organisations.

With reference to the research methodology developed, further research will concern the construction and development of a tool designed to support designing of software agent societies in accordance with its assumptions. In the case of the method for examining usability, further research will concern its development towards analysis of not only usability but also ergonomics of software agents. In the context of the developed model of trust and reputation, research will concentrate on the aspect of its use with reference to mobile agents operating in numerous agent systems.

References

1. Sołtysik-Piorunkiewicz, A., Żytniewski, M.: Software agent societies for process management in knowledge-based organization. In: Janiunaite, B., Petraite, M. (eds.) Proceedings of the 14th European Conference on Knowledge Management, vol. 2, pp. 661–669. ACPI, UK (2013)
2. Żytniewski, M.: Application of the software agents society in the knowledge management system life cycle. In: Pańkowska, M., Stanek, S., Sroka, H. (eds.) Cognition and Creativity Support Systems, pp. 191–201. Publishing House of the University of Economics in Katowice (2013)
3. Sołtysik-Piorunkiewicz, A.: The development of mobile Internet technology and ubiquitous communication in a knowledge-based organization. Online J. Appl. Knowl. Manag. (OJAKM) 1(1), 29–41 (2013). A Publication of the International Institute for Applied Knowledge Management
4. Żytniewski, M., Kowal, R., Sołtysik, A.: Creation of software agents' society from the perspective of implementation companies. The advantages of their use, the problems of construction and unique features. In: Research Papers of the Wroclaw University of Economics. Business Informatics, vol. 3, issue no. 29, pp. 162–171. Publishing House of Wroclaw University of Economics (2013)
5. Żytniewski, M., Kowal, R., Sołtysik, A.: The outcomes of the research in areas of application and impact of software agents societies to organizations so far. Examples of implementation in Polish companies. In: Ganzha, M., Maciaszek, L., Paprzycki, M. (eds.) Proceedings of the 2013 Federated Conference on Computer Science and Information Systems, vol. 1, pp. 1181–1187. IEEE Computer Society Press, Los Alamitos (2013)
6. Żytniewski, M., Klement, M.: Analiza porównawcza wybranych platform wieloagentowych. In: Kisielnicki, J., Chmielarz, W., Parys, T. (eds.) Informatyka 2 przyszłości 30 lat Informatyki na Wydziale Zarządzania, pp. 88–100. Publishing House of the Faculty of Management of the University of Warsaw (2015)
7. Żytniewski, M.: Comparison of methodologies for agents' software society modeling processes in support for the needs of a knowledge-based organization. In: Kiełtyka, L., Niedbał, R. (eds.) Wybrane zastosowania technologii informacyjnych zarządzania w organizacjach, vol. 296, pp. 15–26. Publishing House of University of Technology in Czestochowa (2015)
8. Żytniewski, M.: Modelowanie systemów agentowych wspomagających organizacje oparte na wiedzy. In: Żytniewski, M. (ed.) Technologie agentowe w organizacjach opartych na wiedzy, pp. 92–119. Publishing House of the University of Economics in Katowice (2015)
9. Żytniewski, M.: Wprowadzenie do teorii społeczności agentów programowych oraz ich zastosowania w organizacjach opartych na wiedzy. In: Żytniewski, M. (ed.) Technologie agentowe w organizacjach opartych na wiedzy, pp. 52–69. Publishing House of the University of Economics in Katowice (2015)
10. Żytniewski, M., Klement, M.: Trust in software agent societies. Online J. Appl. Knowl. Manag. 3(1), 93–101 (2015). A Publication of the International Institute for Applied Knowledge Management
11. Żytniewski, M.: Integration of knowledge management systems and business processes using multi-agent systems. In: Proceedings of the Cooperative Online Organizations conference (Presented at the AAMAS 2015 Workshop), Turkey (2015)
12. Żytniewski, M., Kowal, R.: Using software agents to enhance the functionality of social knowledge portal. In: Abramowicz, W. (ed.) BIS Workshops 2013. LNBIP, vol. 160, pp. 23–34. Springer, Heidelberg (2013)

13. Kopka, B., Żytniewski, M.: The system ergonomics and usability as measurement of the software agent impact to the organization. In: Rebelo, F., Soares, M. (eds.) Proceedings of Advances in Ergonomics in Design, Usability and Special Populations, pp. 21–34. AHFE (2014)

14. Żytniewski, M., Kopka, B.: The proposition of agents' usability analysis method based on an analysis of Polish enterprises. In: Proceedings of the Human Agent Interaction Design and Models Conference (Presented at the AAMAS 2015 Workshop), Turkey (2015)

15. Żytniewski, M., Kopka, B.: Indicators of software agents usability and ergonomic. In: Proceedings of First Medial International Scientific Conference of the Series Decisions Situations of Endangerment, The Journal of Science of the Gen. Tadeusz Kosciuszko Military Academy of Land Forces, Wroclaw (2015)

16. Klement, M.: Zastosowanie zaufania w społcczności agentów programowych. In: Żytniewski, M. (ed.) Technologie agentowe w organizacjach opartych na wiedzy, pp. 120–137. Publishing House of the University of Economics in Katowice (2015)

17. Klement, M., Żytniewski, M.: Metodyczne aspekty modelowania zaufania i reputacji w społecznościach agentów programowych dla potrzeb wspomagania procesów biznesowych organizacji. In: Technologie wiedzy w zarządzaniu organizacją. Scientific Papers of the University of Economics in Katowice (2015) (after positive review)

18. Żytniewski, M.: Rozwój koncepcji społeczności agentów programowych. In: Buko, J. (ed.) Europejska przestrzeń komunikacji elektronicznej, pp. 481–493. Scientific Papers of Szczecin University (2013)

19. Drucker, P.: Post-capitalist Society. Harper Business, New York (1993)

20. Turban, E., Leidner, D., McLean, E., Wetherbe, M.: Knowledge management. In: Information Technology for Management: Transforming Organizations in the Digital Economy, pp. 365–405. Wiley, Hoboken (2006)

21. Jennex, M.E.: Knowledge Management: Concepts, Methodologies, Tools and Applications. IGI Publishing, Hershey (2009)

22. Kwiig, M.: Knowledge Management Foundations. Schema Press, Arlington (1993)

23. Nonaka, I., Takeuchi, H.: Knowledge-Creating Company. Oxford University Press, New York (1995)

24. Davenport, T., Prusak, L.: Working Knowledge How Organizations Manage What They Know. Harward Business School Press, Boston (1998)

25. Van der Spek, R., Spijkervet, A.: Knowledge management: dealing intelligently with knowledge. In: Liebowitz, J., Wilcox, L. (eds.) Knowledge Management and its Integrative Elements. CRC Press, New York (1997)

26. Grudzewski, W.M., Hejduk, I.: Knowledge Management in Enterprises. Difin, Warszawa (2004)

27. Sołtysik-Piorunkiewicz, A.: The Telecom Business Strategies: A Comparative Study of Corporate Blogs. MIDI, Warszawa (2014)

28. Ziemba, E., Eisenbardt, M.: Aktywności prosumenckie z wykorzystaniem technologii informacyjno-komunikacyjnych w świetle badań bezpośrednich. In: Nowicki, A., Jelonek, D. (eds.) Wiedza i technologie informacyjne w kreowaniu przedsiębiorczości, pp. 101–113. Publishing House of Managment Departament, University of Technology, Czestochowa (2013)

29. Ziemba, E., Wielki, J.: The use of corporate portals in managing knowledge on entities operating in the electronic space. In: Wrycza, S. (ed.) Proceedings of the Seventh International Conference on Perspectives in Business Informatics Research, BIR 2008, pp. 143–157. Gdansk University Press (2008)

30. Furmankiewicz, M., Sołtysik-Piorunkiewicz, A., Ziuziański, P.: Artificial intelligence systems for knowledge management in e-health: the study of intelligent software agents. In: Latest Trends on Systems: The Proceedings of 18th International Conference on Systems, Santorini Island, Greece, pp. 551–556 (2014)

31. Sołtysik, A.: Wspieranie procesów zarządzania kapitałem ludzkim z wykorzystaniem agentów programowych. In: Żytniewski, M. (ed.) Technologie agentowe w organizacjach opartych na wiedzy, pp. 284–307. Publishing House of the University of Economics in Katowice (2015)

32. Sołtysik-Piorunkiewicz, A., Furmankiewicz, M., Ziuziański, P.: The method of evaluation of multi-agent software for knowledge management in e-health. In: Kiełtyka, L., Niedbał, R. (eds.) Wybrane zastosowania technologii informacyjnych zarządzania w organizacjach, vol. 296. Publishing House of University of Technology in Czestochowa (2015)

33. Sołtysik-Piorunkiewicz, A., Furmankiewicz, M., Ziuziański, P.: Rola systemów wieloagentowych do zarządzania wiedzą w e-zdrowiu. In: Żytniewski, M. (ed.) Technologie agentowe w organizacjach opartych na wiedzy, pp. 268–283. Publishing House of the University of Economics in Katowice (2015)

34. Żytniewski, M., Sołtysik, A., Kowal, R.: Creation of software agents' society from the perspective of implementation companies: the advantages of their use, the problems of construction and unique features. Bus. Inf. 3(29), 162–171 (2013). Publishing House of the University of Economics in Wroclaw

35. Żytniewski, M., Kopka, B.: Użyteczność Systemów agentowych oraz analiza propagacji Wiedzy. In: Żytniewski, M. (ed.) Technologie agentowe w organizacjach opartych na wiedzy, pp. 138–156. Publishing House of the University of Economics in Katowice (2015)

36. Żytniewski, M., Kopka, B.: Social aspects of the impact of software agents on participants of business processes in knowledge based organisations. In: Pańkowska, M. (ed.) Creativity Support Systems, Publishing House of the University of Economics in Katowice (2015) (after positive review)

37. Cortés, U., Annicchiarico, R., Urdiales, C.: Agents and healthcare: usability and acceptance. In: Annicchiarico, R., Garcia, U.C., Urdiales, C. (eds.) Agent Technology and e-Health, pp. 1–3. Birhauser Verlag, Basel (2008)

38. Żytniewski, M., Klement, M., Skorupka, D., Stanek, S., Duchaczek, A.: Application of the AHP method in modeling the trust and reputation of software agents. In: Proceedings of International Conference of Numerical Analysis and Applied Mathematics, Greece (2015)

39. Gołuchowski, J.: Wprowadzenie do inżynierii wiedzy. Difin, Warszawa (2011)

40. Sołtysik, A., Kostrubała, S., Sołtysik-Piorunkiewicz, A., Stanek, S.: Wspieranie procesu rekrutacji pracowników w przedsiębiorstwie z wykorzystaniem systemów wieloagentowych. In: Knosala, R. (ed.) Innowacje w Zarządzaniu i Inżynierii Produkcji. Publishing House Polskie Towarzystwo Zarządzania Produkcją Opole (2012)

41. Sołtysik, A.: Wspieranie procesów pozyskiwania, kreowania i utrzymania kapitału ludzkiego w organizacji opartej na wiedzy: Wstępne wyniki badań. In: Technologie wiedzy w zarządzaniu publicznym. Publishing House of the University of Economics in Katowice (2015) (under review)

42. Sołtysik-Piorunkiewicz, A.: Knowledge management impact of information technology Web 2.0/3.0. The case study of agent software technology usability in knowledge management system. In: AIP Conference Proceedings, vol. 1644, p. 219 (2015). http://dx.doi.org/10.1063/1.4907840

43. Sołtysik-Piorunkiewicz, A., Furmankiewicz, M., Ziuziański, P.: Artificial intelligence and multi-agent software for e-health knowledge management system. Bus. Inf. 2(32), 51–63 (2014). Publishing House of the University of Economics in Wroclaw

Fuzzy Logic as Agents' Knowledge Representation in A-Trader System

Jerzy Korczak$^{(\boxtimes)}$, Marcin Hernes, and Maciej Bac

Wrocław University of Economics,
Komandorska 118/120, 53-345 Wrocław, Poland
{jerzy.korczak,marcin.hernes,maciej.bac}@ue.wroc.pl

Abstract. The paper presents the application of a fuzzy logic in building the trading agents of the A-Trader system. A-Trader is a multi-agent system that supports investment decisions on the FOREX market. The first part of the article contains a discussion related to the use of fuzzy logic as representation of an agent's knowledge. Next, the algorithms of the selected fuzzy logic buy-sell decision agents are presented. In the last part of the article the agent performance is evaluated on real FOREX data.

Keywords: Multi-agent systems · Financial decision support systems · Fuzzy logic · Knowledge representation

1 Introduction

Financial decisions are made under conditions of risk and uncertainty that influence their level of performance. These decisions are usually supported by decision support systems and various computational models. Among them, there are multi-agent systems [1] which use various methods based on mathematics, statistics, finance or artificial intelligence [2–13]. Currently there is a large number of FOREX (Foreign Exchange Market) software platforms offering real-time services [14]. Examples are AvaTRADE and FinEXo based on MetaTrader4 platform, EXsignals, FXPro, Trade360, Trade Chimp, XTRADE. This paper presents the system called A-Trader, which belongs to the category of trading signal generators that provide recommended open and close positions for online FOREX traders. The trading opportunities are generated by consensual advice, computed by multiple software agents that use technical and fundamental analysis as well as behavioral sentiments.

The quotes, economic data and behavioral data are provided online from various financial services. Currencies are traded against one another in pairs, for instance EUR/USD, USD/PLN. Trading on FOREX relies on opening/closing long/short positions. A long position is a situation in which one purchases a currency pair at a certain price and hopes to sell it later at a higher price. This is also referred to as the notion of "buy low, sell high" in other trading markets. On FOREX, when one currency in a pair is rising in value, the other currency is declining, and vice versa. If a trader thinks a currency pair will fall, he will sell it and hope to buy it back later at a lower price. This is considered a short position, which is the opposite of a long position.

© Springer International Publishing Switzerland 2016
E. Ziemba (Ed.): FedCSIS 2015, LNBIP 243, pp. 109–124, 2016.
DOI: 10.1007/978-3-319-30528-8_7

The quotes, economic data and behavioral data are provided online from various financial services. The A-Trader receives tick data which are grouped to minute aggregates (M1, M5, M15, M30), hourly aggregates (H1, H4), daily aggregates (D1), weekly aggregates (W1) and monthly aggregates (MN1). The A-Trader supports a High Frequency Trading (HFT) and puts strong emphasis on price formation processes, short-term positions, fast computing, and efficient and robust indicators. The economic and behavioral data are collected from different experts' portals and social media portals.

High frequency traders are constantly taking advantage of very small quote changes with a high rate of recurrence to generate important profit rates. As many HFT experts underline, the traders seek profits from the market's liquidity imbalances and short-term pricing inefficiencies. Hence, the minimization of time from the access to quote information, through the entry of an order until its execution, is vital. Generally speaking, to support traders, the systems must provide as soon as possible advice as to which position should be taken: buy, sell or do nothing. Time series forecasting is more difficult while online trading has to be served.

The architecture of a-Trader and the description of the different groups of agents have already been detailed [15–17]. In general, the agents possess their own knowledge, they can continuously learn and change their knowledge in order to improve their performance.

Different methods of agents' knowledge representation can be applied in a-Trader. In our previous work [15, 16] we were focused on three-valued knowledge representation of this group of agents. Value "1" denoted "buy" decision, value "−1" denoted "sell" decision, value "0" denoted "leave unchanged". Agents are implemented using the C# environment and MQL4 language.

The key part of the system is the Supervisor agent. Its task is, among others, to coordinate the work of agents on trading strategy and it presents the final strategy (suggestions of open/close positions) to the trader. The Supervisor uses various strategies and evaluates their performance.

The a-Trader allows also for making arbitrarily independent decisions by traders (experts) on the basis of their knowledge and experience. The traders' decisions can be stored in a database, evaluated, and compared with strategies provided automatically by agents.

The purpose of this paper is to present a manner of applying a fuzzy logic as the agents' knowledge representation and evaluates the performance of selected agents and trading strategies in the a-Trader system.

This paper is organized as follows: the first part briefly presents the state-of-the-art in the considered field; the algorithms of three selected agents; and the final part that discusses the results of the performance evaluation of these agents.

2 Related Works

The literature on the subject presents many different methods for agents' knowledge representation. The main ones include first-order predicate logic, production systems, artificial neural networks, frame representation, ontologies such as semantic web and semantic networks, multi-attributes and multi-values structures, and multi valued logic [18–27]. Some of these methods are closely related to fuzzy logic.

The first-order predicate logic that is one common knowledge representation is founded on the following general assumptions [28]:

- the knowledge representation is independent of physical media,
- agents' internal states are related to the objects of the external environment,
- the knowledge representation consists of symbols forming the structure,
- reasoning is based on the manipulation of these structures to derive other structures.

Often agents' knowledge is represented as multi-attribute and multi-value structures which allow representation of the real world environment in a wide scope of objects features.

Multi-valued logic and fuzzy logic are more suitable methods for HFT. Three-valued logic is a very simple language consisting of proposition symbols and logical connectives. It can handle propositions that are known true, known false, or completely unknown. The set of possible models, given a fixed propositional vocabulary, is finite, so entailment can be checked by enumerative models. Inference algorithms for three-valued logic include backtracking and local–search methods and can often solve large problems very quickly [29]. Three-valued logic is reasonably effective for certain tasks, but does not scale to environments of unbounded size, because it lacks the expressive power to describe the real world objects.

To reduce this weakness, a fuzzy logic can be applied in HFT. Fuzzy logic is an approach founded on "degrees of truth" rather than the usual "true or false" values (1 or 0). The idea of fuzzy logic was first proposed by Zadeh in the 1960s when he was working on the problem of computer understanding of natural language [30]. Fuzzy logic is a form of multi-valued logic derived from fuzzy set theory [2] to deal with approximate reasoning. In contrast to "crisp logic", where binary sets are processed by binary logic, fuzzy logic variables may have a truth value that ranges between 0 and 1 that allows the user to express imprecision and flexibility in a decision-making system [8, 31, 32]. [33] states that the theory of fuzzy logic is a language which attempts to describe and analyze complex systems, systems of ill-defined mathematical and physical phenomena with accurate mathematical models. This is an approach for expressing operational laws of a system in linguistic terms instead of mathematical equations. [34]. Fuzzy inference copes with imprecise inputs and allows inference rules to be specified using imprecise linguistic terms, such as "very high" or "slightly low" [35]. It also reduces the data-processing complexity of planning interactions between agents [34] extraction [36], energy management [37], robotics [8], e-commerce modeling [38], wireless sensor network [39]. Fuzzy logic allows also for trust modeling in multiagent systems because it offers the ability to handle uncertainty and imprecision effectively, and is therefore ideally suited to reasoning about trust [35]. Fuzzy logic was also used for trading on FOREX, for example, in Expert Advisor [40] or technical analysis system [41] or fuzzy time series forecasting [42–44]. However, in these systems, the probability of decisions is ranged to [0..1]. In trading applications it is unfavorable, because the trader can buy, sell or leave a currency unchanged. Therefore, in the A-Trader system, the confidence of decisions range is

[−1..1], where "−1" level denotes a "strong sell" decision, "0" level denotes a "strong leave unchanged", and decision "1" level denotes a "strong buy" decision. The positions can be open/close with different levels of confidence of decision. For example, the long position can be open, when a level of confidence is 0.6, or a short position can be open, when a level of probability is 0.7. Therefore the timeframe for the opening/closing position is wider than in the case of three valued-logic. An example of this difference is presented in Figs. 1 and 2 (Ai – denotes the ith agent). In the case of three-valued logic (Fig. 1), the green color points denote a "*buy*" decision, the red color ones denote a "*sell*" decision, and the black color points denote a "do nothing" decision. There are often agents that generate buy/sell decisions too fast or too late. In the case of fuzzy logic, the ranges of decisions probability often cover the best point for trading. In Fig. 2, the green triangle denotes the transition from "*do nothing*" decision to "*buy*" decision, and the red inverted triangle denotes transition from "*do nothing*" decision to "*sell*" decision, and the black color denotes a "*do nothing*" decision). Therefore it is possible to place open/close positions closer to the optimal decision than in the case of a three-valued logic.

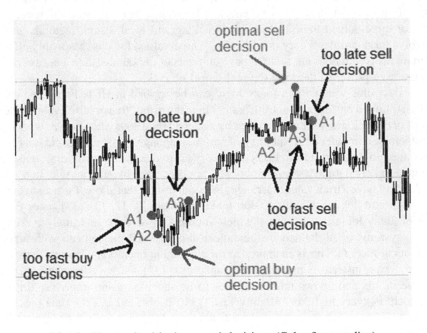

Fig. 1. Three-valued logic agents' decisions (Color figure online)

Of course, the level of probability of decision for open/close position plays a vital role. This level can be determined on the basis of trader experience, or by the Supervisor on the basis of, for example, an evolutionary algorithm.

Using the fuzzy logic as agents' knowledge representation allows the trading decision to be closer to real experts' decisions (made under conditions of risk and uncertainty) that are also taken with a certain level of probability.

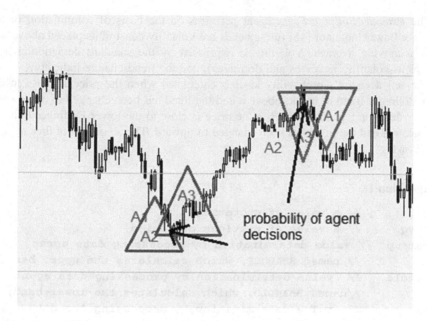

Fig. 2. Fuzzy logic agents' decisions (Color figure online)

Fuzzy logic can be also used by trading advisors for the following tasks:

- forecasting, i.e. to calculate the output value for input data lies outside the scope initially predicted,
- expressing the agent's knowledge in a flexible, intuitive way,
- computation of decisions' probability level,
- implementation of different automated learning algorithms,
- validation and consistency measuring that can speed up automated learning and improve user interpretability,
- taking into consideration ambiguity – the "natural" way for expressing uncertain knowledge.

The next part of the article describes selected fuzzy logic buy-sell decision agents implemented in a-Trader.

3   Description of the Fuzzy Logic Buy-Sell Decision Agents

A-Trader contains approximately 1500 agents, including about 800 processing data agents (they compute different indicators on the FOREX market, for instance trend indicators, oscillators) and 300 agents (running in all time periods) setting the buy-sell decision, including: 200 three valued logic agents and 200 fuzzy logic agents, also 200 agents providing the strategies. In order to illustrate the performance analysis, four agents were chosen: *ExtendedBollingerFuzzy, EvolutionaryFuzzy* and *ConsensusFuzzy*.

The *ExtendedBollingerFuzzy* agent performs on the basis of combination of the Bollinger Bands indicator [45] (these bands are volatility constraints placed above and below a moving average. Volatility is expressed by the standard deviation, which changes as volatility increases and decreases), and the trend change indicator.

The sell decision's probability level is calculated when the price is close to the upper Bollinger Band or breaks above it and the trend has been changed to downward. The buy decision is calculated when the price is close to the lower Bollinger Band or falls below it and the trend has been changed to upward. The algorithm of this agent is the following:

Algorithm 1

```
Input:  q // a value of quotation,
prevq     // a value of previous quotation
bbandup  // value determination by processing data agent
          // named BBANDUP, which calculates the upper band,
bbandlo   //  value determination by processing data agent
          //named BBANDLO, which calculates the lower band,
sma       //  value determination by processing the data
          // agent named SMA,  which calculates the simple
          // moving average of quotation.
Output: The fuzzy logic decision D (value range [-1..1]).
BEGIN
Let D:=0, calcBands:=0; //counter for fuzzification.
maxcount:=0.              //maximum counter limit for fuzzifi
                         // cation.
Δ =Abs((sma-((bbandlo+bbandup)/2))/10).
If q<(bbandlo (+Δ)) and (prevq>q)  then
If (calcBands>0) then calcBands=0, calcBands:=calcBands-1.
  If (calcBands<-maxcount) then calcBands=-maxcount,
        D=calcBands/maxcount;
If q>(bbandup (-Δ)) and (prevq<q) then
If (calcBands<0) then calcBands=0, calcBands:=calcBands+1.
  If (calcBands>maxcount) then calcBands=maxcount;
        D=calcBands/maxcount;
END
```

In a trading system, the fuzzification is understood as a process of conversion of an input variable (i.e. signals determined by processing agents) into a fuzzy set.

The *EvolutionaryFuzzy* agent is created on the basis of an evolutionary algorithm [46, 47]. This agent determines the best thresholds for open/close positions on the basis of following fuzzy logic agents:

1. Based on technical analysis indicators [48]:

- WilliamsFuzzy,
- TrendLinearRegFuzzy,
- RSIFuzzy,
- CCIFuzzy,
- BollingerFuzzy,
- ExtendedBollingerFuzzy.

2. Based on behavioral data - behavioral agent described in details in [49].

The *ConsensusFuzzy* agent (detailed in [17]) is founded on the consensus theory [50–52] and provides the decisions on the basis of the set of decisions generated by other fuzzy logic agents in the system.

The algorithm is as follows:

Algorithm 2

```
Input:  A= {D⁽¹⁾, D⁽²⁾, .... D⁽ᴹ⁾ } //The profile consists of M
    // fuzzy logic agents` decisions, where M – number of
    // fuzzy logic agents in the system,
    D⁽¹⁾, D⁽²⁾, .... D⁽ᴹ⁾ //decisions of particular agents
Output:  // The Fuzzy logic consensus CON (value range
        // [-1..1]) according to A.
BEGIN
Let CON:=0.
    Determine a sequence B by sorting elements of A
    profile in an increasing order.
    k₁=(M+1)/2 the element of B.
    k₂=(M+2)/2 the element of B.
    Set CON as any value from interval [k₁, k₂].
END.
```

It should be noted that currently in the system there are 100 agents using fuzzy logic representation. The evaluation of the performance of presented fuzzy logic agents will be shown further in the article. It is worth noting that this set of trading agents may be easily extended if required.

4 Experiments

The agents performance analysis is carried out with data within the M1 period of quotations from the FOREX market. For the purpose of this analysis, a test was performed in which the following assumptions were made:

1. USD/PLN quotes were selected from randomly chosen periods, notably:

- 9-11-2015, 00:00 am to 10-11-2015, 23:59 pm, (1440 quotations),
- 11-11-2015, 12:00 am to 13-11-2015, 21:59 pm (2160 quotations),
- 16-11-2015, 0:00 am to 18-11-2015, 23:59 pm (2880 quotations).

2. At the verification, the strategies (signals for open long/close short position-equals to 1, close long/open short position-equals to −1) of the Supervisor are based on different decisions' probability levels calculated by fuzzy logic agents described in Sect. 3 (the example of strategy is presented in Fig. 3, where the green line means the "long position" and the red one the "short position").

3. It was assumed that decisions' probability levels for open/close position are determined by the evolutionary algorithm (on the basis of earlier periods).

4. It was assumed that the unit of performance analysis ratios (absolute ratios) is pips (a change in price of one "point" in Forex trading is referred to as a pip, and it is equivalent to the final number in a currency pair's price).

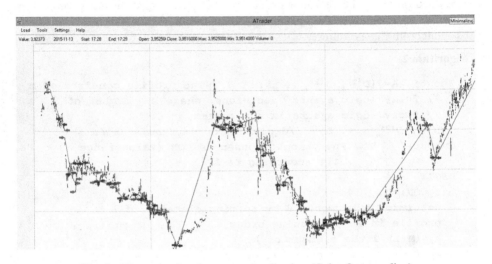

Fig. 3. The example of strategy visualization (Color figure online)

5. The transaction costs are directly proportional to the number of transactions.

6. The capital management - it was assumed that in each transaction the investor engages 100 % of the capital held at the leverage 1:1. It should be pointed out that the investor may define another capital management strategy.

7. The performance analysis was performed with the use of the following measures (ratios):

- rate of return (ratio x_1),
- the number of the transactions,
- gross profit (ratio x_2),
- gross loss (ratio x_3),
- the number of profitable transactions (ratio x_4),
- the number of profitable transactions in a row (ratio x_5),
- the number of unprofitable transactions in a row (ratio x_6),
- Sharpe ratio (ratio x_7).

$$S = \frac{E(r) - E(f)}{O(r)} \cdot 100 \ \% \tag{1}$$

where:

$E(r)$ – arithmetic average of the rate of return,

$E(f)$ – arithmetic average of the risk-free rate of return,

$O(r)$ – standard deviation of rates of return.

- the average coefficient of volatility (ratio x_8) is the ratio of the average deviation of the arithmetic average multiplied by 100 % and is expressed:

$$V = \frac{S}{|E(r)|} \cdot 100 \ \% \tag{2}$$

where:

V – average coefficient of variation,

s – average deviation of the rates of return,

$E(r)$ – arithmetic average of the rates of return.

Value at Risk (ratio x_9) – the measure known as value exposed to the risk - that is the maximum loss of the market value of the financial instrument possible to bear in a specific timeframe and at a given confidence level [53]

$$VaR = P * O * k \tag{3}$$

where:

P – the initial capital,

O – volatility - standard deviation of rates of return during the period,

k – the inverse of the standard normal cumulative distribution (assumed confidence level 95%, the value of k is 1,65),

- the average rate of return per transaction (ratio x_{10}), counted as the quotient of the rate of return and the number of transactions.

8. For the purpose of the comparison of the agents' performance, the following evaluation function was elaborated:

$$y = a_1 x_1 + a_2 x_2 + a_3 (1 - x)_3 + a_4 x_4 + a_5 x_5 + \ldots$$
$$+ a_6 (1 - x)_6 + a_7 x_7 + a_8 (1 - x)_8 + a_9 (1 - x)_9 + a_{10} x_{10} \tag{4}$$

where x_i denotes the normalized values of ratios mentioned in item 6 from x_1 to x_{10}. It was adopted in the test that coefficients a_1 to $a_{10} = 1/10$.

It should be mentioned that these coefficients may be modified with the use of, for instance, an evolutionary/genetic method or determined by the trader (investor) in accordance with his/her preference (for instance the user may determine whether he/she is interested in the higher rate of return with a simultaneous higher risk level or lower risk level, but simultaneously agrees to a lower rate of return). The function is given the values from the range [0..1], and the agent's efficiency is directly proportional to the function value.

9. The results obtained by the tested agents were compared with the results of the Buy-and-Hold benchmark (a trader buys a currency at the beginning and sells a currency at the end of an investment period) and the EMA benchmark (Exponential Moving Average – a type of moving average that is similar to a simple moving average, except that more weight is given to the latest data).

Table 1 presents the results obtained in the particular periods.

Table 1. Performance analysis results

Ratio	ExtendedBollingerFuzzy			EvolutionaryFuzzy			ConsensusFuzzy			EMA			B & H		
	Period 1	Period 2	Period 3	Period 1	Period 2	Period 3	Period 1	Period 2	Period 3	Period 1	Period 2	Period 3	Period 1	Period 2	Period 3
Rate of return [Pips]	-28	844	164	69	253	-503	324	1081	435	256	241	106	-256	8	324
The number of transactions	37	57	37	2	4	4	34	38	107	284	727	248	1	1	1
Gross profit [Pips]	152	427	152	191	180	179	172	421	175	38	188	65	0	0	0
Gross loss [Pips]	54	162	85	122	185	153	36	177	143	27	204	125	-256	8	324
The number of profitable transactions	10	26	26	1	3	1	14	24	44	54	220	117	0	0	0
The number of profitable consecutive transactions	3	8	6	1	2	1	5	8	8	6	10	11	0	0	0
The number of unprofitable consecutive transactions	5	3	2	1	1	3	3	5	6	8	10	3	1	1	1
Sharpe ratio	0.84	1.4	1.62	2.8	1.16	2.5	0.84	2.02	3,07	0.3	0.68	0.9	0	0	0
The average coefficient of volatility	1.00	2.63	0.63	0.54	0.73	0.70	0.39	2.18	0.14	2.32	3.36	3.72	0	0	0
The average rate of return per transaction	-0,76	14.81	4.43	34.5	63,25	-125,7	9.52	28.44	4.07	0.90	0.33	0.43	-256	8	324
Value of evaluation function (y)	0.19	0.28	0.43	0.32	0.38	0.02	0.66	0.35	0.43	0.20	0.18	0.43	0.01	0.04	0,18

In the performance analysis, not only the rate of return was taken into consideration, but also other ratios, including the level of risk involved in the investment. In general, it may be noticed that the fuzzy logic agents generated not only profitable decisions. It may be noticed that the values of efficiency ratios of particular agents differ in each period: for instance the estimated values of such ratios as *Gross Profit* and the *Number of Profitable Consecutive Transactions*. The values of *Rate of Return*,

Sharpe Ratio and *Average Rate of Return per Transaction* show significant dispersion among particular agents; this was observed in the case of the agents *ExtendedBollingerFuzzy*, *EvolutionaryFuzzy* and *EMA*.

The evaluation function provides the immediate recommendation of the best agent. It may be noticed that the values of the evaluation function oscillate in the range from 0.01 to 0.66. Thus, the use of this function reduces the deviation of the values of the ratios. The results of the experiment allow us to state that the ranking of agents' evaluation differs in particular periods. In the first period, the *ConsensusFuzzy* was the best agent, the *EvolutionaryFuzzy* agent was ranked higher than *ExtendedBollingerFuzzy*, and *EMA* benchmark was ranked higher than the *B&H*. In the second period, the *EvolutionaryFuzzy* was the best agent, and the *ConsensusFuzzy* and *TrendLinearReg* agents were ranked higher than the *EMA* and *B&H*. Considering the third period, it may be noticed that the *ExtendedBolingerFuzzy* was the best agent and *ConsensusFuzzy* agent was ranked higher, but *EvolutionaryFuzzy* was ranked lower than the *EMA* and *B&H*. The *B&H* benchmark was ranked lowest in two periods, and in the first period it generated the losses. It should be noticed that in the second and third period, the upward trend was observed, therefore *B&H*'s *Rate of Return* was positive. The first period shown a downward trend, and therefore the *B&H*'s *Rate of Return* is negative.

Taking into consideration all the periods, it may be stated that there is no agent ranked highest most often. Also, agents achieving the highest Rate of Return were not always ranked in the highest positions. The low level of risk was influenced by the ranks of the *ConsensusFuzzy* and *EvolutionaryFuzzy* agents. And, on the other hand, the *EMA* was often ranked low because of a high risk level (low value of *Sharpe Ratio*). Moreover, it generated a high number of transactions, so transaction costs were very high. It is also worth noting that in the case of the *EvolutionaryFuzzy* agent, despite the fact that the *Rate of Return* in particular periods was not highest, the high value of evaluation function results was achieved with very low transaction costs in comparison to the other agents. Often, *the average rate of return per transaction* was very high.

In the case of fuzzy logic agents, the value of buy-sell decision agents' evaluation was most often higher than the value of *EMA* and *B&H* benchmarks (see last row of Table 1). In the case of three-valued logic agents, instead, there were many cases where the value of buy-sell decision agents' evaluation was lower than the value of *EMA* and *B&H* (see [16, 17]). Also, the values of such ratios as *Rate of Return* and *Number of profitable transactions* were about several percent higher in the case of fuzzy logic. The risk measuring ratio values (*Sharpe ratio, the average coefficient of volatility*) were similar using fuzzy and three-valued logic.

The fuzzy logic has also demonstrated the better performance of the Supervisor strategies, because the opening/closing positions were generated closer to the optimal point determined on the basis of analysis historical data. In order to analyse the fuzzy logic agents' decisions efficiency it was also necessary to take into consideration the thresholds for open/close positions (Table 2). In the system, the *EvolutionaryFuzzy* agent was in charge to determine the thresholds for individual agents, therefore there was no general threshold value.

Table 2. Thresholds for open/close positions

Agent	Open long	Close long	Open short	Close short
ExtendedBollingerFuzzy	0.65	−0.55	−0.65	0.55
ConsensusFuzzy	0.6	−0.5	−0.65	0.6

The generated thresholds for opening/closing long/short positions differ in the case of particular agents. However, these levels often were not equal to 1, 0 or −1 (as in the case of three-valued logic). In addition, the levels for the open long position were different that levels for the close short position, and levels for the open short position were different than levels for the close long position.

In addition to the agents based on the currency quotes and the technical analysis, in A-Trader system the agents using the fundamental analysis and behavioral data were implemented. A decent fundamental analysis comprises the examination of macro-economic indicators, asset markets and political considerations when evaluating a nation's currency. Macroeconomic indicators include figures such as growth rates, as measured by Gross Domestic Product, interest rates, inflation, unemployment, money supply, foreign exchange reserves, and productivity. Asset markets comprise stocks, bonds and real estate. Political considerations impact the level of confidence in a nation's government, the climate of stability, and level of certainty. Other indicators that may be considered are the Purchasing Manager's Index (PMI), Consumer Price Index (CPI), Durable Goods Orders, Producer Price Index (PPI), and retail sales. Briefly speaking, FOREX fundamental analysis concerns the economic, political and social powers driving supply and demand at the market currencies. There are two major factors affecting supply and demand balance: interest rates and international trade. Interest Rates can have either a strengthening or weakening effect on a particular currency. High interest rates attract foreign investment which will strengthen the local currency. The international trade balance which shows a deficit (more imports than exports) is usually an unfavorable indicator. Deficit trade balances mean that money is flowing out of the country to purchase foreign-made goods, and this may have a devaluing effect on the currency.

The problem is that, frequently, online forex fundamental analyses do not provide sharp entry and exit points. Huge amounts of information come out at regular intervals and only a part of it is of some importance.

The user of A-Trader may also confirm buy/sell decisions related to a currency pair (e.g. PLN/USD) by using other quotations, such as:

- gold price ratios: when gold goes up, the USD often goes down (and vice versa); that means gold prices tend to have an inverse relationship to the USD, offering several ways for currency traders to take advantage of that relationship.
- oil price ratios: oil-dependent countries weaken as oil prices rise; if oil prices continue to rise, that can be a consideration for buying a commodity.

The example of visualization of such considerations is presented on Fig. 4.

The different quotation pairs are not yet integrated in the performance evaluation window in a-Trader, but the user can confirm his/her decisions by using charts.

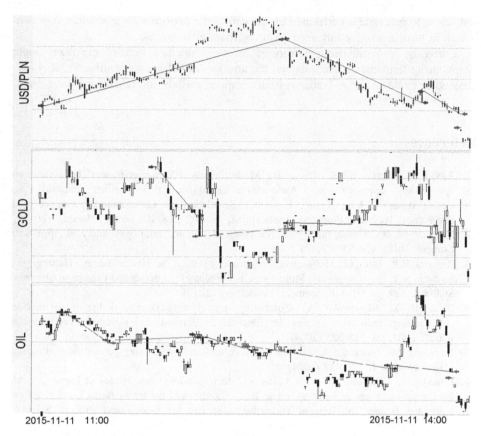

2015-11-11 11:00   2015-11-11 14:00

Fig. 4. Relationships between quotations of USD/PLN pair and gold and oil prices

5 Conclusions

The fuzzy logic agents in the A-Trader system take independent buy-sell decisions with a certain level of probability. The analysis results presented in this article allow us to draw the conclusion that the application of fuzzy logic as an agents' knowledge representation allows for opening/closing and long/short positions closer to the optimal points than the agents based on the three-valued logic.

In consequence the predictions performed by A-Trader were more precise, in periods with both upward and downward trends.

The implementation of fuzzy logic entailed the development of new agents and new trading strategies. The computational complexity of fuzzy logic algorithms is not higher than in the case of three-valued logic, so the computing time for trading positions was almost the same.

It can be also concluded that depending on the current situation on the FOREX market, the level of performance of a particular agent changes. There is no one agent which definitely dominates over the others. The automatic setting of the best agent in time close to real time is performed by the use of the performance evaluation function. It has, in turn, a positive influence on investment effectiveness.

Currently, tests are being performed on the implementation of the fuzzy logic agents using fundamental analysis and the analysis of behavioral sentiments. It is also planned to evaluate the A-Trader system on more periods and other quotations pairs.

References

1. Aloud, M., Tsang, E.P.K., Olsen, R.: Modelling the FX market traders' behaviour: an agent-based approach. In: Alexandrova-Kabadjova, B., Martinez-Jaramillo, S., Garcia-Almanza, A.L., Tsang, E. (eds.) Simulation in Computational Finance and Economics: Tools and Emerging Applications, pp. 202–228. IGI Global, Hershey (2012)
2. Arabacioglu, B.C.: Using fuzzy inference system for architectural space analysis. Appl. Soft Comput. 10(3), 926–937 (2010)
3. Barbosa, R.P., Belo, O.: Multi-agent forex trading system. In: Hakansson, A., Hartung, R., Nguyen, N.T. (eds.) Agent and Multi-agent Technology for Internet and Enterprise Systems. SCI, vol. 289, pp. 91–118. Springer, Heidelberg (2010)
4. Badawy, O., Almotwaly, A.: Combining neural network knowledge in a mobile collaborating multi-agent system. In: Electrical, Electronic and Computer Engineering, ICEEC 2004, pp. 325–328 (2004)
5. Dempster, M., Jones, C.: A real time adaptive trading system using genetic programming. Quant. Finance 1, 397–413 (2001)
6. Franklin, S., Patterson, F.G.: The LIDA architecture: adding new modes of learning to an intelligent, autonomous, software agent. In: Proceedings of the International Conference on Integrated Design and Process Technology. Society for Design and Process Science, San Diego (2006)
7. Glattfelder, J.B., Dupuis, A., Olsen, R.: Patterns in high-frequency FX data: discovery of 12 empirical scaling laws. Quant. Finance 11(4), 599–614 (2011)
8. Kazar, O., Ghodbane, H., Moussaoui, M., Belkacemi, A.: A multi-agent approach based on fuzzy logic for a robot manipulator. JDCTA 3(3), 86–90 (2009)
9. Kirkpatric, C.D., Dahlquist, J.: Technical Analysis: The Complete Resource for Financial Market Technicians. Financial Times Press, Upper Saddle River (2006)
10. Korczak, J., Lipinski, P.: Systemy agentowe we wspomaganiu decyzji na rynku papierów wartościowych. In: Stanek, S., Sroka, H., Paprzycki, M., Ganzha, M. (eds.) Rozwój informatycznych systemów wieloagentowych w środowiskach społeczno-gospodarczych, pp. 289–301. Wydawnictwo Placet, Warszawa (2008)
11. LeBaron, B.: Active and passive learning in agent-based financial markets. East. Econ. J. 37, 35–43 (2011)
12. Martinez-Jaramillo, S., Tsang, E.P.K.: An heterogeneous, endogenous and co-evolutionary GP-based financial market. IEEE Trans. Evol. Comput. 13(1), 33–55 (2009)
13. Żytniewski, M., Kowal, R., Sołtysik, A.: The outcomes of the research in areas of application and impact of software agents societies to organizations so far. examples of implementation in polish companies. In: Ganzha, M., Maciaszek, L., Paprzycki, M. (eds.) Proceedings of Federated Conference Computer Science and Information Systems (FedCSIS), Kraków, pp. 1165–1168 (2013)
14. http://www.forexfraud.com/forex-trading-software-reviews.html

15. Korczak, J., Hernes, M., Bac, M.: Risk avoiding strategy in multi-agent trading system. In: Ganzha, M., Maciaszek, L., Paprzycki, M. (eds.) Proceedings of Federated Conference Computer Science and Information Systems (FedCSIS), Kraków, pp. 1131–1138 (2013)
16. Korczak, J., Hernes, M., Bac, M.: Performance evaluation of decision-making agents in the multi-agent system. In: Ganzha, M., Maciaszek, L., Paprzycki, M. (eds.) Proceedings of Federated Conference Computer Science and Information Systems (FedCSIS), Warszawa, pp. 1171–1180 (2014)
17. Korczak, J., Bac, M., Drelczuk, K., Fafuła, A.: A-Trader - consulting agent platform for stock exchange gamblers. In: Ganzha, M., Maciaszek, L., Paprzycki, M. (eds.) Proceedings of Federated Conference Computer Science and Information Systems (FedCSIS), Wrocław, pp. 963–968 (2012)
18. Fikes, R., Kehler, T.: The role of frame-based representation in reasoning. Commun. ACM 28(9), 904–920 (1985)
19. Kadhim, M.A., Alam, M., Harleen, K.: A multi-intelligent agent architecture for knowledge extraction: novel approaches for automatic production rules extraction. Int. J. Multimedia Ubiquitous Eng. 9(2), 95 (2014)
20. Palit, I., Phelps, S., Ng, W.L.: Can a zero-intelligence plus model explain the stylized facts of financial time series data? In: Proceedings of the Eleventh International Conference on Autonomous Agents and Multi-Agent Systems (AAMAS), vol. 2, pp. 653–660. International Foundation for Autonomous Agents and Multi-agent Systems, Valencia (2012)
21. Piunti, M., Ricci, A.: Cognitive use of artifacts: exploiting relevant information residing in MAS environments. In: Meyer, J.Ch., Broersen, J. (eds.) KRAMAS 2008. LNCS, vol. 5605, pp. 114–129. Springer, Heidelberg (2009)
22. Chen, X.L., Li, L.M., Wang, Y.Z., Ning, W., Ye, X.: ERPBAM: a model for structure and reasoning of agent based on entity-relation-problem knowledge representation system. In: IEEE/WIC/ACM International Joint Conferences on Web Intelligence and Intelligent Agent Technologies, WI-IAT 2009, vol. 3, pp. 365–368 (2009)
23. Zhang, X.F., Wang, G.J., Meng, G.W.: Theory of truth degree based on the interval interpretation of first-order fuzzy predicate logic formulas and its application. Fuzzy Syst. Math. 20(2), 8–12 (2006)
24. Zhu, G.J., Xia, Y.M.: Research and practice of frame knowledge representation. J. Yunnan Univ. (Natural Sciences Edition) 28(S1), 154–157 (2006)
25. Zeng, Z.: Construction of knowledge service system based on semantic web. J. China Soc. Sci. Tech. Inf. 24(3), 336–340 (2005)
26. Martin, J., Odell, J.J.: Object Oriented Methods: The Foundations. Prentice Hall, Englewood Cliffs, New York (1994)
27. Li, S.P., Yin, Q.W., Hu, Y.J.: Overview of researches on ontology. J. Comput. Res. Dev. 41(7), 1041–1052 (2004)
28. Ferber, J.: Multi-Agent Systems. Addison-Wesley Longman, Boston (1999)
29. Russell, S.J., Norvig, P.: Artificial Intelligence: A Modern Approach, 2nd edn. Pearson Education, London (2003)
30. Zadeh, L.A.: Fuzzy Sets, Fuzzy Logic. Fuzzy Systems. World Scientific Press, New York (1996)
31. Wang, X.Z., An, S.F.: Research on learning weights of fuzzy production rules based on maximum fuzzy entropy. J. Comput. Res. Dev. 43(4), 673–678 (2006)
32. Valiant, L.: Probably Approximately Correct: Nature's Algorithms for Learning and Prospering in a Complex World. Basic Books, New York (2013)
33. Novák, V., Perfilieva, I., Močkoř, J.: Mathematical Principles of Fuzzy Logic. Kluwer Academic, Dordrecht (1999)

34. Gharbi, A., Samir, B.A.: Fuzzy logic multi-agent system. Int. J. Comput. Sci. Inf. Technol. **6**(4), 273 (2014)
35. Aref, A., Tran, T.: using fuzzy logic and q-learning for trust modeling in multi-agent systems. In: Ganzha, M., Maciaszek, L., Paprzycki, M. (eds.) Proceedings of Federated Conference Computer Science and Information Systems (FedCSIS), Warszawa, pp. 59–66 (2014)
36. Ropero, J., Gómez, A., Carrasco, A., León, C.: A fuzzy logic intelligent agent for information extraction: introducing a new fuzzy logic-based term weighting scheme. Expert Syst. Appl. **39**(4), 4567–4581 (2012)
37. Lagorse, J., Simoes, M.G., Miraoui, A.: A multiagent fuzzy-logic-based energy management of hybrid systems. IEEE Trans. Ind. Appl. **45**(6), 2123–2129 (2009)
38. Balachandran, B.M., Mohammadian, M.: Development of a fuzzy-based multi-agent system for e-commerce settings. Procedia Comput. Sci. **60**, 593–602 (2015)
39. Shamshirband, S., Kalantari, S., Bakhshandeh, Z.: Designing a smart multi-agent system based on fuzzy logic to improve the gas consumption pattern. Sci. Res. Essays **5**(6), 592–605 (2010)
40. Oyemade, D.A., Godspower, O., Ekuobase, O., Chete, F. O.: Fuzzy logic expert advisor topology for foreign exchange market. In: Proceedings of the International Conference on Software Engineering and Intelligent Systems, Ota, Nigeria (2010)
41. Cheung, W.M., Kaymak, U.: A fuzzy logic based trading system. In: Proceedings of the Third European Symposium on Nature inspired Smart Information Systems, St. Julians, Malta (2007)
42. Aladag, H.C., Yolco, U., Egrioglu, E.: A new time invariant fuzzy time series forecasting model based on particle swarm optimization. Appl. Soft Comput. **12**(10), 3291–3299 (2012)
43. Chen, M.Y.: A high-order fuzzy time series forecasting model for internet stock trading. Future Gener. Comput. Syst. **37**, 461–467 (2014)
44. Singh, P., Borah, B.: Forecasting stock index price based on M-factors fuzzy time series and particle swarm optimization. Int. J. Approximate Reasoning **55**(3), 812–833 (2014)
45. Bollinger, J.: Bollinger on Bollinger Bands. McGraw Hill, New York (2001)
46. Karjalainen, R.: Using genetic algorithms to find technical trading rules. J. Financ. Econ. **51**, 245–271 (1999)
47. Eiben, A.E., Smith, J.E.: Introduction to Evolutionary Computing. Springer-Verlag, Heidelberg (2003)
48. Lento, C.: A combined signal approach to technical analysis on the S&P 500. J. Bus. Econ. Res. **6**(8), 41–51 (2008)
49. Korczak, J., Fafuła, A.: A method to discover trend reversal patterns using behavioral data. In: Wrycza, S. (ed.) SIGSAND/PLAIS 2011. LNBIP, vol. 93, pp. 81–91. Springer, Heidelberg (2011)
50. Hernes, M., Nguyen, N.T.: Deriving consensus for hierarchical incomplete ordered partitions and coverings. J. Univ. Comput. Sci. **13**(2), 317–328 (2007)
51. Hernes, M., Sobieska-Karpińska, J.: Application of the consensus method in a multi-agent financial decision support system. Inf. Syst. e-Business Manag. **14**, 167–185 (2015). doi:10.1007/s10257-015-0280-9. Springer, Heidelberg
52. Nguyen, N.T.: Using consensus methodology in processing inconsistency of knowledge. In: Last, M., Szczepaniak, P.S., Volkovich, Z., Kandel, A. (eds.) Advances in Web Intelligence and Data Mining, Studies in Computational Intelligence, vol. 23, pp. 161–170. Springer-Verlag, Heidelberg (2006)
53. Chan, L., Wong, W.K.: Automated trading with genetic-algorithm neural-network risk cybernetics: an application on FX markets. Finamatrix J., 1–28, February 2012

Data Mining Approach to Assessment of the ERP System from the Vendor's Perspective

Ilona Pawełoszek[✉]

Faculty of Management, Częstochowa University of Technology,
Armii Krajowej 19b, 42-201 Częstochowa, Poland
ipaweloszek@zim.pcz.pl

Abstract. The paper presents an approach to analysis and assessment of benefits brought by an implementation of an Enterprise Resource Planning system. The research has been conducted on a sample of 10 Polish companies using the Xpertis software, which is one of the popular applications for supporting the business activities of small and medium companies. The approach presented hereby aims at elaboration of the assessment method which can be easily applied by the software vendor, moreover it is acceptable by the customers because it does not disclose the confidential business information and still gives the results informative enough to be valuable as well for the software company as for its customers. Analysis conducted through the Orange Data Mining tool was described. The comparative study of the Xpertis ERP features and the customers' characteristics has been briefly presented and the directions of the future development of the considered software have been proposed.

Keywords: ERP implementation · Assessment · Usability · Data mining

1 Introduction

The assessment of benefits brought by an implementation of an ERP system is important from the point of view of two groups of stakeholders. The first group are companies which choose to use the system, incur costs of its implementation and maintenance. The other group's members are the system creators and vendors for which the system is a commodity for sale and a product covered by information and promotion campaigns. The aims of both groups of stakeholders are somehow similar. In both cases there is a need for a forecast how the implementation of integrated information system will influence the functioning of the user-company in different areas. That information is crucial for a customer who buys the ERP system and wants to know whether the investment will bring him operational effectiveness and competitive advantage. On the other hand the ERP vendors are strongly interested in effectiveness and usability of their system to use that knowledge in further development of their product and improvement of the level of their services (customer support, training, helpdesk applications etc.). The domain of information systems analysis and assessment is a broad field related to many aspects of the company's functioning.

© Springer International Publishing Switzerland 2016
E. Ziemba (Ed.): FedCSIS 2015, LNBIP 243, pp. 125–143, 2016.
DOI: 10.1007/978-3-319-30528-8_8

The ERP assessment issues are well grounded in the literature, however most of the approaches represent the customer's perspective.

The critical success factors (CSFs) for an ERP implementation, with the number of over 80 [1] have been well documented in the literature [2]. The factors such as: top management support, project team competence, interdepartmental cooperation, clear goals and objectives, project management, are considered to be monitored during the implementation of the system [3]. But the question arises how to assess the system that has already been implemented and in the same time to check whether the successful implementation directly translates into the overall performance of the system during the consecutive years of its exploitation [4].

The main problem that confronts the current measurement frameworks is the fact that much of the benefits are strategic, therefore they are hard to quantify and may only appear several years after the implementation of the solution [5].

The aim of this paper is to present an approach that can be taken by software companies to create a method for assessment of their products in terms of customer needs and identification of areas for the product's improvement.

The presented approach aims at bringing relevant and informative results that can also be presented to future customers to show them the usefulness of the system and reduce the information asymmetry which is cited as an important factor of ERP implementation failure [6]. The approach used in this study is based on the example of Xpertis ERP system offered by Macrologic Inc.

The structure of the paper is as follows. Section 2 introduces a context for the study which is rooted in Polish market of ERP systems. The main focus has been on small and medium software companies and the issues they face in competing on highly demanding Polish market. Section 3 briefly describes the problems of ERP evaluation from the vendors perspective with special focus on software usability. Section 4 provides the description of research approach and design. Section 5 presents the data analysis approach based on clustering and classification methods. This section also presents the research results, respectively, the system features and the customers' characteristics. The conclusion section summarizes the outcome of the work, and suggests future research directions.

2   Polish Market of ERP

For today's companies the support from well-tuned IT solution seems absolutely necessary, although according to Central Statistical Office of Poland the share of Polish companies using ERP was only 18 % in the year 2013 and grew to 22 % in 2014, which is around 9 % points less than average for 28 EU countries [7].

Most of the small and medium Polish companies built their own systems (almost 40 % of manufacturers with 100 to 1000 employees) or do not have the integrated IT system at all. The lack of integrated enterprise system hinders and delays information flow within an organization because the data is kept in many loosely coupled applications. Such a situation negatively impacts the company's competitiveness [8].

An analysis of the numerous reports from ERP market brings the reader to the conclusion that the market capacity is high. The potential target group are small and medium companies that do not have the ERP, but also large companies that need to replace or modernize their legacy system.

However the survey among managers of the Polish SME companies reveals little awareness of the need to implement the ERP and its impact on the company's profitability (only 33 % of respondents declared to see the need to implement the ERP system) [9]. Many companies complain that after their huge investments in ERP systems, they find it does not bring the expected results in terms of new orders, new profits, or competitive advantage [10].

For the majority of small and medium enterprises the decision of adoption as well as the selection of the appropriate ERP system is a difficult task. The main issues are shortage of financial resources, limited qualified IT personnel, lack of resources and time have been cited as the main factors that make this task difficult and risky [11].

The Polish ERP market is a very competitive one. There was 31 ERP vendors in Poland in 2014. The unquestionable market leader is SAP (39.6 % share), which is followed by Comarch, Oracle, IFS and BPSC. The remaining market share of around 26 % is divided among other small companies one of which is Macrologic Inc..

Large companies own enough financial and managerial resources to develop and bring to market new software products and to gain dominant share of the market. Contrarily, small software companies often meet difficulties in finances and staffing while running their businesses. Therefore they often choose to concentrate on a market niche, which is disregarded by large companies. Small companies also opt to build their competitive advantage mainly on the basis of their excellent responsibility and flexibility.

Actually, due to the limitation of resources faced by small and medium companies best practices which have proven in large firms might be too expensive or time consuming to perform. Accordingly, there is a need to find specific solutions to improve small companies' software processes in several aspects [12].

3   Problems of ERP Assessment from the Vendors' Perspective

The software systems today are more than just a commodity, they are strategic asset custom tailored to the issues each company is facing. They provide the ability to precisely adapt the software components to the needs of the organization. They are characterized by the requirement to provide maximum flexibility, understood primarily as a possible use by a variety of organizations [13].

Due to the complexity of enterprise systems, bringing a new product to the market is both expensive and risky for the vendor. Initial investment requires both highly skilled human effort, time and specialized IT tools. While planning and developing a new software product it is necessary to anticipate its complete lifecycle which is of even 10 to 20 years of exploitation.

From the marketing point of view, one of the most important factors is usability of the ERP system, which, according to ISO Standards can be viewed as a set of three factors: effectiveness, efficiency and satisfaction [14]. While users' satisfaction is quite easy to asses, there is more confusion when it comes to actually measure the system's efficiency or effectiveness especially in economic terms. It is hard to say to what degree the system impacts the overall performance of a company. The values to be measured are dynamic and change with the time that has elapsed since the completion of implementation.

Usability can be also described in narrower sense as a set of three following criteria [15]: navigation, presentation and learnability. Learnability is the most tricky to asses because it highly depends on other non-system issues such as users' skills, technical background, previous experiences with similar systems etc. Learnability can be measured as time needed to get basic knowledge to work with the system. Learnability is associated with accessible online or offline help files and additional training offered by the vendor. It often happens that the first implementation of the ERP system in a given company requires changes in business processes in such case the users can report difficulties in understanding the system as it does not correspond with the processes they are used to.

The evaluation of the system always requires cooperation of the stakeholders in determining where the highest probabilities of weak points exist. These observations are valuable as well for the vendor to gain knowledge about the products as for customers to help them improve their businesses.

4   Approach to Assessment of ERP System Implementation

The aim of the study was to evaluate the impact of the ERP system on different areas of the company where the system is supposed to bring improvements in comparison to the situation before the system implementation. The studied product was the ERP system Xpertis developed by Macrologic Inc.. The system has been chosen due to the fact that Macrologic's Executives are substantially interested in continuous improvement of their product and competitiveness on the demanding Polish enterprise software market. The company is searching for new approaches to get valuable product and customer knowledge [16]. To get the whole picture of the complex software system it is necessary to consider the customer's perspective [17]. By acquiring the customers' knowledge the vendor gains deep understanding of the product usability that allows to present the benefits accurately and persuasively.

Competitors on ERP market offer very similar products, therefore it can be hard to recognize the differences between them as well for the customer as for the vendor. In this situation the competitive advantage can be found in the way of communicating with the future and existing customers. The key element of communication seems to be the way of presenting them a value proposition [18].

Gaining the customer's knowledge is a difficult task. Survey practitioners often experience difficulties in collecting reliable data due to various privacy concerns. Some of the companies refuse to take part in the survey as their company policy do not allow sharing internal information with outsiders even for academic purposes [19]. Companies are afraid to conduct the research because it could reveal weaknesses in the management process [20]. Some of the companies' excuse for not taking part in the surveys is that the studies do not seem to bring any value for the respondents. To avoid such situation the goal of the study should be clearly defined and the utility value for the respondents should be the communicated at first.

The presented approach to analysis and assessment of ERP systems addresses the problem of commercially-sensitive information. This could be achieved through an adequate design of the survey questionnaire.

The approach, although it is tailored to fit the needs of the Macrologic Inc. and the Xpertis ERP, can be used by other software companies offering similar systems after some necessary modifications of the survey questionnaire according to the specificity of their product.

The survey has been conducted on the sample of 10 Polish companies, who have recently (during the past three years) completed the implementation of the Xpertis system. The participants for the survey were selected using a non-random decision rule intended to select the set of companies who satisfy the following conditions:

- The surveyed companies localized in different cities representing at least 50 % of Polish voivodships (administrative districts).
- The Company's management board's permission for the employees to undergo the survey.
- The Companies differentiated throughout the branches of industry (furniture, metallurgic, chemical, foundry, services and other).
- There were usually 7–10 persons who were surveyed in each of the companies. The persons are employees who are directly involved in operating the selected system's modules.

The survey questions were brainstormed by the team of three IT and management experts, all of them having experience in using the considered ERP.

The responders were employees operating the system in their daily work. They were asked to evaluate the impact of the system using the Likert-type scale from −2 to 2 (presented in Table 1). The lack of evaluation were also allowed in cases when particular question was not relevant to the scope of the company's activities.

Table 1. Rating scale and its interpretation

Very bad/significant deterioration	Bad/deterioration	Neutral/ no changes	Good/ improvement	Very good/significant improvement	Not applicable*
−2	−1	0	1	2	NA

* The answer in case the given ERP module was not implemented or the company does not operate in the given area.

The reasons for the choice of the Likert scale instead of concrete values were twofold: the chosen scale is easy to interpret and compare because the values are normalized and the Likert-type scale was acceptable to the surveyed companies as a form of the survey that does not disclose their detailed financial and operating information.

The survey questions covered 11 areas of the organization's activity: Manufacturing/ execution of orders, Sales, After-sales services, Recycling, Marketing, Procurement, Warehouse management, Economic analyses, Organization, Human resources and payroll, Accounting and finance.

The questions for all the aforementioned areas are organized into 3 categories and subsequent factors:

1. General factors:

   – Compliance with the business requirements (Pre-implementation analysis)
   – Compliance with business strategy
   – Functional adjustment to the business process specificity

2. User interface factors and usability factors:

   – Overall satisfaction of the user
   – Ease of use
   – Functional adjustment to the user's tasks
   – User friendliness of the interface
   – User assistance in problem solving
   – User's autonomy (necessity of the system's administrator assistance)
   – Visual attractiveness of the printed documents.

3. Specific factors – different for each area of company, associated with specific business operations.

The dataset yields a matrix containing 10 units of observation, each one is described by 205 factors. The first aim of analysis was to extract the factors which are important and influence the functioning of the Xpertis ERP system, usability and effectiveness of the users' work and at the same time eliminating those factors which appear to be irrelevant (mainly assessed as 0 and NA).

The second aim was to find similarities between evaluations made by 10 surveyed companies. These similarities and differences can be useful to create the profiles of features and needs of different groups of customers. This research will allow to get knowledge about the needed future adjustments of the ERP system to the customers' needs. The next interesting issue is verification of the selected methods to determine to what degree the data mining techniques are appropriate to the problem. This can be done, inter alia, by comparing the results delivered by data analysis methods with an opinion of a human-expert.

From the point of view of the vendor the implementations can be considered as successful or less successful. The opinion about the implementation of the ERP system is highly qualitative and subjective. The process of implementation renders artifacts that can be evaluated positively or negatively by the customer. However also social relations arise between the project teams of both the vendor's and the customer's companies that can be the subject of evaluation. The overall picture of implementation is thus created by issues such as communication, mutual understanding, coordination of actions, active involvement of employees and executives etc.

An important conclusion regarding the successfulness of the implementation can be drawn by comparing the opinion of the customer and the software vendor. It may be assumed that the implementation is successful when the two opinions are consistent.

5   Data Analysis Method and Key Insights

5.1   Introduction to the Data Analysis Method

The analyses of the collected data could be performed on an intuitive way by a simple method of screening the spreadsheet and selecting those factors which received the highest and the lowest scores in the customers' opinions. However a more detailed approach can be taken using data-mining as it offers statistically based methods for identification of patterns in data sets.

In this case the analysis of important features of ERP was performed through the means of cluster analysis. Then decision trees were used to find patterns and rules leading to successful implementations. For the considered dataset cluster analysis seems to be the appropriate choice because it allows to identify groups of similar records and moreover it is a well described and investigated method that is still being developed and ameliorated up till today [21].

Cluster analysis or clustering is a common technique of statistical data analysis. The objective of clustering is to assign observations to the homogeneous groups (called clusters) in a way that the observations in the same cluster are similar to one another in some sense.

There are many clustering methods based on various algorithms that can be applied depending on the nature of the dataset under consideration. Different clustering algorithms may render different results on the same data. Moreover the same clustering algorithm may bring different results on the same data, if it involves arbitrary initial parameters. However interpreting the results of cluster analysis is not a trivial task, because it requires knowledge of semantic relations between investigated attributes of the ERP system and the domain it supports.

There are three important steps in the preparation of cluster analysis:

1. Selecting a distance measure – The similarity between various objects is defined by a distance measure. The distance measure plays an important role in obtaining semantically meaningful clusters. For simple datasets where the data is multidimensional, Euclidean distance can be used [22]. Moreover the Euclidean distance is appropriate for data measured on the same scale. It should be noted that in this case the qualitative ordered scale was applied so the analysis requires prudent interpretation of distances between observations to draw valid conclusions.
2. Choosing a clustering method and tool. A hierarchical clustering method has been applied to classify the data set. The clustering algorithm was used and analyses were performed with Orange 2.7.1 software[1] [23].
3. Determining the number of clusters. It is still an open problem in the data mining community. There is no generally recognized method to set the right number of clusters. The heuristics, background knowledge, rule of thumb can be recommended. Preserving an informative value of the clusters is most important.

---

[1] Software developed by Bioinformatics Lab at University of Ljubljana, Slovenia, in collaboration with open source community http://orange.biolab.si/.

In the presented case the clustering can be applied to two purposes. The first one is to distinguish groups of the features which received similar ratings from the users of Xpertis ERP system. The analysis will bring general knowledge of strengths and weaknesses of the software perceived by the customers. For this analysis data matrix was prepared with the column names indicating the specific customers and the rows corresponding with the 205 studied features.

The second purpose to which the clustering method was applied was to identify similarities between customers' assessments. The results of this method allowed to identify characteristics of the customers who are satisfied with the implementation of the system. In this case of analysis the matrix should be transposed (customers described by rows, features by columns).

Further, the results of an interview with the vendor will be presented and the method of decision rule discovery will be applied to check which features of the system are characteristic for successful and less successful implementations.

5.2   Clustering Results of the System's Features

In the case of feature clustering the dataset was divided on 6 clusters numbered from 0 to 5. Each of the clusters contains observation with similar values assigned by the users of the Xpertis ERP. Table 2 presents brief statistic characteristics of each cluster. As it can be easily seen from the Fig. 1 (which is graphical representation of the data from the Table 2) the clusters differ markedly from each other. Also discrepancy in the average evaluation for each cluster can be seen. The features assigned to each cluster were described in detail in earlier work [19].

Table 2. The statistics of the clusters.

Cluster	Number of features	Evaluation					
		−2	−1	0	1	2	NA[a]
Cluster 0	87	0.0 %	0.0 %	11.1 %	31.7 %	55.1 %	2.1 %
Cluster 1	13	0.0 %	0.0 %	7.7 %	12.3 %	78.5 %	1.5 %
Cluster 2	36	0.3 %	0.3 %	32.1 %	37.6 %	18.7 %	2.0 %
Cluster 3	36	3.3 %	0.3 %	0.6 %	75.6 %	19.4 %	0.8 %
Cluster 4	11	2.7 %	4.5 %	50.9 %	34.5 %	0.9 %	6.4 %
Cluster 5	22	0.0 %	0.0 %	19.1 %	3.6 %	0.0 %	77.3 %
Sum	205						

[a]The answer in case the given ERP module was not implemented or the company does not operate in the given area.

Cluster 5 contains attributes which are mostly irrelevant for the evaluation of the system or describe the areas that are not influenced by the system. The attributes in this cluster describe the following areas: recycling (all the attributes from this group), human Resources and Payroll, −3 attributes, accounting and finance (2 attributes).

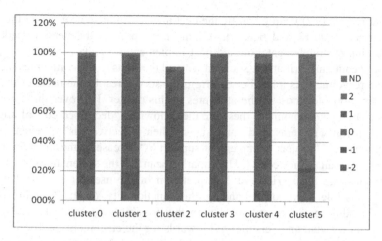

Fig. 1. Visualization of feature clusters statistics (Color figure online).

The aforementioned attributes from the cluster 5 indicate that the companies do not involve in the recycling activities and do not see the need to support this area by ICT tools. The other area in this cluster is human resources management. This one is probably seen as a diverse collection of "soft" skills that can be hardly supported by IT tools. The system could be extended by the functions of replacement workforce management in the area of registering the profiles of employees and job seekers. Additionally the decision support tools could be implemented to the recruitment process to make it more effective at getting the best person for a job or a project.

Cluster 4 represents the areas on which the ERP system does not have the clear impact or the impact is slightly positive.

Analyzing the results of the assessment some recommendations for further development of the system can be drafted. In the areas of manufacturing and after-sales services there is a need for more user autonomy. However the need for the administrator's intervention was mostly indicated by two of the surveyed companies. Creation of e-communities seems to be interesting future development direction of the ERP system. E-communities may focus on different aspects of the company's functioning and also support the knowledge flow and retention. There is a movement taking place in the IT industry that is really driven by major consumer technology vendors like Apple, Google, and Facebook. In fact, employees and managers of almost any business are already communicating with each other through various Web 2.0 technologies. However all of this communication is taking place outside the bounds of formal and secure IT systems [24]. Adding collaborative Web 2.0 technologies to ERP applications could be a way to address these challenges both for business users and IT.

Cluster 3 is characterized by moderately good (75.6 %) and very good (19.4 %) evaluation of the Xpertis ERP features. There are 36 elements in the cluster 3 - mainly the features associated with the user's interface and visual aspects.

Although the overall assessment is positive there are also signals pointing to the problems regarding the users' autonomy in different modules of the system. This may indicate the poor practical skills and theoretical background of some of the users.

The lowest ratings (−2) were given by the customers who have been using the system for the shortest time (3 and 6 months). This may indicate the need for additional training during the implementation and post-implementation phase.

Cluster 2 contains attributes associated with all the areas of the companies' activities (apart from recycling). As it can be seen from the survey results the users evaluation is good or very good for most of the attributes in this cluster. However there are also 5 attributes that received mainly 0, these are the following: "decreased cost of after sales services", "loyalty systems and analysis of their effectiveness", "revenues from after-sales service", "project management support", "increase in the financial revenue and decrease of loan service costs". The 0 marks mean that the system does not influence the aforementioned areas. However interpretation of the users' assessment indicates interesting possible ways of enhancing the functionality of the system modules. The CRM module could be extended with the possibility to create targeted loyalty programs with relevant and personalized rewards for the customers. Also project management is not directly supported by any module of the system. The project management support should be offered as an optional module integrated with Human Resources and financial modules. Although for now not all the customers practice project management, this discipline is becoming more widely recognized and used throughout the world [25]. Therefore it can be expected that the enterprise project management support could be one of the important features distinguishing the ERP product.

Cluster 1 contains features that are considered very positively influencing the business (mainly marks 2 and 1). This cluster mainly describes the areas associated with enterprise-wide communication and information management. The Users reported significant improvement in marketing effectiveness and efficiency relative to the performance before the implementation of Xpertis system.

The Xpertis system has significant impact on acceleration of information flow, document circulation, reporting and analyses. The four companies of the 10 surveyed, claimed that the system does not influence the number of offers sent to their customers and the number of received responses. This fact can be caused by the business specificity and long-term contracts with their customers.

Cluster 0 is the largest one with 87 factors of the system evaluation. The data in this cluster reflect the very positive or moderately positive impact of the system on the surveyed areas of the business. The cluster contains data associated with 10 modules (apart from the recycling module). The most often appearing features are: ease of use, overall satisfaction or the users, support in problem solving, automation and acceleration of the specific operations.

Regarding the large number of factors in this cluster and the limited size of the hereby publication the factors are not listed.

So far the potential areas of weakness seem to be factors from the cluster 5, and 4. Particularly the need for administrator's intervention reported by two of the 10 surveyed companies. To facilitate such analyses in the future some of the factors should be reconsidered in the questionnaire:

- human resources management (probably the problem was framed too broadly),
- creation of replacement workforce and employing the replacement workers in the projects (probably the surveyed companies do not practice project management).

The question about the system's compliance with business strategy is recognized by the surveyed employees as correlated with the support for operational tasks.

5.3 Clustering Method for Identification of the Customers' Characteristics

In practice of marketing segmenting is the popular technique of putting customers into groups based on similarities. This part of the research approach is aimed at identification and analyses of regularities and similarities between companies exploiting the ERP system. The groups generated by the clustering algorithm underwent semantic interpretation which required additional insight to find out the reasons of the similarities between the cluster members.

Although the sample was only 10 companies, the large number of factors taken into consideration made the problem appropriate for the use of statistical methods. This time the clustering based on k-means algorithm was the choice. The dataset was partitioned arbitrarily into 4 clusters having roughly similar number of data points.

The Fig. 2 presents the visualization of the clusters in Orange Data Mining software. The index on the vertical axis refers to the particular customer and the horizontal axis represents the cluster number.

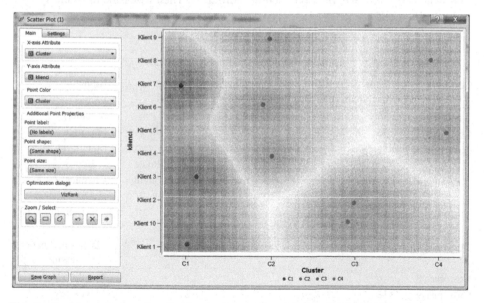

Fig. 2. Customer clusters visualization in Orange Data Mining Software (Color figure online)

By comparing the data on the time that has elapsed since the completion of the implementation with the clusters created by k-means algorithm it is easy to see some regularities in the evaluations made by customers assigned to the same cluster.

It should be noted that the clustering was performed only on the basis of the customers evaluations of the system. Such an approach was taken intentionally to check how far the evaluation depends on the customers' characteristics. The Table 3 presents the features of the surveyed Macrologic's customers along with the division on clusters. As it was mentioned before the customers 5 and 8 reported problems with the users' autonomy, that were caused by little experience because the time after the completion of the system's implementation was relatively short (3 and 6 months). It can be reasonably expected that the evaluation will get better with time. The both observations were located in the cluster 4.

Regarding the data in the Table 3 it can be assumed that the period of 1 year is the threshold time after which the users get enough experience to easily operate the system. Also the one year of exploitation gives the comprehensible view of achievements of targets assumed in pre-implementation phase.

The survey results also show the low evaluation cases in spite of the long post-implementation period (customer 2). In case of this customer the interview and observation showed the classical example of information asymmetry between the buyer and the vendor of ERP system. By considering available data regarding the specificity of the surveyed companies along with the evaluations of the ERP system it can be found that there is no clear dependence between branch of industry and the customer perception of the system. For example the customer 1 and 8 both represent the metallurgic industry, however their production is different. Their assessments of the system are very divergent.

Table 3. The Customers' characteristics

Customer	Time since ERP implementation (months)	Cluster	Number of IT staff	Branch
Customer 1	36	1	1	Metallurgy
Customer 2	36	3	1	Furniture
Customer 3	12	1	Casual employee	Metallurgy
Customer 4	18	2	Additionally acting	Chemical
Customer 5	3	4	1	Services, projects
Customer 6	30	2	9	Services
Customer 7	20	1	1	Plastics and paper processing
Customer 8	6	4	1	Metallurgy
Customer 9	18	2	2	Metallurgy, molding
Customer 10	12	3	1	Manufacturing, plastics

Another example that proves the hypothesis of interdependence of time factor and the user's evaluation of the system is cluster 2 which contains two customers (9 and 4). Both customers evaluations were similar and the time after the completion of implementation is 18 months in both cases. The clear correlation between the number of IT staff, the form of employment and the customers' evaluations could not be identified.

5.4   Discovery of Key Factors of Successful Implementations

The last part of the study focused on the assessment of the vendor's satisfaction regarding the implementation of the system. For this purpose the executives of Macrologic Inc. were asked to evaluate the ten examined implementations of the Xpertis ERP. Table 4 presents the marks assigned by Macrologic to each of the implementations with the short comment justifying the mark in each case. The chosen marking scale was [2...5], where 2 means the implementation was not successful, and 5 – very successful. To clearly divide the successful implementations from the less successful ones the observations were arbitrarily assigned by Macrologic executives into two classes: 0 (successful implementations, marks 4 and above), and 1 (less successful mark below 4).

Table 4. Results of the interview with Macrologic's executives

Customer	Mark (According to Macrologic, scale [2...5] pts.)	Class 0/1	Macrologic's comments on implementation
Customer 1	5	0	Very demanding customer, aware of his needs and able to define the goals of implementation. Problems during the implementation solved cooperatively by means of compromise
Customer 2	3	1	A "difficult customer", often unaware of his needs. Often using the statement "I thought it should be like that". After implementation of subsequent modules the customer's knowledge and awareness of workflow in ERP increased. Thus the cooperation got better
Customer 3	4	0	Implementation n accordance with the schedule. Less initiative from the customer in initial phase which was followed by "recovery" of needs. Implementation was successful but far from perfect
Customer 4	4	0	The implementation was efficient, mainly due to involvement of one of the executives of the company. Good knowledge of ERP modules and skills

(Continued)

Table 4. (*Continued*)

Customer	Mark (According to Macrologic, scale [2…5] pts.)	Class 0/1	Macrologic's comments on implementation
			of the Project Leader enabled quick achievement of goals. Lack of involvement by the rest of the users was important negative issue
Customer 5	3	1	Lack of precisely defined goals of implementation caused the implementation dragging along in the phase of project completion. Lack of discipline of the system users in terms of timely completion of tasks commissioned by the implementation supervisor, which caused significant delays
Customer 6	5	0	A multi-office company with very precisely defined goals of implementation. Professional project leader from the Customer's company. Very good cooperation with the project leader contributed to the success of the project
Customer 7	4	0	Implementation completed in a short time, after the implementation new requirements from the customers appeared and were fulfilled by Macrologic
Customer 8	2.5	1	Lack of proper project leader from the customer's company. Lack of specified goals, the whole responsibility shifted to Macrologic
Customer 9	3.5	1	Implementation in accordance with the assumptions of Macrologic. The Customer on the initial phase was poorly involved. After the completion of the implementation the specified needs appeared which could be defined earlier, what could save costs and facilitate the implementation
Customer 10	3	1	Lack of precisely specified goals. Lack of discipline of the system users and timely completion of the tasks

As it can be seen the set of observations was divided on two classes each counting 5 observations. The next thing to consider was whether the responses of the customers for the 205 questions described in Sect. 5.2 are related to the evaluations of implementations according to Macrologic.

Formal interpretation supporting the evaluation was performed using decision trees algorithm. The method allows to determine which of the 205 questions in were decisive and what responses were characteristic for the customers who underwent successful or less successful implementations.

In principle, decision trees are used to predict the membership of objects to specific category (class), taking into account the values that correspond to their attributes (predictor variables) [26, p. 159].

The decision tree algorithm was applied separately to the data describing 3 areas of the system. For this part of the study the following areas have been selected: Manufacturing, Sales, Marketing and After-Sales. The choice was governed by the overall frequency of implementations of the ERP modules supporting the selected areas and the fact that they are important for the company's profitability.

For illustration Table 5 presents data input for the area of Manufacturing. The input data contained the customers' evaluations of the features (F1..F20) characteristic for each area which were treated as attributes (columns), the number of the customer (C1..C10, which were meta attributes), and the class – 0 or 1 (coding respectively successful and less successful implementations).

Table 5. The structure of data input to the decision tree algorithm.

F1	F2	F3	...	F14	F15	F16	F17	F18	F19	F20	Meta attr.	Class
2	2	1	...	2	2	2	0	0	1	−1	C1	0
1	1	1	...	2	2	1	1	1	1	1	C2	1
2	1	2	...	2	2	2	1	1	1	0	C3	0
.	.	.	...	.	.	.	.	.	.	.	.	.
.	.	.	.	.	.	.	.	.	.	.	.	.
.	.	.	.	.	.	.	.	.	.	.	.	.
1	1	1	...	2	2	1	1	2	1	1	C10	1

In case of manufacturing area, the application of decision trees algorithm revealed a classification rule based on the attribute F16 – Allocation of labor among supplies and orders. The rule was:

```
if F16<=1 then class 1
if F16=2 or F16=NA then class 0
```

Allocation of labor is a difficult task which, when done manually, requires experience and optimization skills. Thus support for this task is very important for production managers. The semantic interpretation of the rule discovered by the decision tree algorithm allows to assume that the customer's satisfaction of this feature is one of the important conditions of the successful implementation. As it can be seen in the data

Table 4 the implementation was successful also for customer 6 which did not implement the manufacturing module, because the company operates in services industry.

The next area selected for analysis was Sales. The module of Sales was implemented in all the surveyed companies. The most characteristic feature for successful implementation in this area was "Automation of customer control". The customer control encompasses the assessment of customer's reliability and many tasks that can be supported by ERP module, such as defining the pricing models and discounts with their priorities and rules.

The next area analyzed was Marketing, where the ERP software is to support a range of activities such as: contacting customers, automating the sales force activities and competitor assessment, Cross-selling and Up-selling, aiming to raise the value of a single sale transaction, increasing the confidence and reducing the risk of taking over the customer by the competitors [27].

In the area of Marketing six rules were discovered (illustrated on Fig. 3).

The following features were found important by the algorithm of decision trees:

– functional adjustment (whether the system supports all the necessary user tasks) (feature coded as D_F_5),
– new medium of communication (feature coded as D_F_12),
– number of offers sent to customers (feature coded as D_F_16).

Classification Tree	Class	P(Class)	P(Target)	# Inst	Distribution (rel)
◢ <root>	cluster 0	0.500	0.500	10	0.500:0.500
D_F_5 <=1.50	cluster 1	1.000	0.000	4	0.000:1.000
◢ D_F_5 >1.50	cluster 0	0.833	0.833	6	0.833:0.167
◢ D_F_12 <=1.50	cluster 0	0.500	0.500	2	0.500:0.500
D_F_16 <=0.50	cluster 0	1.000	1.000	1	1.000:0.000
D_F_16 >1.00	cluster 1	1.000	0.000	1	0.000:1.000
D_F_12 >1.50	cluster 0	1.000	1.000	4	1.000:0.000

Fig. 3. Decision rules for the area of Marketing.

The first of the abovementioned features turned out to be decisive. If the feature was evaluated 2 the customer was in most cases assigned to the class 0 (successful implementation). Two other rules found by the algorithm appeared to be less important because there was only one instance that followed them.

This exception was the case of the Customer 9, who assessed positively all the considered features. The implementation of the system in case of that customer was marked 3.5 by Macrologic's executives, therefore it was neither a particularly good nor bad. The conclusion can be reached that probably the subjective assumption to assign the case of Customer 9 to the class 1 (less successful) was not correct.

In the area of After-sales there were two important features indicated by decision tree algorithm: information on customer complaints and user support in problem solving. The first one is the decisive feature, if the value was less than 1 the implementation is less successful. User support in problem solving is also the important characteristics it was evaluated on 1 or 2 by all the customers assigned to the class 0 (successful), apart from one exception. As in previous analysis the exception appeared in case of Customer 9, who evaluated this feature as 2. Again there is a proof that the mark 3.5 describing the implementation should be assigned rather to class 0.

The above analysis of the Xpertis ERP system implemented in 10 surveyed companies, shows that the considered software in most of the cases contributes to an improvement of the users' work in various aspects (communication, reporting, acceleration of operational tasks).

6 Conclusion

The study presented in the hereby paper is an attempt to elaborate the easy to use methodology for the software vendors to get more insight about their customers' needs and the possibilities of improvement of their products. The approach presented hereby let the vendor create an insight on the overall system features in a way that does not reveal private information of the investigated companies. Therefore the research results can be presented to potential customers to better illustrate the areas of the impact of the ERP system on business processes.

The cluster analysis is useful and flexible method to discover structures in a data set however it does not provide any explanation itself. The semantic interpretation of clustering effects can be performed by combining the data of each cluster with the knowledge of experienced members of the implementation team. The models of analyses can be used multiple times with different data sets.

The cluster analysis was extended further to identify decisive features which are characteristic to successful and less successful implementations of ERP software. The methods of clustering and decision trees can be performed to analyze the features of each separate module. Such analysis requires to prepare the data set limited to the selected features. The new dataset can be then easily loaded to the model built in Orange Data Mining tool.

The problem of post-implementation analysis of the ERP systems deserves further exploration. The approach presented in this paper could be an inspiration for small and medium software companies to elaborate their own method for products evaluation and comparison of their customers. The advanced assessment approaches based on data mining are often considered as reserved for large businesses with expansive budgets and creative departments. However, with open source data visualization and analysis tools available it is easier than ever for small and medium companies to gain knowledge on their products and customers to let them more effectively compete with larger companies on software market.

Acknowledgments. The survey prepared is a collaborative effort. Therefore the author thanks Cezary Stępniak, Częstochowa University of Technology, Poland, for the idea of the research and cooperation on preparation of the survey questionnaire. The author would like to thank Janusz Jakóbczak consultant to the Management Board of Macrologic Inc. for consulting the survey questionnaire, gathering data and his comments to the draft of the paper.

References

1. Ngai, E.W.T., Law, C.C.H., Wat, F.K.T.: Examining the critical success factors in the adoption of enterprise resource planning. Comput. Ind. **59**, 548–564 (2008)
2. Leyh, C.: Critical success factors for ERP projects in small and medium-sized enterprises – the perspective of selected German SMEs. In: Proceedings of the 2014 Federated Conference on Computer Science and Information Systems, FedCSIS 2014, Warsaw, Poland, pp. 1181–1190 (2014). https://fedcsis.org/proceedings/2014/pliks/243.pdf
3. Somers, T.M., Nelson, K.: The impact of critical success factors across the stages of enterprise resource planning implementations. In: Proceedings of the 34th Hawaii International Conference on System Sciences (HICSS-3), Maui, Hawaii (2001)
4. Jenatabadi, H.S., Noudoostbeni, A.: End-user satisfaction in ERP system: application of logit modeling. Appl. Math. Sci. **8**(24), 1187–1192 (2014)
5. Dyczkowski, M., Korczak, J., Dudycz, H.: Multi-criteria evaluation of BI systems The case study of InKoM dashboard. Bus. Inform. Wroc. Univ. Econ. Res. Pap. **3**(33), 35–60 (2014)
6. Tazyeen, F.: Modeling government ERP acquisition methods using system dynamics. Massachusetts Institute of Technology (2012). http://web.mit.edu/smadnick/www/wp/2012-04.pdf
7. Berezowska, J., Huet, M., Kamińska, M., Kwiatkowska, M., Orczykowska, M., Rozkrut, D, Wegner, M.: Społeczeństwo informacyjne w Polsce: Wyniki badań statystycznych. Główny Urząd Statystyczny Urząd Statystyczny w Szczecinie (2014)
8. Mejssner, B.: Mniejsze przedsiębiorstwa w kolejce po ERP, Computerworld, vol. 16 (2014). http://www.computerworld.pl/artykuly/395608/Mniejsze.przedsiebiorstwa.w.kolejce.po.ERP.html
9. Tchorek-Helm, T.: Dlaczego firmy nie kupują ERP (2011). http://www.komputerwfirmie.pl/informacje/raporty/pelny/4636/dlaczego-firmy-nie-kupuja-erp
10. Hsu, P.: Commodity or competitive advantage? analysis of the ERP value paradox. Electron. Commer. Res. Appl. **12**(6), 412–424 (2013)
11. Stefanou, C.J.: Adoption of free/open source ERP software by SMEs. In: Devos, J., van Landeghem, H., Deschoolmeester, D. (eds.) Information Systems for Small and Medium-Sized Enterprises, pp. 157–166. Springer, Berlin (2014)
12. Shen, Y.: Software Engineering Challenges in Small Companies, Helsinki (2008). http://www.cs.helsinki.fi/u/paakki/Shen.pdf
13. Wieczorkowski, J., Pawełoszek, I., Polak, P.: Software standardization in the context of the innovativeness of enterprise operations. In: Kommers, P., Isaias, P. (eds.) Proceedings of the International Conference e-Society 2015, pp. 215–222. IADIS Press, Lisbon (2015)
14. ISO 9241-11: Ergonomic requirements for Office work with visual display terminals (VDTs) – Part 11: Guidance on usability. International Organization for Standardization, Geneva, Switzerland (1998)
15. Scholtz, B., Calitz, A., Cilliers, C.: Usability evaluation of a mediumsized ERP system in higher education. Electron. J. Inf. Syst. Eval. **16**(2), 148–161 (2013)
16. Hong Tang, S., Homayouni, M., Alaei, H.: The role of intelligent agents in customer knowledge management. Afr. J. Bus. Manage. **5**(16), 7042–7049 (2011)
17. Frauendorf, J.: Customer Processes in Business-to-Business Service Transactions. Deutscher Universitts-Verlag, Wiesbaden (2006)
18. Hutt, M.D.: e-Study Guide for: Business Marketing Management: B2B, 10th edn Study Guide. Cram101 Textbooks Reviews (2012)

19. Senathiraja, R., Fernando, M.D.: An empirical study on the impact of multiple intelligences on team development in the IT industry in Sri Lanka. South East Asia J. Contemp. Bus. Econ. Law **2**(1), 47–58 (2013)
20. Kot, E.M.: How to conduct the audit of intellectual capital in polish tourism business? Electron. J. Knowl. Manage. **7**(4), 459–468 (2015)
21. Nekvasil, M.: Evaluation of Semantic Applications for Enterprises, Prague (2010). http:// nekvasil.eu/files/papers/1012%20-%20dissertation%20thesis%20-%20Evaluation%20of% 20Semantic%20Applications%20for%20Enterprises.pdf
22. Vimal, A., Valluri, S.R., Karlapalem, K.: An experiment with distance measures clustering. Technical report, Center of Data Engineering, Hyderabad (2008). http://www.cse.iitb.ac.in/ ~comad/2008/PDFs/61-ankita.pdf
23. Demšar, J., Curk, J.T., Erjavec, A.: Orange: data mining toolbox in Python. J. Mach. Learn. Res **14**, 2349–2353 (2013)
24. Anderson, D.: Enterprise 2.0 and social media coming to ERP, InfoWorld, 22 December 2010. http://www.infoworld.com/article/2624804/erp/enterprise-2-0-and-social-media-coming-to-erp.html
25. Newell, M.W., Grashina, M.N.: The Project Management Question and Answer Book. AMACOM, New York (2004)
26. Gorunescu, F.: Data Mining; Concepts, Models and Techniques. Springer, Heidelberg (2011)
27. Kubiak, B.F., Weichbroth, P.: Cross- and up-selling techniques in e-commerce activities. eCommerce ePayments New Entrepreneurship **15**(3), 217–225 (2010)

Evaluation of Information Systems

Comparative Analysis of Electronic Banking Websites in Poland in 2014 and 2015

Witold Chmielarz[✉] and Marek Zborowski

Faculty of Management, University of Warsaw,
Szturmowa 1/3, 02-678 Warsaw, Poland
witold@chmielarz.eu, mzborowski@wz.uw.edu.p

Abstract. The main objective of this article is to identify the best e-banking websites in Poland from the point of view of an individual customer in the last two years. Using modern IT tools for communications with customers of banking services, banks create competitive advantages as well as opportunities for providing banking services in a way which would be convenient for consumers. After a short introduction the authors define the assumptions for the study. The methodological approach, based on theoretical and empirical study in the field of e-banking, allows them to build the evaluation model for the construction of high quality e-banking website each year. Subsequently, authors carried out multilateral analyses and presented the conclusions of the study. The identified categories are classified into three groups: economic, technological and anti-crisis. The originality of the work comes down to knowledge of the determinants of customer's quality perception of websites and a starting point for effective quality management of their e-services banking system.

Keywords: Electronic banking · Websites' assessment · Factors in the development of websites

1 Introduction and Literature Review

It appears that the consequences of the worldwide crisis in electronic banking in Poland strengthen the tendencies which show that the crisis, which started in the second half of 2008, does not concern this area. When we compare 2014 results to the second quarter of 2015, the number of individual clients with potential access to account increased more than 7.5 % (the expected growth per year will be more than 16 %) reaching over 27 million users; the number of active individual clients went up – during only the last half year – by over 3 % reaching 13,502 million [1]. Undoubtedly, it is the fastest growing banking sector and – as indicated in earlier articles [2] – nothing points to the fact that something may undermine these positive trends.

The increase in absolute numbers of clients is shown in Fig. 1. The increase in the number of clients with potential access to account via the Internet is accompanied by a continuous increase of active customers (at least one transaction a month). Since the end of 2008 till the second half of 2015 the number increased by over 15 million users, which is an increase by 141 %. Every year the population of new customers using the possibilities offered by the Internet to handle banking transactions is growing. In 2008

© Springer International Publishing Switzerland 2016
E. Ziemba (Ed.): FedCSIS 2015, LNBIP 243, pp. 147–161, 2016.
DOI: 10.1007/978-3-319-30528-8_9

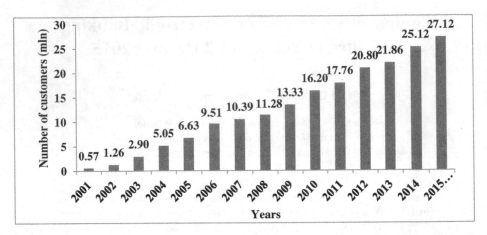

Fig. 1. The evolution of the number of clients with electronic access to account in 2001–2015 in millions (Source: the author's own work on the basis of data from Polish Banks Association (Związek Banków Polskich), [1]

more than 890,000 people started to use e-banking services, and in the first half of 2015 that number was more than 2.5 million. There are nearly 50 % of active users, out of all clients having electronic access to account.

Poland in the European statistics – with regard to penetration - compares quite well – according to ComScore [3] report – it takes the sixth place (52.3 %), while the European average is 40 %. The largest e-banking penetration is in the Netherlands - 66 %, the lowest in Switzerland (18.8 %). France (60 %), Finland (56.4 %), Sweden (54.2 %) are ahead of us, behind are among others: Germany, Spain, Denmark and Norway. The dynamics of the increase in the number of e-banking clients in Poland is still one of the highest on our continent – in recent years we note the increase of over one million every year. So, this is very important area of e-services, and an interesting object of the scientific research.

There are many publications concerning the issue of evaluation of websites and access to e-banking services, but there is no easy solution to the encountered problems [2, 4–11]. The review of the literature shows that e-banking websites (as well as e-commerce websites) may be analysed from the point of view of:

- usability (site map, directory);
- interactivity (availability and responsiveness);
- functionality (search, navigation, relevance of content);
- visualisation (colour scheme, background, graphics, text);
- efficiency (cost of purchase, transport, the difference in prices offered by traditional and online shops); and
- reliability and availability.

Most of evaluation methods are traditional scoring methods based on specific criteria sets, evaluated by means of an applied scale. Technical and functional criteria are most commonly applied. Most of them contain factors which may be evaluated in a very subjective way: text clarity, attractive colours, images and pictures, the speed and intuitiveness of navigation, etc. Moreover, some users do not treat particular criteria sets in an equivalent way. However, on the other hand, there occur frequent problems with determining preferences for particular criteria and the evaluation of relations between them. This part of the work concerns the application of the author's own, though based on the literature, set of criteria for a scoring evaluation and a selection of electronic services of selected banks.

We are carrying out a comparative analysis mainly in three cases, enabling:

- specification and accurate research into the area in which the software works;
- creating a ranking of IT solutions existing on the market; and
- identification of the features which make particular solutions better than others.

This time we are concentrating on the third case.

2   Research Methodology

At the first half of 2014 (March–June), the authors carried out research on the quality of websites offering electronic access to services of the most popular banks among Polish individual clients on a sample of 361 people, where 311 respondents completed surveys correctly. The participants of the survey were students, aged 19–45, Faculty of Management University of Warsaw and Vistula University in Warsaw. Among the respondents, 69 % were women and 31 % men, mainly from Warsaw and surrounding areas. Each of the respondents declared to have at least one electronic access account with one of the banks operating in Poland (fifteen – used e-banking services provided by two banks, two people – of three banks), thus, in total, the authors examined access to 339 active electronic accounts.

In the surveyed population majority of people held accounts in the banks which are considered to be internet banks (mBank, Inteligo PKO BP), or regarded as modern (AliorBank, Millenium), or the largest ones (PKO BP, BZ WBK, CitiBank).

The study was repeated one year later. The results were collected in April and May 2015. Once again the participants of the survey were students of randomly selected groups of Faculty of Management of the University of Warsaw and Vistula University in Warsaw. This time 289 students participated in the study: 1 person filled in three questionnaires, 6 – two questionnaires and 31 participants failed to complete the survey correctly. In total, the study examined the opinions of 251 users of electronic access to individual banking accounts in ten selected banks which were most popular among students. Over 61 % of respondents were women, less than 39 % were men.

Majority of interviewees used electronic access accounts in institutions which are considered to be internet banks (mBank, Inteligo PKO BP, and recently also VW Bank), the banks which are regarded as modern banks (Alior Bank, Bank Millenium, Getin Bank) as well as in the largest banks in Poland (iPKO (PKO BP SA), ING Bank Śląski, BZ WBK). The percentage share of internet account owners in ten most popular banks in Poland is shown in Table 1. The greatest number of clients with active internet access to account among the examined group of clients using the services of ten most popular banks in 2015 was indicated by mBank (18.76 %), Alior Bank (14.13 %) and

Volkswagen Bank (14.01 %). The smallest numbers in the group were reported by Deutsche Bank (3.91 %), Inteligo PKO BP (4.30 %) and Getin Bank (5.47 %). In comparison to the previous year the largest increase was recorded among the clients of VW Bank (11.13 %). Deutsche Bank (3.91 %) joined the group of top 10 banks in the ranking; BPH (1.95 %) and CitiBank (3.85 %) were no longer present in the group.- This does not correspond to the numbers of electronic access accounts declared by particular banks, however, considering the facts that only the active accounts were described and the fact that the surveyed population is relatively young and specific, the structure of the use of accounts is probably closer to reality than the one presented on the basis of official statistics.

Table 1. The percentages of holders of accounts with electronic access in the most popular banks (Source: the author's own work)

Banks	% of bank account users in the selected banks among the examined population in 2014	% of bank account users in the selected banks among the examined population in 2015
mBank	20.04 %	18.76 %
VW Bank	2.94 %	14.01 %
Alior Bank	15.23 %	14.13 %
iPKO (PKO BP SA)	12.02 %	8.99 %
ING Bank Śląski	6.41 %	7.82 %
BZ WBK	7.21 %	6.29 %
Bank Millenium	6.41 %	6.21 %
Getin Bank	6.39 %	5.47 %
Other banks	5.65 %	4.31 %
Inteligo (PKO BP SA)	8.02 %	4.30 %
Deutsche Bank	0.85 %	3.91 %
CitiBank	5.61 %	3.85 %
BPH	3.21 %	1.95 %

This study belongs to a series of cyclical, yearly analyses concerning the factors influencing the usability of websites with online access to individual accounts in the banks [12–14]. The same set of criteria has been applied in the evaluation of e-banking condition at 2014, 2013, 2011 and earlier, before the crisis began in 2008. They were created on the base of internet discussion among leading researchers from some universities in Poland (Uniwersytet Ekonomiczny we Wrocławiu, Uniwersytet Ekonomiczny w Katowicach, Uniwersytet Ekonomiczny w Poznaniu, Uniwersytet Szczeciński, WNE UW).

The respondents filled in the tables evaluating e-banking websites of the banks where they had their accounts, performing the analysis and assessment of the obtained results. The tables which they completed were sent by electronic mail. In the second stage, they imposed preference coefficients on particular criteria and performed further calculations. The obtained findings were supplemented with comments.

All calculations in the present study are carried out with the application of the author's own, though based on the literature and consultations with experts, set of criteria for a scoring evaluation and a selection of electronic access to services of selected banks.

Criteria applied in this study can be divided into two main groups:

- economic – annual nominal interest rate of personal accounts, account maintenance PLN/month, fee for a transfer to a parent bank, fee for a transfer to another bank, payment order, fee for issuing a debit card, fee for a card PLN/month, interest on savings accounts, interest rate on deposits of 10, 000, interest rate on loans 10, 000; and
- technological – additional services (such as: insurance, investment funds, cross-border transfer or foreign currency account), functionality (set of function available for user), access channels to an account (branches, the Internet, Call Centre, mobile phone), security (ID and password, token, SSL protocol, a list of single-use passwords, a list of single-use codes), visualization (colours, fonts, background, photos etc.), navigation, clarity and ease of use.

Considering the situation of the signs of economic crisis spreading, the authors applied a set of psychological criteria in addition to the criteria used previously in the evaluation of e-banking websites which were discussed above. The psychological criteria included the so-called anti-crisis criteria related to – according to the experts cooperating with the authors – all those activities, which were to counteract potential impact of the crisis on the banking sphere [15]. This additional group of criteria was also included in the previous evaluation of e-banking websites. The group of the considered anti-crisis measures includes:

- dynamics of interest rates on deposits (reduction, increase, differences in rates, tendencies);
- dynamics of interest rates on credits (reduction, increase, differences in rates, tendencies);
- stability of the policy related to basic fees (the number and the nature of changes);
- degree of customer confidence (the number of individual clients, its dynamics, how long the bank has been operating in the Polish market); and
- the average places occupied in the rankings in the Internet and trade magazines last year.

In the scoring method the authors collected information on selected criteria; they were assigned values according to the assumed scoring scale and the results were analyzed in a combined table. For the purposes of the evaluation the authors applied – as in previous studies – a typical Likert scale [16]. A scoring method was used in two variations: simple – where criteria were treated equivalently; and one with a preference scale – where sets of criteria were assigned indicator values differentiating their treatment by clients (the total of coefficients = 1).

In a simple scoring method you need to measure the distance from the maximum value to be obtained (according to the assumed scoring scale). It concerns the value of criterion measure and in the sense of a distance it is the same when we measure the distance from one criterion to another as the other way round. However, we do not define the relations between particular criteria. Assigning a preference scale to particular criteria (or sets of criteria) can be regarded as such a measure. A linear preference scale in a normalized form defines in turn the participation of particular criteria in the final score. It establishes a one-time relation between criteria in relation to the final score, it is also a specific "averaged" measure of criteria in particular cases, without the individualization of the evaluation for any of them. However, it does not specify to what degree one criterion is better/worse than the other. It is merely a derivative of the normalized distance.

This round of checking takes place about two weeks after the files have been sent to the Editorial by the Contact Volume Editor, i.e., roughly seven weeks before the start of the conference for conference proceedings, or seven weeks before the volume leaves the printer's, for post-proceedings. If SPS does not receive a reply from a particular contact author, within the timeframe given, then it is presumed that the author has found no errors in the paper. The tight publication schedule of LNCS does not allow SPS to send reminders or search for alternative email addresses on the Internet.

In some cases, it is the Contact Volume Editor that checks all the pdfs. In such cases, the authors are not involved in the checking phase.

3   Research Findings

3.1   Comparative Analysis of Internet Access to E-banking Accounts Using a Scoring Method

To evaluate cost, functional, technological and anti-crisis criteria the authors used a preliminary table presenting bank offers related to internet banking services used by respondents and fees connected with using bank accounts operated via the Internet. The table is filled in by each of the study participants. Then, based on the submitted collection of tables the authors created an averaged combined table for the criteria generated by users (for 2015 see: Table 2).

The spread in the respondents' evaluations of the analysed banks amounts to 10.1 % points (compared to 16.4 % points in 2014, 5.1 % points in 2011, and 2.3 points in 2008), which reflects in the fact growing diversity of evaluations; which confirms the thesis that the period of crisis increased the radicalism of evaluations and heightened expectations concerning the tools used to access an account.

The best in the ranking conducted in 2015 were: ING Bank Śląski (81.12 % of the maximum score; 81.77 % in 2014) and BZ WBK (77.29 %; 77.62 % in 2014) (Fig. 2). Inteligo PKOBP S.A. (75.65 %; 76.25 % in 2014) and mBank (74.88 %; 74.56 % in 2014) took subsequent positions. A surprisingly high position in the ranking was taken by VW Bank (seventh position). In the previously conducted evaluations this bank took the 15th place (in other rankings it took similar positions).

Table 2. The combined table of evaluations in 2015 (Source: the author's own calculations)

Criteria/Banks	ING Bank Śląski	BZ WBK	Inteligo PKO BP S.A.	mBank	Alior Bank	Bank Millennium	VW Bank	Deutsche Bank S.A.	iPKO PKO BP S.A.	Getin Bank	Total	%
Annual nominal interest rate of personal accounts	0.20	0.22	0.27	0.22	0.29	0.30	0.75	0.23	0.24	0.29	3.01	30.15
Account maintenance PLN/month	1.00	0.95	0.93	0.93	0.83	0.75	0.88	0.85	0.70	0.70	8.51	85.12
Fee for a transfer to a parent bank	0.99	1.00	0.91	0.95	0.97	0.86	1.00	0.95	0.96	1.00	9.58	95.76
Fee for a transfer to another bank	0.90	0.92	0.82	0.94	0.92	0.89	1.00	0.95	0.92	0.89	9.16	91.57
Payment order	1.00	0.97	0.95	0.90	0.87	0.89	0.63	0.95	0.85	0.88	8.88	88.76
Fee for issuing a debit card	0.95	0.97	0.95	0.98	0.87	0.92	1.00	1.00	0.97	0.98	9.60	95.97
Fee for a card PLN/month	0.63	0.83	0.71	0.78	0.66	0.81	0.88	0.60	0.75	0.57	7.21	72.10
Additional services	0.89	0.84	0.77	0.85	0.76	0.80	0.63	0.70	0.73	0.62	7.58	75.85
Access channels to an account	0.96	0.92	0.73	0.88	0.86	0.86	0.75	0.83	0.88	0.86	8.52	85.20
Security	0.91	0.89	0.82	0.81	0.81	0.88	0.75	0.88	0.79	0.79	8.33	83.29
Visualization	0.89	0.75	0.83	0.80	0.72	0.69	1.00	0.63	0.73	0.66	7.69	76.93
Navigation	0.89	0.82	0.85	0.73	0.72	0.72	0.88	0.78	0.78	0.68	7.83	78,30
Clarity and ease of use	0.89	0.80	0.85	0.68	0.76	0.67	0.75	0.78	0.74	0.68	7.59	75.86
Functionality	0.91	0.87	0.83	0.85	0.80	0.69	0.50	0.69	0.75	0.61	7.50	75.01
Interest on savings accounts	0.75	0.52	0.55	0.50	0.72	0.60	0.75	0.69	0.46	0.77	6.31	63.13
Interest rate on deposits of 10,000	0.61	0.54	0.59	0.64	0.63	0.53	0.88	0.57	0.55	0.80	6.35	63.53
Interest rate on loans 10,000	0.63	0.58	0.50	0.50	0.62	0.60	0.00	0.50	0.52	0.52	4.97	49.71
Anti-crisis measures	0.62	0.51	0.76	0.55	0.44	0.55	0.00	0.38	0.50	0.48	4.78	47.84
Total	14.60	13.91	13.62	13.48	13.26	13.00	13.00	12.93	12.82	12.78	133.41	
% of the maximum score	81.12	77.29	75.69	74.88	73.68	72.25	72.22	71.82	71.22	70.98		

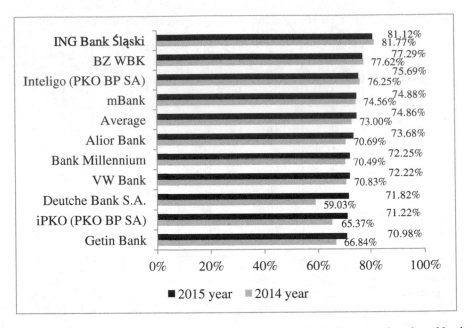

Fig. 2. Ranking of banks for assessing electronic access to individual accounts in selected banks in Poland in 2014 and 2015 (Source: the author's own work)

The general scores in the assessment of websites' quality are still on the increase, and as a consequence, those banks which met and exceeded the clients' optimal assessment requirements last year ranked lower in 2015. The lowest scores within the top 10 positions were assigned to Getin Bank (70.98 %; 66.84 in 2014, one position lower in the ranking than in the previous year) and iPKO Bank PKO S.A. (71.22 %, 65.37 % in 2014 – decline of 6 positions). Compared to 2014, the order in the ranking of the evaluation of banking electronic websites did not undergo any significant changes. BPH, which hardly ever appears in the students' questionnaires in 2015, left the group of top ten banks and Citi Bank ranked below the tenth position. This year Getin Bank ranked lower than last year as a result of the fact that it offered worse economic conditions to their clients in comparison to other banks. The greatest positive changes were reported by Deutsche Bank (almost 13 % points) and iPKO PKO BP S.A. (almost 6 % points). The differences in minus were minimal – the biggest in the case of Inteligo PKO BP S.A., and they amounted to a half of a percentage point.

Generally speaking, there occurred a reversal of the situation from three years ago – the banks which two years ago fell in the rankings, at present, are trying to make up for the previous losses. Another issue which seems to be characteristic of this study – general scores for the quality of the websites increased (see Fig. 3.).

In the majority of analysed cases there are no obligatory payments for issuing a debit card; transfers to the parent bank are usually free of charge. The level of security can be regarded as satisfactory for clients and steadily increases every year. Based on the compilation, we can conclude that a fee for issuing a card (usually there is no fee for

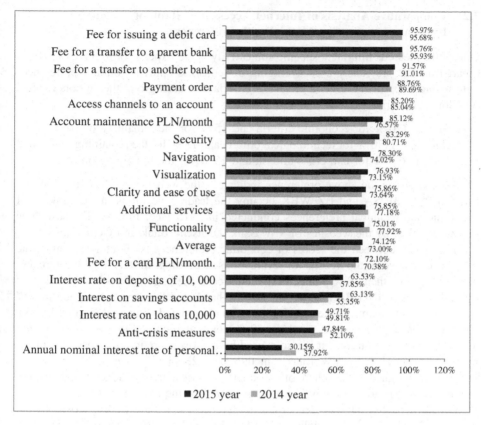

Fig. 3. Ranking of criteria for assessing electronic access to individual accounts in selected banks in Poland in 2014 and 2015 (Source: the author's own work)

such a service) reached a level which, at present, may satisfy clients' needs almost in 100 % (96 %), similarly to the fee for transfer to another bank. Undoubtedly, the worst indicator in 2014 was interest rate on savings accounts functionality (evaluated by the majority of users as too low – 37.92 % of the maximum scores), which in 2015 obtained even lower scores of 30.15 %. The factors which scores below 50 % of points were: the interest rates on loans (49.71 %) and anti-crisis measures – 47.84 % (see: Fig. 3). From the factors not listed within the criteria clients paid attention to the lack of possibility to make a cross-border transfer (e.g. SWIFT in Inteligo) or no possibility of fully automatic obtaining a credit – via the Internet. In 2008 there were no anti-crisis measures among the criteria; however, if we compare this study with the research carried out in 2011, we have to admit that during the crisis e-banking clients neither noticed any signs of the crisis nor were able to define anti-crisis measures undertaken by the banks, and at present they sometimes suggest criteria to be applied for their evaluation.

3.2   Comparative Analysis of Internet Access to E-Banking Accounts by Means of a Scoring Method with Preferences

One of the methods limiting a specific subjectivity in the experts' or users' evaluations (apart from the previously used averaging of scores) is applying unitary preferences with regard to particular criteria or sets of criteria. For each group the authors applied one dominant variant:

- economic (70 % for economic criteria and 15 % for the remaining ones);
- technological (70 % for technological criteria and 15 % for the remaining ones); and
- anti-crisis (70 % for anti-crisis criteria and 15 % for the remaining ones).

After applying the above preference indicators, the websites of ING Bank Śląski, Inteligo PKO BP SA and BZ WBK occupy the leading positions in the ranking of economic and technical preferences conducted in 2015 (see: Fig. 4). The last three places are taken by the websites of VW Bank, Deutsche Bank and Getin Bank.

The spread between the scores of economic preferences is about 7 % points; the differences between the results of evaluations according to technical preferences amounts to more than 18 % points. In the latter case, the large differences were caused by high scores of ING Bank Śląski on the one hand, and low scores assigned to VW Bank website on the other (the website was seen as outdated compared to other banks). An even greater difference of shocking 52 % points is recorded in the case of evaluation of anti-crisis solutions. It is also caused by the low score in the assessment of the measures undertaken by VW Bank's in this area (23.44 %). In general, the lowest scores were assigned to the sphere of anti-crisis measures: among the ten banks leading in the assessment, five of them do not obtain 60 % of the maximum score.

For 2014 in the first case (economic preferences) the three leading positions are taken by ING Bank Śląski, Inteligo PKO BP S.A. and BZ WBK (see: Fig. 5). Next, Bank BPH and mBank are among the best banks with regard to economic factors. iPKO PKO BP S.A., CitiBank, Alior Bank occupy the last positions of the ten analysed banks. In the leading positions (in the relation to research not taking into account preference criteria) Inteligo PKO BP S.A. moves by two places, Bank Millenium by one place. iPKO PKO BP S.A. records the greatest fall. The spread between the highest and the lowest scores in the case of economic preferences was the smallest and amounted to 17 % points. Simultaneously, it was more than twice the value in a correspondent evaluation in 2015.

In the case of technical preferences the leaders are as follows: BPH, ING Bank Śląski and BZ WBK - further positions are taken by: Inteligo PKO BP S.A. and mBank. The last positions were occupied by: Getin Bank, iPKO and Citi Bank. The spread between the largest and smallest score in this variant was 21 % points, mainly due to the low scores in the case of the assessment of Getin Bank website (lack of integration between Getin Online website and the main site of the bank as well as technical problems when using the website). The differences in the evaluation were similar to those indicated a year later.

In the case of anti-crisis preferences the order is very similar to the other evaluations. The first is ING Bank Śląski, next – Millenium Bank and Inteligo PKO BP S.A. The last positions are occupied by Alior Bank, iPKO PKO BP S.A. and Getin Bank.

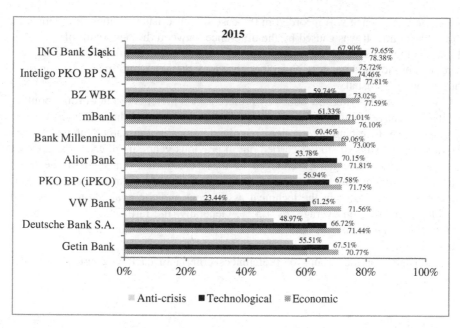

Fig. 4. Ranking of the scores according to various types of preferences for 10 selected banks in Poland in the 2015, according to the order of economic criteria (Source: the author's own work)

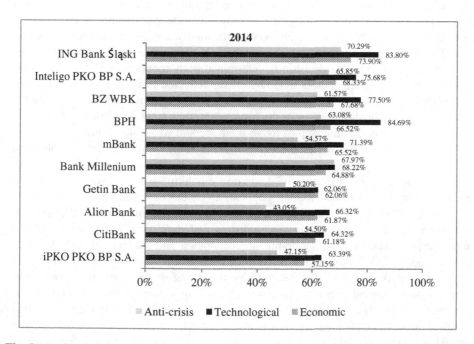

Fig. 5. Ranking of the scores according to various types of preferences for 10 selected banks in Poland in the 2014, according to the order of economic criteria (Source: the author's own work)

The biggest difference was recorded in the case of anti-crisis activities. It amounted to over 27 % points. It was caused by the difference between the best score of ING Bank Śląski and the worst result of Alior Bank. A year later, Alior Bank gained 10 % points more than in the previous year. Even though it took the antepenultimate position, it did not rank tenth as usual.

All in all, multiplying the values by preference coefficients did not bring about any significant changes in the analysed cases, because the order of the examined websites offering access to e-banking services remained basically the same. Interestingly, in contrast to the results of studies carried out in previous years, in all cases the positions of leading banks have hardly changed in these categories. Since 2014 the scores assigned to economic factors increased, on average, by 9.11 % in the case of the first ten websites; the scores in the technical assessment and the evaluation of anti-crisis activities decreased, on average, by 1.5 %. Generally, the farther away from the first year of crisis, i.e. 2008, the less attention is paid to highlighting the importance of anti-crisis criteria in evaluating banking websites.

The results for the groups of preferences criteria in each year are presented in Figs. 4 and 5.

4   Conclusions

The present analysis has shown that the crisis situation 2008, whose signs are visible in various industries, does not apply to electronic banking. While in 2011 it could be a one-off phenomenon, after seven years we may conclude that it starts to be seen as a clear trend. Also, it confirms the changes concerning the banking customers' awareness. The choice of the access to an account starts to be a matter of an informed choice, not a chance or habit. The decision is determined both economic and technical conditions. The result is the choices made by clients reflected in the presented study and commented on in the surveys. It is true that some of the opinions indicate - despite the awareness of certain shortcoming of the bank where they hold an account – resistance to changes, but it is the first step to move their account to another bank.

The selection of the research sample and its limitations affected the obtained findings. Students are a group which have relatively the greatest number of access to e-banking and use it most frequently. And know e-banking websites very well. Taking the above factors into consideration, it appears to be the best sample for carrying out the research. This group in the population also has a wide, and perhaps the greatest, knowledge concerning the newest technologies and their use. The selection of the student groups was random, the dominance of women and students of early years of study are accidental. However, it is a group which does not have considerable financial resources, and this may be the reason why the representatives of this group have relatively the cheapest access to the internet banking websites. Simultaneously, the awareness of the high usability of information technology means that this particular group is able to appreciate the practical (or entertainment) value of the offered e-banking services. In addition, the representatives of this group, after a few years of using e-banking websites designed for them, are less likely to be satisfied with a product or service – in the form of e-banking website for example - of lower quality.

Taking into consideration the conducted analyses, we may draw the following conclusions:

- in the minds of users of electronic banking a clear distinction between the virtual banks (electronic access only) and electronic access services of traditional banks lost its importance, and it appears to be a continued trend. It is caused by the following phenomena (quotation from a student's survey: ... as we can see the results are comparable. This is due to the large similarity of services offered by banks with regard to visualisation and "starting package", that is all for 0zł...):
  - virtual and traditional banks try to maximally increase the number of communication channels,
  - it is difficult to separate a virtual bank from a traditional one,
  - e-banking websites of traditional banks are just as technologically advanced and modern as those of virtual banks,
  - we observe lowering of that prices of basic e-banking services in traditional banks, sometimes below the prices of virtual banks,
  - we have a more possibility of access – phenomenon of mobile banking via mobile applications (smartphones, tablets), in the coming years mobile access to banks (through applications for smartphones or tablet) may dominate the present market [17];
- users have higher expectations with regard to the quality of e-services. The averages from the rankings – previously relatively constant – have become dynamic and fluctuate;
- entering the market (for example - the case of Alior Bank) and allocating significant resources to a clever advertising campaign does not guarantee an automatic promotion to the top position in the rankings (for example - Credit Agricole);
- having two or more accounts in two or more banks to perform various financial transactions is still a rare phenomenon;
- too few clients dynamically respond to changes in banking services market; nevertheless, the m-banking operations performed using smartphone and tablet banking applications is becoming increasingly important in the market of electronic banking services;
- vast majority of active bank customers consider economic criteria to be the most important criteria in the evaluation of electronic access to banking services – usually the prices of the most frequently used services. More and more people admit, however, that when selecting a website, to a certain degree, they tend to focus on user-friendliness and intuitiveness as well as the visual attractiveness of the website[1]; and

---

[1] quotation from a student's survey (original phrasing): ... *personally, when selecting banking services, I am more influenced by economic factors than the visualization or the simplicity or complexity of navigation. Visual qualities depend on a personal taste, and I think they should not be a decisive factor in the selection of a financial institution, to which we entrust our own money. With regard to the technical and functional level of the service, it does not determine my choice - especially since the current market seems to have developed a certain standard, below which banks can no longer operate because customers are bound to verify it quickly and leave...*

- users of electronic banking services more frequently notice anti-crisis measures of banks and even though they do not influence their choices in any considerable degree, they can note and identify them.

This confirms the author's thesis about the inadequacy and a specific superficiality of standard, unified, quantitative methodologies used for evaluation and selection of e-banking websites. It also points to the need of further studies into constructing multi-dimensional, multi-criteria, hierarchical and multi-faceted system for websites' evaluation, with the consideration of additional, more specific information, e.g. customer profile [18].

Nevertheless, despite the problems related to using e-banking services, which the article presents, we observe that the Internet tends to assume the role of the main (also for an individual client) channel of communication with the bank. Undoubtedly, this development irrevocably changes the expectations, perceptions and habits related to using banking services which users have had so far, and also, simultaneously, it urges the banks to introduce quick changes of the medium which would take into account holders' requirements. However, its reign in the market may be threatened by the emergence of new IT solutions that will satisfy the requirements of Internet banking customers to a greater extent than the present internet solutions. The research into new tools and relevant applications will be the area of interest for further studies in the future.

References

1. NETB@nk Raport Bankowość internetowa i płatności bezgotówkowe. Podsumowanie IV kwartału 2014, April 2015. http://www.zbp.pl/Netbank_Q4_2014v3.pdf
2. Chiou, W.C., Lin, C.C., Perng, C.: A strategic framework for website evaluation based on a review of the literature from 1995–2006. Inf. Manag. 47(5–6), 282–290 (2010)
3. ComScore Report, April 2014. http://www.egov.vic.gov.au/focus-on-countries/europe/trends-and-issues-europe/statistics-europe/internet-statistics-europe/comscore-releases-2014
4. Bauer, H.H., Hammerschmidt, M., Falk, T.: Measuring the quality of e-banking portals. Int. J. Bank Market. 23(2), 153–175 (2005)
5. Mateos, M.B., Mera, A.C., Gonzalez, F.J.M., Lopez, O.R.G.: A new web assessment index: Spanish universities analysis. Internet Res. Electron. Netw. Appl. Policy 11(3), 226–234 (2001)
6. Migdadi, Y.K.A.: The quality of internet banking service encounter in Jordan. J. Internet Bank. Commer. 13(3) (2008). http://www.arraydev.com/commerce/jibc/. Accessed 13 June 2015
7. Miranda, F.J., Cortes, R., Barriuso, C.: Quantitative evaluation of e-banking web sites: an empirical study of Spanish banks. Electron. J. Inf. Syst. Eval. 2(9), 73–82 (2004)
8. Sikorski, M.: Usługi on-line. Jakość, interakcje, satysfakcja klienta. Wydawnictwo PJWSTK, Warszawa (2013)
9. Webb, H.W., Webb, L.A.: SiteQual: an integrated measure of web site quality. J. Enterp. Inf. Manag. 17(6), 430–440 (2004)
10. Wielki, J.: Modele wpływu przestrzeni elektronicznej na organizacje gospodarcze. Wydawnictwo UE we Wrocławiu, Wrocław (2012)

11. Yang, Z., Cai, S., Zhou, Z., Zhou, N.: Development and validation of an instrument to measure user perceived service quality of information presenting web portals. Inf. Manag. **42**(4), 575–589 (2005)
12. Chmielarz, W., Zborowski, M.: Comparative analysis of electronic banking websites in selected banks in Poland in 2014. In: Ganzha, M., Maciaszek, L., Paprzycki, M. (eds.) Proceedings of the 2015 Federated Conference on Computer Science and Information Systems, Łódź, Poland, September 13–16, pp. 1499–1505 (2015)
13. Chmielarz, W.: Methodological aspects of the evaluation of individual e-banking services for selected banks in Poland. In: Pańkowska, M. (ed.) Infonomics for Distributed Business and Decision-Making Environments: Creating Information System Ecology, pp. 201–216. IGI Global, Business Science Reference, Hershey, New York (2010)
14. Chmielarz, W.: Comparative analysis of electronic banking services in selected banks in Poland in 2013. In: Gospodarowicz, A., Wawrzyniak, D. (eds.) Current Problems of Banking Sector Functioning in Poland and East European Countries, Prace Naukowe Uniwersytetu Ekonomicznego we Wrocławiu, Wrocław, no. 316, pp. 16–29 (2013)
15. Chmielarz, W.: Metody oceny elektronicznych usług bankowych dla klientów indywidualnych w Polsce. In: Gospodarowicz, A. (ed.) Bankowość detaliczna – idee, modele, procesy, Prace Naukowe Uniwersytetu Ekonomicznego we Wrocławiu, Wrocław, no. 54, pp. 9–26 (2009)
16. Likert, R.: A technique for the measurement of attitudes. Arch. Psychol. **140**, 1–55 (1932)
17. Chmielarz, W., Łuczak, K.: Mobile banking in the opinion of users of banking applications in Poland. Appl. Mech. Mater. **79**(5), 31–38 (2015)
18. Chmielarz, W.: Koncepcja ekspertowego systemu oceny i selekcji witryn internetowych. In: Gołuchowski, J., Filipczyk, B. (eds.) Wiedza i komunikacja w innowacyjnych organizacjach. Systemy ekspertowe – wczoraj, dziś, jutro, Wydawnictwo UE w Katowicach, Katowice, pp. 183–190 (2010)

The Impact of Enhancing a Performance Measurement System on the Israeli Police

Marina Vugalter and Adir Even[✉]

Department of Industrial Engineering and Management,
Ben-Gurion University of the Negev, POB 653, 8410501 Beersheba, Israel
vugalter@post.bgu.ac.il, adireven@bgu.ac.il

Abstract. The Performance Measurement System (PMS) explored in the study was implemented by public police forces, using advanced Business Intelligence (BI) technologies. The study examines the impact of enhancing that PMS, through analysis of metric results over an 8-year period that covered a transition between two major system versions. The analysis results indeed show a significant impact of transitioning to the new PMS in most (75 %) performance metrics. A noticeable impact of the transition is the temporary performance decline, followed by some improvement that can be attributed in part to the redefinition of some metrics. Further, the results confirmed the preliminary assumptions that the improvement in the measured performance is positively and significantly associated with human-resource allocation; however, with some mediation effects of the crime category and the organization unit.

Keywords: Performance measurement systems (PMS) · Key performance indicators (KPI) · Business intelligence (BI) · IS adoption

1 Introduction

Today, performance measurement systems (PMS) are broadly adopted across all industries and business domains. Their implementation is often supported by Business Intelligence (BI) technologies [1, 2]. PMS implementation is motivated by the need for consistent and well-organized measurement, reflecting past behavior and current state, toward supporting decisions and driving continuous performance improvement [3]. PMS may back these goals by providing solutions for gathering, analyzing, and distributing relevant information [4]. Much of the PMS research so far was not supported by rigorous evidence [5]. Further, PMS studies mostly focus on for-profit businesses [6, 7], but less on organizations that are not necessarily driven by profit goals, such as governmental agencies or community-based groups [8, 9].

This study explores the impact of a PMS in a governmental agency – the Israeli Police Forces. The research examines the transition between two PMS: the "MENA-HEL" that was used between 2006 and 2010, and the "MIFNE" that replaced it in 2010. Both PMS were implemented with advanced Business Intelligence (BI) technologies and embedded a number of performance metrics that reflect the police strategy and activities. Beyond enhancement of BI technologies, a key difference between the systems was the re-design of the metrics structure. While the "MENAHEL" offered

© Springer International Publishing Switzerland 2016
E. Ziemba (Ed.): FedCSIS 2015, LNBIP 243, pp. 162–178, 2016.
DOI: 10.1007/978-3-319-30528-8_10

a large number of metrics (over 150), some with low relative weights, the "MIFNE" offered a reduced and more focused set, developed based on the knowledge and insight that were gained during the operation of the "MENAHEL".

The focus of "MIFNE" is not on the quantity of measures, as on their quality and essence. The newer system exposes police officers not only to performance measures in their own stations, but in other stations as well for the sake of comparison. Further, the newer performance measurement system serves not only police stations, but rather all organizational police units. One new main module that is part of "MIFNE" is "internal services" - as part of the comprehension of the importance of police officer's and his family's social satisfaction. Moreover, "MIFNE" is targeting every organizational unit specifically, compared to "MENAHEL" that defined a uniform target for all units. The new PMS offers interactive investigation capabilities, and several options for "drilling-down" from high-level presentation of metrics to a more detailed and seg-mented view. It enables identification of exceptional trends or events that required an attention. Both PMS are managed and operated by the Israeli police research and statistics unit. Representatives of this unit, who collaborated with this research, claim that the "MIFNE" system introduced a significant change in perception in police performance evaluation and measurement, as part of a broader 3-years transition program under the same name that started in 2011. The broader "MIFNE" program is motivated by the need to improve the public trust of the police, and the PMS is seen as a major strategic tool for enhancing public trust through continuous and visible improvement efforts.

A question that motivates this study is whether or not the transition to a new PMS promoted the desired improvement in police-units performance. Was the influence positive, or rather negative in some cases? Is the influence moderated by certain characteristics of the organizational unit? This study suggests that these questions may have important implications for performance measurement in the Israeli police as for the adoption of PMS in other organizations. To examine these questions, this study performed in depth analysis of performance metric results that were covered by the PMS over an 8-year time period during which the transition between the two major system versions occurred. The reminder of this work starts with a review of relevant literature on the key topics issues that this study deals with. We then proceeded to development of a theoretical model that guides the investigation, as well as the asso-ciated set of hypotheses. This is followed by a detailed description of the empirical evaluation – data collection procedures, statistical analysis, and discussion of the results that were obtained. To conclude, we summarize the study's key achievements and contributions, highlight its limitations, and propose possible directions for future research.

2   Literature Review

"When you can measure what you are speaking about, and express it in numbers, you will know something about it, otherwise your knowledge is of a merge and un satisfactory kind" [10].

The concept of Performance measurement systems (PMS), as a tool for aiding strategic management and organizational decision-making has started emerging in the 1960s, and kept developing ever since. Initially, PMS focused on productivity management and control and later the scope was extended to cover financial control. Over the years the concept has developed further to an integrative multi-dimensional perspective that covers all managerial aspects, and can serve not only commercial firms, but also the public sector, non-profit organizations, healthcare providers, and many others [11]. PMS have captured research attention in various contexts such as economic, human-resources, information- systems, industrial and management and more. Systems as such are implemented today in a broad range of organizations of all types and from all industries [12]. Organizations aim at accomplishing their goals by matching between strategy and performance, and their success depends on tracking and monitoring performance in comparison to the objectives that were defined.

Several approaches for forming and managing PMS have emerged over the years [13, 4], aim at addressing shifts in focus in that field – e.g., shifts from financial measures to integrated measures, from operational perspectives to strategic perspectives, and from a narrow to a broad set of stakeholders. The field has developed in response to global and business trends [11]. The limitations of traditional PMSs, together with intense competitive pressures and changing external demands, have led to the increased advocacy of non-financial measures [14, 15].

A leading paradigm in the field of PMS is the Balanced Scorecard (BSC). The BSC aims at supporting accounting, decision-making and management as a whole. It rose to the challenge of the limitations of accounting measures [16]. Its basic idea is to translate strategy into measures, and into action. The BSC, when introduced originally, suggested measuring along four interlinked perspectives, each reflecting a set of organizational concerns and managerial goals: (a) Financial: the ability to fulfil the expectation of external stakeholders, such as investors and regulators, (b) Customer: the ability to satisfy customer needs and adapt to shifts in market demands and trends, (c) Internal: effectiveness and efficiency of business processes that the firm, implements toward supporting stakeholder and customer needs, and (d) Innovation and Learning: the ability to promote organizational learning and build human and knowledge resources. Quantification of BSC efficiency is still a challenge, since cause-effect relationship that it represents are not clear or empirical based. The relationship in this model are logical, however not necessarily casual. From these reasons researches proposed some options to improve the current model [11].

The Performance Prism (P-P) paradigm offers a more comprehensive view of different stakeholders (such as employees, suppliers, alliance partners or intermediaries). It suggests organizing the PMS around five linked perspectives of performance [17]: (a) Stakeholder satisfaction, (b) Strategies, (c) Processes, (d) Capabilities, (Combination of people, practices, technology and infrastructure that together enable execution of the organization's business processes), and (e) Stakeholder contributions. A key strength of that approach is the innovation in common belief that performance measures should be strictly derived from strategy is incorrect. It is the wants and needs of stakeholders that must be considered first.

PMS are often built using Business Intelligence (BI) technologies. BI systems provide the ability to analyze information for supporting decision making, toward gaining competitive advantage [7]. The broad adoption of BI is driven by the notion that fact-based decisions are necessary for successful management [3]. As PMS rely on access to data resources and effective presentation of key performance indicators (KPI's), BI systems appear to be a natural fit for PMS implementation [5]. Although performance measurement is extensively discussed in academic research, the PMS domain has developed outside the organizational impacts in practice [13]. Obviously, investment in PMS technologies alone does not guarantee performance improvement. The success depends much on interaction of end-users and their use for improving performance [18]. Surveys of PMS studies reflected positive effects [1, 7]; however, suggest that such claims should be further supported by evidence in a rigorous manner, through evaluation with real-world data. This study contributes to that end by evaluation of the data collected in a BI-supported PMS in a real-world setting.

3   Research Methodology

The transition between the two PMS systems in the Israeli police raised questions that this study aims to explore: did the transition indeed gained the desired effect on performance measurement? What factors may possibly affect the actual contribution of replacing a PMS? One could expect that the contribution will be affected by factors such as the size of police station, socio-economic characteristics, or the activity or crime category that the performance metrics reflect. These questions are reflected in the model that guides this study (Fig. 1), which observes the following constructs:

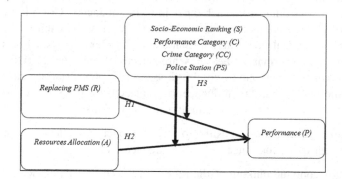

Fig. 1. Research model

Performance (P): The dependent variable is the organizational performance as reflected in the values of the PMS metrics. Positive and/or negative trends in metric values reflect the influence transitioning to a new PMS and possibly other factors.

PMS Replacement (R): Transition to a new PMS is expected to have a significant impact on performance. Accordingly, the first set of hypotheses reflects possible manifestations of that impact:

- **H1a:** PMS Replacement will significantly affect performance.
- **H1b:** PMS Replacement significantly improves performance over time.
- **H1c:** PMS Replacement will cause temporary performance decline during the transition period.

Resources Allocation (A): An alternative, or possibly complementary, explanation to the effect of PMS replacement on performance is the allocation of resources. Performance could have been enhanced not only by PMS replacement, but also by extending human-resource allocation, where the effect is expected to be positive:

- **H2:** Increasing human resource allocation will improve the measured performance.

The study assumes that the effect on performance will be affected by a few organizational and environmental factors:

- **Socio-Economic Ranking (S):** The common assumption in literature is that socio-economic ranking may influence on the dependent variable in some researches as in politics and government [13] and entrepreneurship [16]. Certain demographic characteristics, such as the socio-economic ranking of the region in which the police station acts, are expected to moderate the effect of PMS replacement.
- **Performance Category (PC):** PMS commonly arrange the performance metrics in clusters. For example, in PMS that are based on the Balanced Score Card (BSC) methodology [16], the measurements are categorized under four key clusters. Such categorization could be detected in the police PMS as well, and the model assumes that this categorization will have some effect.
- **Crime Category (CC):** The police typically characterize different types of crime along different categories.
- **Police Station (PS):** There is a different effect on measures among different police stations so stations differ from each other in PMS enhancing. Considering common qualities of police stations assist to divide them to clusters. Each Cluster is differ from other in internal and external characters. This examination helps assessing whether or not performance measures are effected from internal (HR allocation, socio-economic ranking) and external (crime records) police stations characteristics. The assumption is that the influence of replacement PMS on performance is expected to be different between different police stations.

Accordingly, the model assumes the following moderation effects: the influence of PMS replacement on performance will be moderated by:

- **H3a:** Socio-economic ranking of the region in which the station acts
- **H3b:** Performance category
- **H3c:** Crime category
- **H3d:** Police station characteristics

4   Research Findings

This section describes the empirical evaluation, along the suggested model and the associated hypotheses, with real-world data received from the Israeli police.

4.1 Data Preparation and Preliminary Analysis

The study was based on performance measurements that were retrieved from the police database, with some additional pieces of data that were retrieved from other sources. The measurements covered an 8-year period (January 2006 to December 2013), 146 organizational units (districts, regions, special units, etc.), and 33 performance metrics - 8 annual measures, per metric and per unit. The 33 metrics can be classified to 3 main categories: (a) crime records, (b) charges, and (c) arrests. Each category includes 11 items. Three of these 11 (weapons, illegal stay, and drugs) are typically defined as exposure offenses - crimes with no previous complaint or report; hence, exposed only by initiated activity. Exposure-based crimes are typically more challenging to handle than others; hence, often get higher attention. A key target is to increase the probability of exposure-based crimes to be resolved. Another data source provided by the police included human resource per organizational unit and year. That dataset also contain geography-based socio-economic ranking per station. After removing records with missing or inconsistent values and keeping only stations with full information on HR allocation and performance measures for the entire period- 2006–2013, 60 stations remained.

A preliminary analysis of 3 main categories (crime records, charges and arrests) shows an improvement in metrics after the switch to the new system (2012); however, with some period of instability during the transition in 2011 (Fig. 2). In addition, the ratio between arrests and crime records has a positive trend, and the ratio between arrests and charges is increasing as well over time. For 15 performance measures out of 33 (45.45 %) there is an increase in performance following the switch and among the 33 measures, only for 2 (6 %) transition period (2011) is followed by improvement in performance, the rest of measures (94 %) are followed by decline in performance. Furthermore, a preliminary analysis shows a positive relationship between HR allocation (number of police officers in a station) and performance measures: crime records, arrests and charges. A preliminary examination shows a strong correlation between crime records and arrests especially (Fig. 3); however, the correlation with charges measure appears to be weaker.

4.2 Evaluation Results

H1: The Impact of Enhancing Performance Measurement Systems. The first hypothesis (H1) suggests that replacing the PMS will result in significant decline in performance during the transition period and also significant performance improvement following the replacement; the results support it partially. The datasets that were examined for this hypothesis is 3 year period between 2010 and 2012. In 2010 the former PMS was active. The transition to the new PMS system began in 2011. Then, the first version was active, followed by a year of the actual transition. By 2012, the transition was over and the new system became live in the organization.

The three derived hypotheses - H1a, H1b, and H1c - were tested by examining the rate of measures that had a significant effect (P-Value < 0.05) (Table 1). The H1a

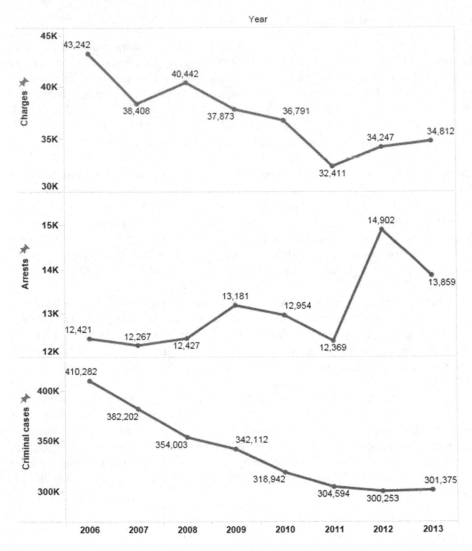

Fig. 2. Preliminary performance analysis

assumption, suggesting that measures show significant change over time, is largely supported, as for 25 out of 33 measures (75.7 %). The H1b assumption suggesting that measures will significantly improve following replacement was not supported as 24 out of 33 measures have no significant improvement (72.7 %). However, most of the measures that were improved significantly are included in the arrests category. The H1c assumption suggesting that measures will temporarily decline during transition is supported in part. 31 measures among 33 had some decline in performance during the transition period (93 %), however, 10 only (30 %) had a statistical significant decrease.

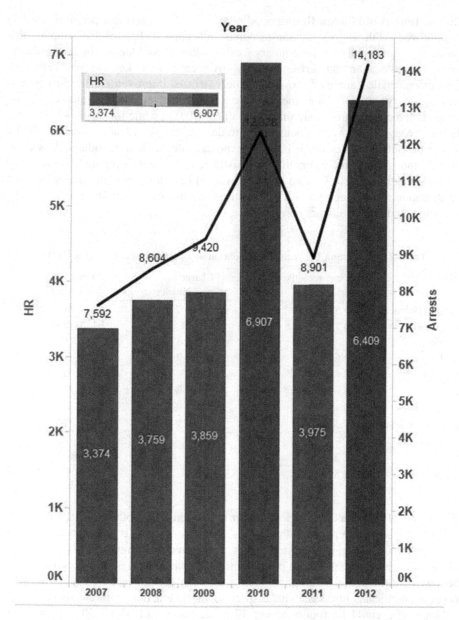

Fig. 3. Arrests versus investment in human resources (Color figure online)

Table 1. Change in performance measures (H1)

Hypothesis	Significant measures	Ratio
H1a	25	75.75 %
H1b	9	27.27 %
H1c	10	30 %

H2: The Impact of Human Resource Allocation. H2 suggests that performance will be improved with higher human-resource allocation. The results support this assumption significantly. A preliminary analysis shows consistently-high correlation between HR allocation and performance improvement in three key metrics (Tables 2).

A more detailed analysis shows that the extent of improvement varies between performance types. For some measures (e.g., violence, aggravated attack, regular attack, etc.), the correlation is significant (P-Value < 0.05), while for others – "exposure offenses" (e.g., illegal stay, weapons, drugs trade) it is less significant (P-Value > 0.05). The most significant difference is between exposure offenses and the others. As seen in Table 2, among the 30 indicators that demonstrated in 3 categories (a table is presented for each category), 7 (70 % of all crime measures) have a significant correlation with HR allocation in all categories. All 3 exposure measures (30 % of all crime measures) have a low and not significant correlation.

Table 2. Correlation between HR allocation and performance measures (H2)

Crime metric	Crime records performance	Charge performance	Arrests performance
Regular violence	83.58 %	57.98 %	61.22 %
Aggravated violence	73.7 %	62.1 %	61.70 %
Total violence	83.61 %	59.89 %	60.86 %
Property	63.81 %	51.86 %	53.86 %
Sex	54.67 %	43.60 %	39.73 %
Regular attack	78.74 %	54.45 %	56.56 %
Aggravated attack	69.53 %	61.20 %	50.67 %
Weapons	1 %	22.1 %	0 %
Illegal stay	11.2 %	0 %	21.0 %
Drugs	48.52 %	57.2 %	30.30 %

H3a: Moderation Effects of Socio-Economic Ranking. Hypothesis H3a, suggesting that the impact of replacing the PMS on performance is moderated by the socio-economic ranking, is supported in part. A repeated-measures ANOVA test shows influence of replacing the PMS on performance measures for the 3 key measures (H1a). The test confirmed the assumption H1a with high significance (P-Value = ~ 0). However significant influence with respect to the interaction with Socio-Economic Ranking (H3a) could be found among 17 measures out of 33 (~ 50 %). In crime records, high significance (P-Value = ~ 0) interaction was found in 7 out of 10 categories (~ 70 %), however for arrests category only among 3 out of 10 (30 %) the interaction is significant, and for charges 5 out of 10 have highly significant interactions (50 %). This interaction is found to be significant in all categories for violence and attack more than the others. A possible conclusion is that different stations will show difference in the influence of replacing PMS, based on the socio-economic characteristics of the region under their control and crime category.

H3b: Moderation Effects of Performance Category. Hypothesis H3b suggests that the impact of enhancing PMS on performance will be moderated by performance category. This assumption relates to H1, which argues that replacing PMS has an impact on the performance. Replacing the PMS will result in significant decline in performance during transition period and also significant performance improvement following the replacement is dependent on performance category. The results associated with the testing of this assumption are presented in Table 3. For most crimes in all categories some significant change in performance measures could be detected (P-Value < 0.05). For arrests, the 90 % ratio of crimes with a significant change is the highest, and for the other two categories the ratio 70 % is relatively high as well. Regarding the increase in performance following the replacement, for crime-records and charges categories, the ratio is 10 %, however for arrests category the improvement ratio of 70 % is significant. No significant decrease in performance could be detected during the transition period for none of the category in all crimes. For crime records category, 50 % of crimes had a significant decline in performance, for charges category 40 % and for arrests only 10 % from crimes.

Table 3. Ratios between significant performance measures (H3B)

Impact	Category	Significant metrics	Ratio
Total change	Crime records	7	70 %
	Charges	7	70 %
	Arrests	9	90 %
Increase	Crime records	1	10 %
	Charges	1	10 %
	Arrests	7	70 %
Decrease	Crime records	5	50 %
	Charges	4	40 %
	Arrests	1	10 %

H3c: Moderation Effects of Crimes Category. Hypothesis H3c suggests that the impact of enhancing PMS on performance will be moderated by the crime category. This assumption is derived from H1 as well, which suggests that replacing the PMS will result in temporary decline in performance during the transition period. Examination results of the impact on performance show that for sex and aggravated attack crimes there is no significant change in performance in none of the categories (Table 4). For illegal stay, crime records category and for drugs charges, the change in performance is no significant; however, for rest of crimes (80 %) the change is significant in all categories for 6 crimes and for the rest 2, is significant in 2 categories out of 3. None of the above crimes has a significant improvement or a significant decline in all categories.

H3d: Moderation Effects of Station Characteristics. Hypothesis H3d suggests that the impact of enhancing PMS on performance will be moderated by characteristics of the police station. This is based on the assumption that the influence of replacing PMS

Table 4. Comparison between crime categories

Category	Crime Records	Charges	Arrests
Regular violence	0.00	0.00	0.00
Aggravated violence	0.01	0.08	0.01
Total violence	0.00	0.00	0.00
Property	0.02	0.316	0.05
Sex	0.588	0.55	0.115
Regular attack	0.05	0.01	0.00
Aggravated attack	0.11	0.14	0.187
Weapons	0.06	0.06	0.01
Illegal stay	0.00	0.00	0.638
Drugs	0.00	0.14	0.00
Total	0.00	0.00	0.00

differs between stations. In order to test this assumption, all 57 police stations were divided to clusters by cluster analysis method k-medoids. Cluster analysis was made according to measures: HR allocation, socio-economic ranking, and criminal charges in crimes: regular violence, aggravated violence, aggravated attack and property. Some divisions were tested as for 4 clusters, 5 clusters and 6 clusters. One cluster included all police stations in regions with a high population of citizens of a certain religion, and the rest were classified to k clusters by k-medoids algorithm. The best clustering division was accepted by 5 clusters. The next step after cluster analysis was testing this sub-hypothesis on the clusters. This classification shows a partial support to the assumption; for sex crimes and illegal stay- charges and arrests categories there is a significant interaction with clustering (Table 5). Also, for aggravated attack crimes – charges, the interaction is significant. Results of repeated measures ANOVA show that the only crime category with significant interaction is criminal charges. However this result is obvious since the cluster analysis is based on criminal charges measures, as mentioned above. Moreover it is clear (Table 5) that for some measures as sex and illegal stay in arrests and charges categories and also in aggravated attack charges, the influence on performance measures is dependent on the cluster attribute.

Table 5. Significance of variance between station clusters

Crime metric	Crime records	Charges	Arrests
Regular violence	0.00	0.14	0.76
Aggravated violence	0.00	0.14	0.98
Total violence	0.00	0.09	0.90
Property	0.00	0.09	0.12
Sex	0.43	0.00	0.00
Regular attack	0.09	0.09	0.47
Aggravated attack	0.00	0.03	0.71
Weapons	0.69	0.985	0.92
Illegal stay	0.13	0.02	0.02
Drugs	0.08	0.498	0.11

Following repeated measures ANOVA, determining directionality of measures is defined as next step. Tukey HSD test was done in order to determine what police stations clusters achieved better performance in each year and who improved over time. Results of Tukey HSD test for illegal stay arrests measure show that cluster 2 is in total better than clusters 3 and 4; police stations that relate to cluster 2 perform better than those that relate to clusters 3 or 4. In addition, the performance is higher in 2012 than in 2010. Results of Tukey HSD test for illegal stay charges measure show that cluster 1 is in total better than clusters 4 and 5, so the number of illegal stay charges is higher in stations from cluster 1 than clusters 4 or 5. For conclude illegal stay crimes, one can say that there is significant difference between police stations that relate to different clusters in performance. Regarding sex arrests measure, cluster 1 is seen to be better than 4 and 5 in 2010–2012. Moreover, cluster 2 is better than 3, 4 and 5 and 3 is better than 4 and 5. Police stations that related to cluster 3 improved in sex arrests measure significantly over time. Regarding sex charges measure, the results show that clusters 1 and 2 have higher performance than 3, 4 and 5. Moreover cluster 3 is better than 5 and also than 4 in 2011–2012. In sex charges, as in sex arrests, cluster 3 has improved in 2012. These results support partially the assumption that influence of PMS replacement on performance is different between different police stations, however there are some limitations that have to be considered as:

- Different police stations have a different illegal stay crimes rate, so this measure is depends on the geographical area. Therefore it is misleading to compare illegal stay crime measure between police stations.
- Although the clusters were defined according to police stations input measures, one can recognize a high variance in output measures. The crime measures are not distributed union since the deviation is high inside each cluster. The police stations in each cluster are differ from each other hence the comparison between clusters to test the hypothesis is limited.
- Each police station has a different point of start, so there are "strong" stations that accomplish their targets and achieve high scores and on the other edge there are "weak" stations that achieve low scores and their performance is considered as low. For "strong" stations the improvement rate would probably be lower than "weak" stations that have a high potential for improvement in performance. From this reason, one should considered the improvement rate as more significant than the performance actual measures when comparing between police stations.

To avoid the negative consequences identified above, the improved measures ratio following the enhancing of PMS was compared between all police stations. The average, minimum, maximum and Standard deviation of ratio of improved measures and ratio of deteriorate measures are shown in (Table 6). For some police stations the influence is strong (88 % of measures were improved and 82 % of measures were decreased), however some police stations were less influenced by the transition (18 % of measures were improved and 18 % of measures were decreased). This examination can suggest is that the influence of enhancing PMS in organization is different among police stations, hypothesis as hypothesis H3d suggests.

Table 6. Ratio changes for each police station (H3d)

	Deterioration	Improvement
Average	58 %	53 %
Minimum	18 %	18 %
Maximum	88 %	82 %
Standard deviation	0.17	0.15

5 Conclusions

Our research examined the impact of enhancing PMS and factors that are possibly involved in that impact. This section summarizes and discusses the key findings, highlight the research contributions, and points out limitations and possible directions for future research.

5.1 Summary of Findings

The level of support that was gained for the different hypotheses is summarized in the Table 7. Some of the assumptions were strongly supported by the empirical findings, but others were supported only in part.

Table 7. Summary of results

Hypothesis			Support
H1	a	PMS Replacement will significantly affect performance	Strong
	b	PMS Replacement significantly improves performance over time	Partial
	c	PMS Replacement may result in a temporary performance decline during the transition period	Partial
H2		Increasing HR allocation will improve measured performance	Partial
H3	a	Stations that act in regions with different socio economic ranking will show difference in the influence of replacing PMS on the performance	Strong
	b	Different performance categories will show different influence of PMS replacement on performance	Strong
	c	Different crime categories will influence of PMS replacement on performance differently	Partial
	d	Influence of PMS replacement on performance is different between different police stations	Strong

The study shows that, generally, there is a significant change in performance in most of crime categories following enhancing PMS. The only categories that were not affected from PMS enhancing are sex, aggravated violence, drugs trade charges and illegal stay records. The study shows that the improvement in performance following the change is mostly expressed in terms of crimes from the arrests category (an output measure): violence, attack, and illegal stay. Furthermore, for most crime categories a decrease in performance during transition period could be detected. The decrease was statistically significant only for 30 % of measures. For violence and aggravated attack crimes there is a significant decrease in performance for arrests and charges, while for drugs trade there is a significant decrease in crime records and arrests.

The evaluation confirmed that performance improved with higher human-resource allocation in most crimes categories, except for exposure crimes; main conclusion for the police is that no matter how resource allocation is high, the impact on performance wasn't significant. We can conclude that without any consideration in size of human-resource in a police station, its performance in dealing with crimes like illegal stay, drugs trade and weapons remains the same. Police officers can learn from this study that the quantity of the police force staff in a police station will not dramatically improve the quality of those measures, so the focus should be on the quality of HR and less the quantity.

Moreover, as suggested previously, the socio-economic ranking is shown to have a strong moderating effect on performance in the crime-records category; however, for output measures as charges and arrests, it seems that changes in performance are not affected by socio-economic ranking. The baseline assumption that a PMS system and, in particular, a BI-supported one has an influence on organizational change and improvement in performance has been confirmed. However, the possible decline in performance during the transition period cannot be neglected.

5.2 Research Contribution

The findings obtained from this research contribute to a better understanding of our existing knowledge on PMS. The main goal of this research was to enrich the existing literature about enhancing performance system measurement in organizations and its influence on performance in particular. This goal was accomplished by supporting the claim that enhancing PMS in organizations ay influence the performance measures. Understanding the consequences of enhancing PMS in organizations is critical to the process and it's important to understand those before enhancing process begins. Enhancing PMS process requires a broad variety of resources - human, time and budgets. Hence, the process of implementing a PMS mandates in-depth understanding of the expected challenges and the associated difficulties.

Many prior researches had focused on the importance developing, implementing, use and review PMS in organizations, however almost no evidence was seen to the influence of enhancing PMS. Very little empirical and theoretical research had been carried out on enhancing PMS. This research is innovative due to its contribution to academic literature in a field that had never been investigated before, even though it's very meaningful and relevant. One of main conclusions that arise in this research is that enhancing PMS in an organization by itself is not influence on performance measures, but the combination with other factors as well. Some of these variables are controlled and some are internal and are not controlled. Managers of enhancing PMS process have to be aware to those factors that may moderate the influence on performance measures.

Through this paper, we have predicted and identified performance-measurement challenges of the future, thus presenting the research community with an opportunity for developing proactive research programs in anticipation of these challenges.

One meaningful accomplishment in this research may refer to understanding the different factors that may moderate the influence of enhancing PMS. This study indicates that for some of the crime categories the influence on performance measures was significant and for some is not, especially in violence crimes. Furthermore, the influence is moderated by the socio-economic ranking of cities that under a police station responsibility, mostly in illegal stay and violence crimes categories.

A significant improvement was detected in the arrests category. This was shown to be meaningful and valuable for senior police officers. The results show that the influence on performance is moderated by police station characteristics as well; hence, not all police stations were influenced same way. Moderation effects examination revealed some interesting conclusions with practical implications that may assist and serve police officers that manage enhancing PMS process for next transition. There is an increasing consensus of the perception that PMS are not leading to an automatic improvement in performance. In contrast, PMS planning, development and use may affect the improvement in measures. The enhancing process by itself is not contributing to improvement in performance, but the integration with other factors as indicates in this research has an influence. The literature claims that there is a need to a right management of performance measurement systems in both public and non-public sectors. Many researches are focusing on developing methodologies and reviewing the literature on PMS, however little empirical research has been carried out to assess their influence on performance measures, especially in the public sector.

5.3 Directions for Future Research

In order to better understand performance measurement in general and in the public sector in particular, this study can be extended in a few possible directions. Some limitations are ought to be further addresses and explored since the study explores only a few variables that can influence the effect of replacing a PMS.

- Are the moderate variables that were analyzed are the only main ones that can influence performance or other variables need to be considered? Other moderated variables can relate to human aspect as PMS use and user characteristics such as experience, seniority, age and gender. Other influences can possibly be attributes to internal factors such as employee motivation, prior experience, organizational structure, organizational culture and strategic capabilities. Other external variables that can be examined are market uncertainty and possible competition. Some of these factors had already tested in other studies; however, their influence on organizational performance should be further explored.
- Is enhancing PMS improves performance over long period? How performance is influenced in the long term?

- Do other public organizations show similar behavior to the Israeli police? Is the influence of enhancing PMS is specific to this case study or common in other organizations as well?
- Is the influence on performance similar for measures that were not included in the test set but are still part of the PMS?
- Is the influence of enhancing PMS on different police stations shows a variance in intensity change? Further research could also explore whether or not police stations vary in their intensity of change in performance and in which crime categories.

Answering these questions required additional research is required, toward deeper understanding of performance measurement systems and their impact.

References

1. Bourne, M.: Performance management: learning from the past and projecting the future. Measur. Bus. Excellence **12**, 67–72 (2008)
2. Bourne, M., Neely, A.: Implementing performance measurements systems: a literature review. Bus. Perform. Manage. **5**(1), 1–24 (2003)
3. Brynjolfsson, E., Hitt, L., Kim, H.: Strength in numbers: how does data-driven decision-making affect firm performance? In: Proceedings of the 32nd International Conference on Information Systems, Shanghai, China (2011). Paper 13
4. Yadav, N., Sagar, M.: Performance measurement and management frameworks - research trends to the last two decades. Bus. Process Manage. J. **19**(6), 947–970 (2013)
5. Vuksic, V., Bach, M., Popvic, A.: Supporting PM with business performance and business intelligence: a case analysis of integration and orchestration. Int. J. Inf. Manage. **33**, 613–619 (2013)
6. Micheli, P., Kennerley, M.: Performance measurement frameworks in public and non-profit sectors. Prod. Plann. Control **16**(2), 125–134 (2005)
7. Franco-Santos, M., Bourne, M.: An examination of the literature relating to issues affecting how companies manage through measures. Prod. Plann. Control **16**(2), 114–124 (2005)
8. Elbashir, M.Z., Collier, P.A., Davern, M.J.: Measuring the effects of business intelligence systems: the relationship between business process and organizational performance. Int. J. Acc. Inf. Syst. **9**(3), 135–153 (2008)
9. Franco-Santos, M., Lucianetti, L., Bourne, M.: Contemporary performance measurement systems: a review of their consequences and a framework for research. Manage. Acc. Res. **23**(2), 79–119 (2012)
10. Fisher, T.: Business Productivity measurement using standard cost accounting information. Int. J. Oper. Prod. Manage. **10**(8), 61–69 (1990)
11. Nudurupati, S.S., Bititci, U.S., Kumar, V., Chan, F.T.: State of the art literature review on performance measurement. Comput. Ind. Eng. **60**(2), 279–290 (2011)
12. Garengo, P., Biazzo, S., Bititci, U.S.: Performance measurement systems in SMEs: a review for a research agenda. Intl. J. Manage. Rev. **7**(1), 25–47 (2005)
13. Marchand, M., Raymond, L.: Researching performance measurement systems: an information systems perspective. Int. J. Oper. Prod. Manage. **28**(7), 663–686 (2008)
14. Neely, A., Gregory, M., Platts, K., Richards, H., Kennerley, M., Bourne, M.: Performance measurement system design: developing and testing a process-based approach. Int. J. Oper. Prod. Manage. **20**(10), 1119–1145 (2000)

15. Tung, A., Baird, K., Schoch, H.P.: Factors influencing the effectiveness of performance measurement systems. Int. J. Oper. Prod. Manage. **31**(12), 1287–1310 (2011)
16. Kaplan, R.S., Norton, D.P.: The balanced scorecard-measures that drive performance. Harv. Bus. Rev. **70**, 71–79 (1992)
17. Neely, A., Adams, C., Crowe, P.: The performance prism in practice. Measur. Bus. Excellence **5**, 6–13 (2001)
18. Norreklit, H.: The balance on the balanced scorecard a critical analysis of some of its assumptions. Manage. Acc. Res. **11**(1), 65–88 (2000)

Evaluating Efficiency of ArchiMate Business Processes Verification with NuSMV

Piotr Szwed[(✉)]

AGH University of Science and Technology,
Mickiewicza Av. 30, 30-059 Kraków, Poland
pszwed@agh.edu.pl

Abstract. The motivation for our work was an idea of integrating formal verification with business processes modeling. In the presented approach ArchiMate was selected as a language used for definition of processes. We describe a procedure, which extracts behavioral elements from ArchiMate specification and transforms them into a corresponding representation used by NuSMV model checker. Then, we focus on time efficiency of the verification task. We give results of tests performed on a set of artificial process specifications, as well as on a complex business process, whose development was supported by the implemented solution. We compare three semantics of ArchiMate process definitions and discuss their influence on model complexity and verification time.

Keywords: ArchiMate · Business process verification · Model checking · NuSMV

1 Introduction

The goal of business process verification is to check if processes intended to be used or already implemented within an organization exhibit desired behavioral properties. The analyzed processes may be combinations of manual tasks performed by employees with operations supported by IT tools, as well as fully automated specifications run by process execution engines.

Graphical process modeling tools often offer support for local syntax checking, e.g. correct use of links between elements of the diagram. In spite of this, some structural errors remain undetected, especially those resulting from incorrect use of synchronization mechanisms [1]. Partial analysis of model behavior can be performed by simulation techniques, however, only application of formal methods can give unequivocal answer that the verified system meets formally specified requirements.

Although the most frequently used business process modeling notations are BPMN [2] and EPC [3], in this work we decided to focus on verification of process models defined in ArchiMate, a contemporary, open and independent language intended for description of enterprise architectures [4].

Formal system verification can by done either by *deductive reasoning* or *model checking* [5]. Deductive reasoning consists in formulating theorems specifying

© Springer International Publishing Switzerland 2016
E. Ziemba (Ed.): FedCSIS 2015, LNBIP 243, pp. 179–196, 2016.
DOI: 10.1007/978-3-319-30528-8_11

desired system properties and proving or falsifying them using manual or automated techniques. Unfortunately, deductive reasoning methods gives very little information on causes, if a verified property does not hold. Model checking allows to verify a concurrent system modeled as a finite state transition graph against a set of specifications expressed in a propositional temporal logic. It employs efficient internal representations and quick search procedures to determine automatically, whether the specifications are satisfied along the computational paths. Moreover, if a specification is not met, the verification procedure delivers a counterexample that can be used to analyze the source of the error. The main problem faced by model checking is a state space explosion [6]. At the very beginning only small examples could have been processed. A significant progress in this technique was achieved with application of ordered binary decision diagrams (OBBD) [7] allowing to model systems consisting of millions of states and transitions.

Although formal tools reached the state of the art, they are not commonly used in the engineering practice. According to Huuck [8] three factors decide on successful application of formal tools: they should be simple to use, the time spent on model preparation and verification should be comparable with other user activities, and, finally, a tool should provide a real value, i.e. deliver information that was previously not available.

Motivated by an idea of integrating formal verification with modeling of business processes, we developed a software tool that fully automatically translates behavioral elements of a business model expressed in ArchiMate language to a corresponding finite-state graph required by a model checker. Then, after running the verification and possibly detecting errors, valuable information about specifications not met and counterexamples can be returned to a process designer. The goals of the presented approach are: (1) an automation of business process verification tasks and (2) short times required to obtain verification results. In particular, we find the second issue crucial for an integration with an interactive modeling tool.

The concept of verification system is presented in Fig. 1. The business model is defined within Archi [9], a well known ArchiMate modeling tool. As a verification platform the state of the art symbolic model checker NuSMV [10] is used. We have developed an Archi plugin that extracts a subgraph of ArchiMate behavioral elements and transforms it into NuSMV model descriptions. Specifications of desired properties should be defined by a user, however, a part of them can be generated automatically by an analysis of the process structure.

This paper is a continuation and extension to our previous works: [11] describing the concept of verification system dedicated to ArchiMate business processes and [12] giving results of initial tests related to verification efficiency. In this work we describe tests conducted in a more systematic manner, performed by generating models according to three semantics, which combine two approaches to translation of ArchiMate behavioral elements: as state machines or synchronous gates that map directly inputs to outputs. We also examine influence of variable ordering on the time efficiency and memory consumption. The tests were

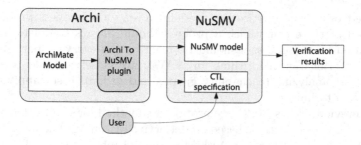

Fig. 1. The concept of the verification system

performed on a set of artificial process specifications and on a complex business process, whose development was supported by the implemented verification tool.

The paper is organized as follows: next Sect. 2 discusses various approaches to the verification of business models. Section 3 presents basic concepts of ArchiMate language. It is followed by Sect. 4, which describes details of the NuSMV model generation procedure. Section 5 reports results of time efficiency tests. Section 6 provides concluding remarks.

2   Related Works

Application of formal methods to verification of business processes was surveyed by Morimoto [1]. Author distinguished three prevalent approaches: based on automata, Petri nets and process algebras. The first approach consists in translating the process description into a set of communicating automata (state machines) and performing model checking with such tools, as SPIN or UPPAAL. In analysis of Petri net models, basically simulation techniques are used, especially in the case of more expressive colored Petri nets.

Model checking has an established position in verification of business processes. It was applied in [13] to BPMN models extended with temporal and resource constraints. In [14] verification of e-business processes was achieved by translation to CSP language and checking refinement between two specifications. In [15] authors implemented a system that translated BPEL specification into NuSMV language, what allowed them to check properties defined as CTL formulas. Three types of correctness properties were analyzed: invariants, properties of final states and temporal relations between activities. The first two can be classified as *safeness*, the last as the *liveness* property. Similarly, in work by Fu et al. [16] CTL was applied to the verification of e-services and workflows with both bounded and unbounded numbers of process instances. The work [17] discusses verification of data-centric business processes. The correctness problem was expressed in the LTL-FO, an extension to the Linear Temporal Logic, in which propositions were replaced by First Order statements about data objects.

Wynn et al. [18] discuss verification tools developed for models in YAWL language [19], with a special focus on OR-joins and cancellation constructs.

The verified process properties are predefined. e.g. a soundness property is a combination of three conditions: a process should always complete, after the completion all its subprocesses should be inactive and every its part should be executable. Verification algorithms for YAWL are closely related to those of Petri nets, i.e. analyzing reachability graphs and in hard cases applying Petri nets reduction techniques.

In our previous works [20, 21] we proposed a method for verification of Archi-Mate behavioral specifications based on deductive reasoning. The described app-roach consisted in transforming ArchiMate model into a set of LTL formulas, then extending it with formulas defining desired system properties and formally proving them using semantic tableaux method. Similar approach to workflow verification was proposed in [22]. The discussed workflow language allowed to combine a few basic workflow patterns: sequences, parallel activities, loops and branches.

Although verification of business processes has been investigated for at least 15 years, surprisingly, there is very little information provided about efficiency of applied techniques. This in particular concerns the formal verification with the model checking approach. However, quantified results for a quite complex process specified in YAWL are given in the work [18] entitled remarkably "Business Process Verification - Finally a Reality!". Without reductions the soundness verification of the process stages took about a few dozen seconds; applying reductions decreased the verification time of the whole process below ten seconds.

NuSMV [10] is a state of the art model checker that has been succesfully used for various verification tasks including formal protocol analysis [23], verification of requirements specification [24] or planning tasks [25]. The package uses a special language (named also NuSMV) to define the verified model as a set of linked finite state machines, as well as its specification in form of temporal logic formulas. The model submitted to the verification tool must be manually coded in NuSMV language or generated from another language amenable to a finite state transition system, e.g. state charts [26] or reachability graphs of Petri nets [27]. Properties to be checked with NuSMV can be expressed in Computational Tree Logic (CTL) or Linear Temporal Logic (LTL). In this work we use CTL as a specification language. CTL allows to define properties that should be satisfied within a tree of computations (paths) starting from a given state. As the tree defines a set imaginable futures, CTL is called the branching time logic. CTL formulas are combinations of two types of operators *path quantifiers* and *linear-time operators*. The path quantifiers are: A (for every path in a tree) and E (there exists a path in a tree). Temporal operators include: G ($G\,p$ means that p holds true globally in the future) and F ($F\,p$ means that p holds true sometime in the future).

NuSMV uses internally ordered binary decision diagrams (OBDD) as a rep-resentation of a state transition system. It is well known, that the size of OBDD depends heavily on the variable ordering [7, 28, 29]. Selecting an optimal ordering is a NP-hard task, however several heuristics can be used to improve the ordering and in consequence reduce the model size, as well as the processing time.

3   Archimate

ArchiMate [4] is a contemporary, open and independent language intended for description of enterprise architectures. It comprises five main modeling layers shortly characterized below. The *Business* layer includes business processes and objects, functions, events, roles and services. The *Application* layer contains components, interfaces, application services and data objects. The *Technology* layer gathers such elements as artifacts, nodes, software, devices, communication channels and networks. Elements of the *Motivation* layer allow to express business drivers, goals, requirements and principles. Finally, *Implementation&Migration* layer contains such elements, as work package, deliverable and gap.

ArchiMate provides a small set of constructs that can be used to model behavior. It includes *Business Processes, Functions, Interactions, Events* and various connectors (*Junctions*), which can be attributed with a logical operator specifying, how inputs should be combined or output produced. According to language specification casual or temporal relationships between behavioral elements are expressed with use of *triggering* relation. On the other hand, ArchiMate models frequently use *composition* and *aggregation* relations, e.g. to show that a process is built from smaller behavioral elements (subprocesses or functions).

Although the set of behavioral elements seems to be very limited when compared with BPMN [2], after adopting a certain modeling convention its expressiveness can be similar [30]. An advantage of the language is that in allows to comprise in a single model a broad context of business processes including roles, services, processed business objects and elements of lower layers responsible for implementation and deployment.

The internal structure of an ArchiMate model constitutes a graph of nodes linked by directed edges. Both nodes and edges are attributed with information indicating the type of element or relation. While generating NuSMV code describing behavioral aspects of ArchiMate model, we focus on components of the *Business layer*: processes (interactions, functions), events and various junctions.

It should be noted that ArchiMate behavioral constructs have no precisely defined semantics. In fact, translation from ArchiMate specification to NuSMV assigns a semantics, which, although arbitrarily selected, follows a certain intuition, e.g. how to interpret an activity or an event.

Definition 1 (Archimate model). ArchiMate model AM is a tuple $\langle V, E, C, R, v, e \rangle$, where V is a set of vertices, $E \subset V \times V$ is a set of edges, C is a set of ArchiMate element types, R is a set of relations, $vt \colon V \to C$ is a function that assigns element types to graph vertices $et \colon E \to R$ assigns relation types to edges.

As we focus on business layer elements that are used to specify behavior, it is assumed that $C = \{Process, Function, Interaction, Event, Junction, AndJunction, OrJunction, Other\}$ and $R = \{triggering, association, composition, other\}$.

4   NuMSV Model Generation

This section discusses language patterns that can be used to model ArchiMate elements in NuSMV, as well as details of the translation procedure.

The basic structural unit in NuSMV language is a *module* understood as a set of variables and statements that assign initial values to variables and define a transition relation. Depending on the module definition, we may distinguish input variables corresponding to stimuli, internal state variables and output variables (actions).

Definition of a module introduces a new type that can be instantiated. Hence, it is possible to declare a variable of a module type and bind it during declaration resembling a constructor call to a number of input variables. Subsequent variables definitions may reference outputs of other modules instances as their inputs. This allows to define a system of communicating state machines of desired complexity, which propagates input stimuli to its components causing subsequent state changes and generation of output signals. Typically, the model integration is achieved within the special *main* module, however, it can be distributed among lower level modules, which are referenced from *main*.

4.1   Modeling ArchiMate Behavioral Elements

We will discuss the idea of translation of ArchiMate behavioral specification into corresponding NuSMV model on a small process example presented in Fig. 2. The whole process is activated upon occurrence of the event *Start*. Then the subprocess *P1* is launched, which is followed by *P2*. If *P2* terminates correctly, a decision is made whether additional subprocess *P3* should be executed or the control flow leads to event *End* directly. However, execution of *P2* can be interrupted by the event *Interrupt*, which redirects back to the process *P1*.

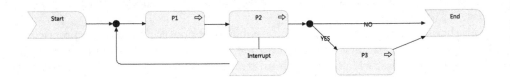

Fig. 2. Sample ArchiMate process specification

Figure 3 shows the structure of NuSMV model corresponding to the process in Fig. 2. Although the presented business process is clearly sequential, it can be realized by a number of concurrent state machines (modules) linked by their output and input variables. The reusable modules correspond to the ArchiMate language constructs: processes, events, forks, joins, etc.

After conducting an analysis of components appearing in ArchiMate behavior specifications the following basic modules were identified and implemented:

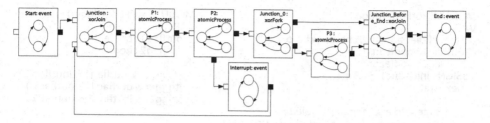

Fig. 3. Linked NuSMV modules used to model the process in Fig. 2

- $atomicProcess_n$: n-ary atomic process has exactly one input, one primary output and n additional outputs, which can be activated if one of n exceptions occurs. The exception should be modeled in ArchiMate as an event linked with the process by the association relation.
- *event*: has only one input and one output (a boolean flag). Multiple recipients may use this flag as trigger.
- *andFork*: used to model AndJunction in Archmate. The module construction is analogous to event.
- $andJoin_n$: n-ary andJoin produces output signal, if all n inputs are set to TRUE.
- $xorFork_n$: n-ary xorFork have one input and n outputs. Upon module activation, only one among possible outputs will be triggered.
- $xorJoin_n$: n-ary xorJoin has n inputs and sets the output flag if any of them is set. Moreover it tracks the number of inputs, e.g. if two from n inputs are activated, the output flag will be set twice.

Figure 4 shows the state diagram of the module xorFork. The module is activated by an input signal *trigger*. Upon the signal arrival, the machine changes the state from *idle* to *started*. Then one of two states can be selected *choice1* or *choice2*. Synchronously, a corresponding output variable is set to *TRUE*: either *outflag1* or *ouflag2*. The output variable, whichever is set, will be cleared during the transition to *idle* state.

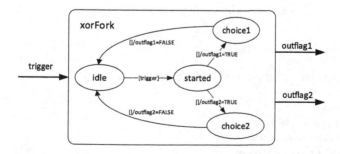

Fig. 4. State machine modeling an xorFork junction with two outputs

```
MODULE xorFork(trigger)                    MODULE xorFork(trigger)
VAR                                        VAR
   state : {idle, signaled, choice1, choice2};   outflag1 : boolean;
   outflag1 : boolean;                        outflag2 : boolean;
   outflag2 : boolean;                     INVAR
ASSIGN   init(state) := idle;                 (!trigger & !outflag1 & !outflag2) |
   next(state) :=                             (trigger & outflag1 & !outflag2 ) |
      case                                    (trigger & !outflag1 & outflag2 )
         state = idle & trigger: {signaled};
         state = signaled : {signaled, choice1,choice2};
         state = choice1 : {choice1, idle};
         state = choice2 : {choice2, idle};
         TRUE : state;
      esac;
INVAR
   (state = choice1 <-> outflag1 = TRUE)
INVAR
   (state = choice2 <-> outflag2 = TRUE)
FAIRNESS
   state = choice1
FAIRNESS
   state = choice2
                        a                                        b
```

Fig. 5. NuSMV code of the module `xorFork` (a) FSM implementation (b) synchronous implementation

Figure 5 gives two NuSMV implementations of the xorFork module. Version (a) is a true state machine, which receives an input signal, changes its internal state and produces outputs. The definition introduces interleaving between state transitions, e.g. a successor of the state *signaled* is one of the states *choice1* or *choice2*, but also the state *signaled*. This enables other model components to change their state, before the selection is made. Alternative implementation, referred as *synchronous*, is shown in Fig. 5. In this case selection of one of output signals (*output1* or *output2*) is done synchronously with setting the input *trigger* to true. We have provided both types of implementations for all elements, including atomicProcess (see [12]). Basically, synchronous implementations allow to reduce interleaving, what makes the internal model representation in NuSMV smaller and speeds up the verification process.

4.2   Generation Procedure

The generation procedure consists of the following stages:

1. Refactoring
2. Assigning representation
3. Main module generation
4. Generation of specification

Refactoring. With relation to the numbers of inputs and outputs, it is expected that elements fall into one of two classes: $1 : m$ (one input and m outputs) or $n : 1$ (m inputs and one output). Hence elements with the arity $n : m$ are replaced by two elements: the first is an appropriate xorJoin or andJoin of arity $n : 1$. The second is the original element with the arity changed to $1 : n$.

Assigning representation. For each ArchiMate element an appropriate NuSMV module type is selected and configured based on element type and numbers of inputs/outputs. Only required modules are generated, e.g. for the process shown in Fig. 2 the code of the following modules will be added: event (for *Start* and *End*), atomicProc (for *P1* and *P3*), atomicProc1 (process with one exeptional output for *P2*), xorFork for the junction following *P2* and xorJoin for the junctions before *P2* and before the event *End* (the last one was added during the refactoring phase.

Main module generation. This step comprises declaration of variables and linking them. For roots (modules without inputs) appropriate initial variables and transitions are added as well. The generated NuSMV code for the *main* module is presented in Fig. 6. It can be noticed that variables definition are unordered and the code contains forward references, e.g. the output variable Junction.output is referenced before P1 definition.

```
MODULE main
VAR
    P1 : atomicProcess(Junction.output);
    P2 : atomicProcess1(P1.outflag);
    P3 : atomicProcess(Junction_0.outflag2);
    Start : event(Start_trigger);
    End : event(Junction_Before_End.output);
    Junction : xorJoin(Interrupt.outflag,Start.outflag);
    Junction_0 : xorFork(P2.outflag);
    Interrupt : event(P2.excptflag1);
    Junction_Before_End : xorJoin(P3.outflag,Junction_0.outflag1);
    Start_trigger : boolean;
ASSIGN
    init(Start_trigger) := FALSE;
    next(Start_trigger) := {FALSE,TRUE};
```

Fig. 6. Generated NuSMV main module code for the process in Fig. 2

Generation of specification. Usually a specification expressing formal requirements should be entered by a user. However, we tried to derive some *liveness* requirements based on control flows within ArchiMate model (see Definition 1). The implemented procedure performs a depth-first search starting from *roots* (ArchiMate elements having no predecessors). It returns a set of paths $\Pi = \{\pi_i\}$ comprising ArchiMate elements linked by control flow relation. For a path $\pi_i = (e_{ib}, \ldots, e_{ie})$, its last element e_{ie} is either a final element in the model (without successors) or a branching element (already present in π_i). In the next step, the sets of elements in paths π_i are restricted to events only and, finally, specifications referencing first and last events in the paths are generated. For the process in Fig. 6 the following eight specifications can be generated:

$$\mathcal{G}(\texttt{Start.outflag-} >\mathcal{F}(\texttt{Interrupt.outflag}\,\mathcal{O}\,\texttt{End.outflag})),$$

where $\mathcal{G} = \{\texttt{AG}, \texttt{EG}\}$, $\mathcal{F} = \{\texttt{AF}, \texttt{EF}\}$ and $\mathcal{O} = \{\&, |\}$. To give an example, the specification AG (Start.outflag -> EF (Interrupt.outflag | End.outflag)). is equivalent to the statement: *for every path, starting with Start event, it is possible to reach a state, where End or Interrrupt events occur.* Details of the algorithm can be found in [12].

5   Experiments

The goal of the conducted experiments was to assess a relationship between the process complexity and the time required to check CTL specifications with NuSMV. During the experiments NuSMV was launched as an external process in the interactive mode, then commands to load models, report numbers of variables and check automatically generated specifications were issued. The NuSMV output was grabbed and information on models processed, as well as the execution times were collected.

During a model generation the implemented Archi plugin can be configured to select a state machine or a synchronous implementation for each ArchiMate element type. Depending on the implementation used, various models differing in semantics can be obtained. In the tests we applied three configurations (and corresponding semantics): *FSM* – all elements are modeled as state machines, *FSM Proc* – state machine based code is used only for atomic processes, other implementations are synchronous and *Sync* – all elements are implemented in the synchronous way.

5.1   Artificial Test Cases

Process specifications can form very diverse structures, however, we assumed that key features characterizing the process complexity are the numbers of branches and loops in the control flow. Hence, the basic process pattern, which was analyzed, comprised several branches and loops placed between two events *Start* and *Stop*. Figure 7 shows an example, in which four subprocesses (activities) are arranged to form two branches and two loops. We have prepared a number of test cases being variations of this pattern and performed tests for two model semantics: *FSM Proc* and *Sync*. Their results are summarized in Table 1. Analogous results for models generated from the same process specifications, but applying *FSM* semantics have been already published in [12].

Each case name in Table 1 is encoded as a string: $n\,\mathrm{p}\,m\{\mathrm{b}|\mathrm{ab}\}\,k\,\mathrm{l}$, where n– number of processes, m–number of branches and k–number of loops. Symbol 'b' appearing in the case name means that the XOR branches (*xorJoins*) were used, wheras 'ab' corresponds to parallel branches placed between two *AndJoins*.

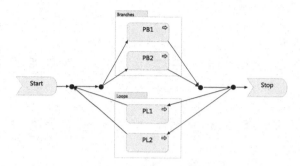

Fig. 7. Test case 4p2b2l: a process consisting of four subprocesses forming two branches and two loops

The column marked as *CC* gives the value of cyclomatic complexity, a commonly used measure that can be interpreted as the number of independent paths in the specification [31]. The measure is basically applicable to sequential processes. For processes containing parallel activities the number of independent paths can be smaller, hence, corrected values of cyclomatic complexity are added in parentheses. Subsequent columns give numbers of state variables, total numbers of states and numbers of reachable states. *Dia* is a system diameter, i.e. the longest path from the initial state. Column *TPS* give total execution time divided by the number of specifications (For each case 8 specifications were automatically generated and tested.) Column *TPSD* gives the processing time one specification after applying dynamic variable ordering (the sift algorithm described in [32] was used).

The test cases are arranged into three groups. The first comprises process specifications with various numbers of branches, however without any loops. As it can be observed, in spite of growing problem sizes, the numbers of reachable states and processing times remain relatively small.

The second group contains hard cases, i.e. those with several OR branches and loops. This makes both the numbers of reachable states very high and for the most complex case 24p12b12 (24 processes, 12 branches and 12 loops) the time spent to check one specification ranges to 80 s.

The third group includes cases with parallel branches that are synchronized at an *AndJoin*. In this case the space of reachable states is much smaller and the execution times are relatively short (up to 560 ms for the case 24p12ab12l). It can be noticed that for the cases 7p2ab5l, 8p3ab5l, 9p4ab5l and 10p5ab5l the numbers of reachable states are equal. This is a natural consequence of the model structure. Regardless of the number of parallel subprocesses, they all start and finish in the same states synchronized by the *AndJoin*.

Table 1 shows that applying dynamic variable ordering can improve processing time for complex models (e.g. 24p12b12l) using *FSM Proc* semantics. However, for smaller models or synchronous semantics, it was inefficient.

Table 1. Results of performance tests.

Name	CC	Semantics: FSM Proc						Semantics: Sync					
		Vars	Total states	Reachable	Dia	TPS [ms]	$TPSD$ [ms]	Vars	Total states	Reachable	Dia	TPS [ms]	$TPSD$ [ms]
2p2b0l	2	10	2304	52	5	9.57	1.79	8	256	3	2	7.91	1.12
3p3b0l	3	13	27648	170	5	7.91	4.34	10	1024	4	2	4.10	3.07
4p4b0l	4	16	331776	438	5	7.92	4.20	12	4096	5	2	3.01	3.17
5p5b0l	5	19	3981310	952	5	7.33	8.05	14	16384	6	2	3.21	3.32
8p8b0l	8	28	$6.87 \cdot 10^9$	5290	5	25.21	17.74	20	1048580	9	2	3.10	3.17
12p12b0l	12	40	$1.42 \cdot 10^{14}$	24542	5	37.93	40.42	28	$2.68 \cdot 10^8$	13	2	3.41	3.50
4p2b2l	4	18	1327100	1632	8	7.49	4.65	14	16384	11	2	3.04	3.31
6p3b3l	6	24	$1.91 \cdot 10^8$	27494	8	15.87	20.83	18	262144	22	2	3.38	3.92
8p4b4l	8	30	$2.75 \cdot 10^{10}$	215118	8	75.28	29.97	22	4194300	37	2	4.01	8.13
10p5b5l	10	36	$3.96 \cdot 10^{12}$	1131380	8	37.75	46.57	26	$6.71 \cdot 10^7$	56	2	5.07	6.60
16p8b8l	16	66	$2.45 \cdot 10^{23}$	$2.35 \cdot 10^8$	8	134.01	540.53	46	$7.03 \cdot 10^{13}$	211	2	7.19	12.78
20p10b10l	20	66	$2.45 \cdot 10^{23}$	$2.35 \cdot 10^8$	8	136.37	541.19	46	$7.03 \cdot 10^{13}$	211	2	6.26	13.90
24p12b12l	24	78	$5.08 \cdot 10^{27}$	$9.83 \cdot 10^8$	8	1172.25	494.22	54	$1.80 \cdot 10^{16}$	301	2	7.60	22.09
7p2ab5l	7 (6)	26	$1.14 \cdot 10^9$	170	8	11.16	11.06	19	524288	12	2	3.40	3.38
8p3ab5l	8 (6)	28	$6.87 \cdot 10^9$	170	8	13.76	12.36	20	1048580	12	2	8.51	3.43
9p4ab5l	9 (6)	30	$4.12 \cdot 10^{10}$	170	8	12.86	10.75	21	2097150	12	2	4.77	3.55
10p5ab5l	10 (6)	32	$2.47 \cdot 10^{11}$	170	8	10.41	11.82	22	4194300	12	2	3.53	3.58
16p8ab8l	16 (9)	47	$9.24 \cdot 10^{16}$	314	8	29.65	38.73	31	$2.14 \cdot 10^9$	18	2	5.23	9.91
20p10ab10l	20 (11)	57	$4.79 \cdot 10^{20}$	430	8	17.25	52.98	37	$1.37 \cdot 10^{11}$	22	2	5.09	9.47
24p12ab12l	24 (13)	67	$2.48 \cdot 10^{24}$	562	8	17.77	68.65	43	$8.79 \cdot 10^{12}$	26	2	5.32	12.16

5.2   Business Process Example

In this section we present results of performance tests for a business process from the health care domain. The analyzed process, namely *Telemonitoring*, was implemented within a prototype system, whose goal was to help patients in self-management of chronic disease through monitoring of symptoms, self-assessment and informing about necessary actions, when symptoms levels indicate a problem [33,34]. The process description was prepared with Archi based on the BPMN model used internally during the system design and implementation. The definition of the Telemonitoring process in ArchiMate language comprises five views, which in BPMN were assigned to two lanes: the first grouping actions performed by a patient and the second comprising fully automated tasks executed within the implemented system.

The goal of the first process stage, presented in Fig. 8, is to collect data related to subjective symptoms and selected control parameters, e.g. PEV (peek expiratory flow) for asthma. The latter are measured with sensors connected by Bluetooth to patients' smartphones, which transmit them automatically to system servers responsible for data storage.

The second process stage, shown in Fig. 9, comprises activities related to data validation and sending an acknowledgement or an error notification on their reception. As it is assumed, that a patient enters data on a regular basis, typically once a day, this stage also include an activity consisting in sending a reminder (triggered by the *Data not received on time* event).

The key activity within the next process stage (Fig. 10) is data analysis. It results in three decisions related to patients condition assessment: *Controlled disease state*, *Exacerbation* and *Critical exacerbation*. The first two are followed by a notification transmitted to a patient, whereas the third corresponding to a severe patient's condition, rises up an *Alert*. Typically, an alert is accompanied by an information to contact immediately a leading physician and/or use a relief medication.

The fourth process stage is related to notification or alert processing at the patient side. This part of the process is depicted in Fig. 11. It is expected that reception of an alert would be notified by a patient by sending appropriate acknowledgment (*Alert Ack*).

Finally, the last stage of the process is shown in Fig. 12. The automated system makes a decision whether an alert should be repeated (*Resend alert*) or escalated to a call center (*Call center emergency notification*).

Based on this specification, three NuSMV models were obtained for *FSM*, *FSMProc* and *Sync* process semantics. As the process can be started with two events: *Patient decides to measure parameters* or *Data not received on time*, sixteen CTL specifications were automatically generated.

During the tests we collected data related to model size, execution time and memory consumption. They are summarized in Table 2. In can be observed that the test for the *FSM* semantics without variable ordering (row 1) failed. The verification processes did not terminate in an acceptable time consuming a few gigabytes memory. The performance was better after applying dynamic

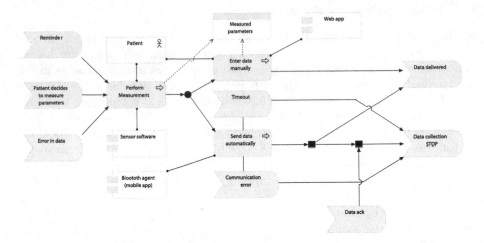

Fig. 8. Collect data

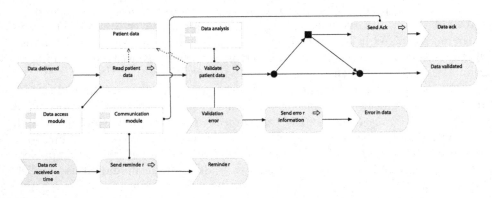

Fig. 9. First stage of patient data analysis

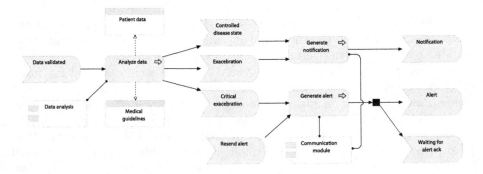

Fig. 10. Second stage of patient data analysis

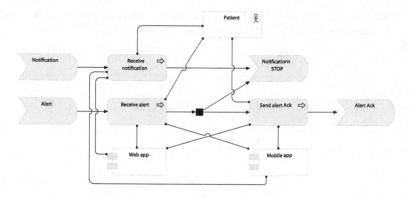

Fig. 11. Receiving notifications

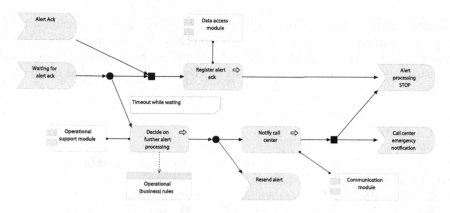

Fig. 12. Alert processing

variable ordering (row 2), however, the total execution time ranged at about 7 min. For the *FSM Proc* semantics a great influence of dynamic variable ordering on processing time can be observed: 82 min vs. 30 s. Finally, for the *Sync* semantics (rows 5 and 6) the verification is very fast.

Table 2 shows also relationships between the assumed semantics and a model complexity. Simplifying the semantics results in reduction of number of system variables, reachable states, as well as the model diameter (maximal trace length). For the *Sync* semantics the whole control flow within the process, including alternative paths, is reduced into an input-output relation between an initial state and one of reachable states. This makes the verification very efficient, however in some circumstances may produce different results, when comparing to models using other semantics.

Transformation of the source BPMN diagram into corresponding ArchiMate representation was performed incrementally. Being equipped with a verification tool, we used it as a support during the process modeling. We performed several reachability tests by generating NuSMV process definitions and (usually

Table 2. Results of performance tests. Dia – diameter (maximimum length of paths), TT – total execution time. TPS – time per specification ($TPS = TT/16$)

No	Semantics	Dynamic Var. Ord	Vars	Total states	Reachable states	Dia	Mem	TT [ms]	TPS [ms]
1	FSM	No	135	$2^{114}.3^{15}.4^5.5^1 = 1.53 \cdot 10^{45}$	$4.20 \cdot 10^{12}$	62	> 3.6 GB	∞	∞
2	FSM	Yes	135	$2^{114}.3^{15}.4^5.5^1 = 1.53 \cdot 10^{45}$	$4.20 \cdot 10^{12}$	62	$\sim$ 56 MB	428 886	26 805
3	FSM Proc	No	84	$2^{67}.3^{15}.4^1.5^1 = 4.24 \cdot 10^{28}$	$3.40 \cdot 10^9$	27	$\sim$1 GB	4 934 098	308 381
4	FSM Proc	Yes	84	$2^{67}.3^{15}.4^1.5^1 = 4.24 \cdot 10^{28}$	$3.40 \cdot 10^9$	27	$\sim$26 MB	30 526	1 907
5	Sync	No	67	$2^{67} = 1.46 \cdot 10^{20}$	66	2	$\sim$10 MB	124	8
6	Sync	Yes	67	$2^{67} = 1.46 \cdot 10^{20}$	66	2	$\sim$10 MB	430	27

manually) adding specifications to be checked. As the process specification is distributed among five views and several branches cross the views boundaries, performing on the fly verification allowed to fix a few hard to notice errors and inconsistencies. Typically, the models to be checked were generated using *Sync* semantics.

6   Conclusions

This paper investigates the problem of automatic verification of behavioral specification embedded within ArchiMate models. We propose an approach consisting in fully automatic translation of ArchiMate specification into a model in NuSMV language and then verifying it with the NuSMV model checker. Requirements specification in form of CTL formulas can be entered by a user, but the implemented tool is capable of generating specifications based on analysis of control flows. The main concern of our work was the time efficiency of the verification tasks. We evaluated it examining a set of artificial business process specifications, as well as a real business process example.

In our opinion the ArchiMate process specification presented in previous section represents quite a convincing proof that various BPMN constructs can be ported to the ArchiMate language. This in particular regards message events between parallel process flows. To model them, *AndJunctions* (represented by filled squares) were used.

The results show, that the described approach can be applied in an interactive verification tool, however, due to state space explosion problem, verification of complex business process specifications, especially using rich in interleaving *FSM* semantics, can still be a challenge for symbolic model checkers. From the three analyzed semantics: *FSM*, *FSM Proc* and *Sync* we find the two last the most useful, as they allow to significantly reduce the complexity of generated models and provide useful verification results obtained in relatively small time.

References

1. Morimoto, S.: A survey of formal verification for business process modeling. In: Bubak, M., van Albada, G.D., Dongarra, J., Sloot, P.M.A. (eds.) ICCS 2008, Part II. LNCS, vol. 5102, pp. 514–522. Springer, Heidelberg (2008)
2. OMG: Business Process Model and Notation (BPMN) version 2.0. Technical report, OMG, January 2011
3. Scheer, A.-W., Nüttgens, M.: ARIS architecture and reference models for business process management. In: van der Aalst, W.M.P., Desel, J., Oberweis, A. (eds.) Business Process Management. LNCS, vol. 1806, pp. 376–389. Springer, Heidelberg (2000)
4. The Open Group: Open Group Standard. Archimate 2.1 Specificattion. Van Haren Publishing, Zaltbommel (2013)
5. Clarke, E.M., Wing, J.M.: Formal methods: state of the art and future directions. ACM Comput. Surv. (CSUR) 28(4), 626–643 (1996)
6. Clarke, E.M., Klieber, W., Nováček, M., Zuliani, P.: Model checking and the state explosion problem. In: Meyer, B., Nordio, M. (eds.) LASER 2011. LNCS, vol. 7682, pp. 1–30. Springer, Heidelberg (2012)
7. Bryant, R.E.: Symbolic boolean manipulation with ordered binary-decision diagrams. ACM Comput. Surv. (CSUR) 24(3), 293–318 (1992)
8. Huuck, R.: Formal verification, engineering and business value. In: Olveczky, P.C., Artho, C. (eds.) Proceedings First International Workshop on Formal Techniques for Safety-Critical Systems, Kyoto, Japan, November 12, 2012, Electronic Proceedings in Theoretical Computer Science, vol. 105, pp. 1–4. Open Publishing Association (2012)
9. Beauvoir, P.: Archi, archimate modelling tool (2015). Accessed March 2015
10. Cimatti, A., Clarke, E., Giunchiglia, E., Giunchiglia, F., Pistore, M., Roveri, M., Sebastiani, R., Tacchella, A.: NuSMV 2: an opensource tool for symbolic model checking. In: Brinksma, E., Larsen, K.G. (eds.) CAV 2002. LNCS, vol. 2404, pp. 359–364. Springer, Heidelberg (2002)
11. Szwed, P.: Verification of archimate behavioral elements by model checking. In: Saeed, K., Homenda, W. (eds.) Computer Information Systems and Industrial Management. Lecture Notes in Computer Science, vol. 9339, pp. 132–144. Springer International Publishing, Warsaw (2015)
12. Szwed, P.: Efficiency of formal verification of archimate business processes with nusmv model checker. In: Federated Conference on Computer Science and Information Systems (FedCSIS), pp. 1427–1436 (2015)
13. Watahiki, K., Ishikawa, F., Hiraishi, K.: Formal verification of business processes with temporal and resource constraints. In: 2011 IEEE International Conference on Systems, Man, and Cybernetics (SMC), pp. 1173–1180. IEEE (2011)
14. Anderson, B., Hansen, J.V., Lowry, P., Summers, S.: Model checking for e-business control and assurance. IEEE Trans. Syst. Man, Cybern. C Appl. Rev. 35(3), 445–450 (2005)
15. Mongiello, M., Castelluccia, D.: Modelling and verification of BPEL business processes. In: Fourth and Third International Workshop on Model-Based Development of Computer-Based Systems and Model-Based Methodologies for Pervasive and Embedded Software, MBD/MOMPES 2006, p. 5. IEEE (2006)
16. Fu, X., Bultan, T., Su, J.: Formal verification of e-services and workflows. In: Bussler, C.J., McIlraith, S.A., Orlowska, M.E., Pernici, B., Yang, J. (eds.) CAiSE 2002 and WES 2002. LNCS, vol. 2512, pp. 188–202. Springer, Heidelberg (2002)

17. Deutsch, A., Hull, R., Patrizi, F., Vianu, V.: Automatic verification of data-centric business processes. In: Proceedings of the 12th International Conference on Database Theory, pp. 252–267. ACM (2009)

18. Wynn, M.T., Verbeek, H., van der Aalst, W.M., ter Hofstede, A.H., Edmond, D.: Business process verification-finally a reality!. Bus. Process Manag. J. **15**(1), 74–92 (2009)

19. Van der Aalst, W.M., Ter Hofstede, A.H.: YAWL: Yet Another Workflow Language. Inf. Syst. **30**(4), 245–275 (2005)

20. Klimek, R., Szwed, P.: Verification of ArchiMate process specifications based on deductive temporal reasoning. In: Ganzha, M., Maciaszek, L.A., Paprzycki, M. (eds.) Proceedings of the 2013 Federated Conference on Computer Science and Information Systems, Kraków, Poland, 8–11 September 2013, pp. 1103–1110 (2013)

21. Klimek, R., Szwed, P., Jedrusik, S.: Application of deductive reasoning to the verification of ArchiMate behavioral elements. Informatyka Ekonomiczna **29**, 76–97 (2013)

22. Klimek, R.: A system for deduction-based formal verification of workflow-oriented software models. Appl. Math. Comput. Sci. **24**(4), 941–956 (2014)

23. Clarke, E.M., Grumberg, O., Hiraishi, H., Jha, S., Long, D.E., McMillan, K.L., Ness, L.A.: Verification of the futurebus+ cache coherence protocol. Formal Methods Syst. Des. **6**(2), 217–232 (1995)

24. Fuxman, A., Pistore, M., Mylopoulos, J., Traverso, P.: Model checking early requirements specifications in tropos. In: Proceedings of the Fifth IEEE International Symposium on Requirements Engineering, pp. 174–181. IEEE (2001)

25. Bertoli, P., Cimatti, A., Pistore, M., Roveri, M., Traverso, P.: MBP: a Model Based Planner. In: Proceedings of the IJCAI01 Workshop on Planning under Uncertainty and Incomplete Information (2001)

26. Clarke, E., Heinle, W.: Modular translation of statecharts to SMV. Technical report, Citeseer (2000)

27. Szpyrka, M., Biernacka, A., Biernacki, J.: Methods of translation of petri nets to NuSMV language. In: Popova-Zeugmann, L. (ed.) Proceedings of the 23th International Workshop on Concurrency, Specification and Programming. CEUR Workshop Proceedings, vol. 1269, pp. 245–256. CEUR-WS.org, Berlin (2014)

28. Andersen, H.R.: An introduction to binary decision diagrams. Lecture notes, IT University of Copenhagen (1997)

29. Szwed, P., Ligeza, A.: Application of OBDD diagrams in verification of tabular rule systems. Schedae Informaticae 14 (2005)

30. Szwed, P., Chmiel, W., Jedrusik, S., Kadluczka, P.: Business processes in a distributed surveillance system integrated through workflow. Automatyka/Automatics **17**(1), 127–139 (2013)

31. McCabe, T.: A complexity measure. IEEE Trans. SE Softw. Eng. **2**(4), 308–320 (1976)

32. Rudell, R.: Dynamic variable ordering for ordered binary decision diagrams. In: Proceedings of the 1993 IEEE/ACM International Conference on Computer-Aided Design, pp. 42–47. IEEE Computer Society Press (1993)

33. Szwed, P.: Application of fuzzy ontological reasoning in an implementation of medical guidelines. In: 2013 The 6th International Conference on Human System Interaction (HSI), pp. 342–349, June 2013

34. Szwed, P., Skrzynski, P., Grodniewicz, P.: Risk assessment for SWOP telemonitoring system based on fuzzy cognitive maps. In: Dziech, A., Czyżewski, A. (eds.) MCSS 2013. CCIS, vol. 368, pp. 233–247. Springer, Heidelberg (2013)

Author Index

Printed in the United States
By Bookmasters